EALING STUDIOS

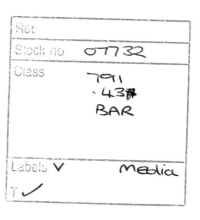

EALING STUDIOS

Charles Barr

CAMERON & HOLLIS
Moffat

A Movie Book

Published by Cameron & Hollis
the publishing imprint of Cameron Books
PO Box 1, Moffat
Dumfriesshire DG10 9SU, Scotland
www.cameronbooks.co.uk
Telephone: 01683 220808
Fax: 01683 220012

Copyright © Movie 1977, 1993, 1998
First edition 1977
Reprinted in paperback 1980
Second edition 1993
Third edition 1998

*British Library Cataloguing-in-Publication
Data*
A catalogue record for this book is
available from the British Library

ISBN 0-906506-11-5

Edited and designed by Ian Cameron

Filmset by SX Composing, Rayleigh,
and Cameron Books, Moffat

Printed and bound in Britain by
MPG Books, Bodmin

Stills appear by courtesy of E.M.I. Elstree
Studios Limited, M.G.M. and the
National Film Archive.

Title spread: Alec Guinness in The Man in
the White Suit.

1977 Acknowledgements
Though this book deals with the films
themselves, and not in any detail with
Ealing as a community or a business
organisation, I am indebted to several
people for their generous help in talking
to me of their work there, and providing
useful background material on the way
Ealing operated: Sir Michael Balcon,
Monja Danischewsky, Thorold
Dickinson, Diana Morgan, and among
actors Derek Bond, Gordon Jackson and
Ralph Michael. I am grateful for other
kinds of insight and information to John
Cutts, John Ellis, Alan Robinson, and
Geoff Brown; and to Sam Rohdie, then
editor of Screen, for encouraging the
work on Ealing published there in 1974
under the title 'Projecting Britain and the
British Character', in effect a first sketch
for the book.
    Then there are three acknowledgements
for technical help going beyond the
requirement of duty. To Jeremy Boulton,
Gillian Hartnoll, and other staff of the
Archive and Information sections of the
British Film Institute; to Jack Middleton,
formerly of Ealing, now Head of Library
Services at E.M.I., for his rapid response
to all requests for help with film viewing
and stills; and to Ian Cameron, for
encouraging this project over several
years, and for some distinctly creative
editing.

1993 Acknowledgements
Since the original publication, I have
benefited from talking at various times to
other Ealing people: T.E.B. Clarke and
Harry Watt (both alas now dead, like
Balcon, Dickinson and Gordon Jackson),
Sidney Cole, Michael Relph, Pat Jackson
and Charles Crichton. Even though none
are quoted in the new final chapter, their
comments have contributed to the
perspective of that chapter, and I hope
that one day they may be used more fully.
I am indebted to Tim Bergfelder for
helping to change my view of *They Came
to a City*. Some further acknowledgements
are specified in the postscript to the new
chapter.

CONTENTS

PROJECTING BRITAIN

In 1929, shortly after sound came to the cinema, the theatre director Basil Dean formed a company to produce films; he called it Associated Talking Pictures. The company's start was promising, and Dean raised the money to build a studio for it. The site chosen was at Ealing Green, in the London borough of Ealing. Construction began and finished in the same year, 1931.

In the next seven years, some 60 feature films were made at Ealing. Half of them were made by Dean's company, ATP, the rest by other companies who simply rented studio space. In publicity, neither set of films was particularly associated with the name Ealing, any more than the products of the nearby Shepherd's Bush studio were known as Shepherd's Bush films: like ATP's, they were given the label not of the studio location but of the producing company, Gainsborough. Gainsborough's head of production at that time was Michael Balcon.

In the late 'thirties, ATP's fortunes declined. Dean left in 1938 to return to the theatre. Ealing was now one of several studios in a precarious position, faced by financial problems, and with the international situation making it hard to plan for the future. Balcon, too, was at a difficult point in his career. After several productive years running both Gainsborough and Gaumont British, with directors like Alfred Hitchcock and Victor Saville working for him, he had been signed up by the American Louis B. Mayer to run the British end of his production. Although the three films made in this new MGM outpost—*A Yank at Oxford*, *The Citadel* and *Goodbye Mr Chips*—had a considerable success, Balcon hated the experience and left as soon as he could, setting up a programme of independent productions, of which the first was to be *The Gaunt Stranger*. No longer having a base of his own, he needed somewhere to shoot it. Ealing provided this. One of the directors of ATP was an old associate of his, Reginald Baker. Very soon, Balcon was invited to take charge of production, filling the place left vacant by Dean.

The studio kept going, employing a combination of people already at Ealing and others whom Balcon brought in with him. To mark this fresh start, there was some juggling with names. Ealing Studios Ltd, a subsidiary of ATP, had hitherto been the company which formally owned the place. Now, ATP was phased out, and Ealing became a *production* company. What might appear to be no more than a boardroom technicality has a wider significance: films were now made not only at Ealing but *by* Ealing, so that it makes sense to use the word as an adjective: Ealing films, Ealing comedies.

Ealing comedies! Surely those come ten years later? The release in quick succession in 1949 of *Passport to Pimlico*, *Whisky Galore* and *Kind Hearts and Coronets* seemed to inaugurate a cycle. Of the eight or nine films which are still, like these, readily identified with the Ealing Comedy label, all except *Kind Hearts* belong very much to both the landscape and the mood of post-war Britain; it is from them that our whole image of Ealing derives.

Asked to invent a typical Ealing comedy plot, one might produce something like this. A big brewery tries to absorb a small competitor, a family firm which is celebrating its 150th anniversary. The offer is gallantly refused, whereupon the boss's son goes incognito from the big firm to infiltrate the small one and sabotage its fortunes. Gradually, he is charmed by the family brewery and by the daughter of the house, saves the company from ruin, and marries into it. Officials and workers unite at the wedding banquet to drink the couple's health in a specially created brew.

To make this really Ealing, lay on the contrasts. The brewery names: Ironside against Greenleaf. Grim offices and black limousines against country lanes, ivy-covered cottages, horses, bicycles. Autocratic rule against the benevolent paternalism of a grey-haired old man who collects Toby Jugs. The beer itself: quantity against quality, machines against craftsmanship. The people and their manners: very harsh, very gentle. Small is beautiful.

This, it will be guessed, is no invention. The film is called *Cheer Boys Cheer*, and Balcon produced it at Ealing in 1939. Whether we should call it an Ealing comedy is a nice academic point. It is a comedy made at Ealing, scripted by Roger Macdougall who, a decade later, would write the much more celebrated *The Man in the White Suit;* it may be less confusing to reserve the actual Ealing comedy label for the set of post-war comedies, that one included, to which historically it has been applied. But *Cheer Boys Cheer* is certainly a startling fore-runner, a reminder that those later films were not a sudden inspiration but had roots and precedents.

Ironside heavies break up a Greenleaf pub in Cheer Boys Cheer.

The celebration of the little man, of the small-scale enterprise, is a traditional theme not confined to Ealing or to England; one need only refer to Frank Capra's Hollywood comedies of the 'thirties. But the *form* of the conflict in this film is rooted in a specifically English tradition that goes back at least to Dickens. Not only did he set idealised small businesses (e.g. in 'Nicholas Nickleby', 'Dombey and Son') against a soulless wider world of commerce, but the very name Greenleaf is a Dickensian one: it belongs to the cheerful little school in 'Bleak House' where Esther Summerson spends six happy years. All the rural associations in the film are a part of this English tradition and are of exactly the kind to be called into play in times of patriotic self-awareness. *Cheer Boys Cheer* was released in August 1939. Greenleaf can clearly stand for England, Ironside for Germany: the verbal reference is implicit, and at one point we are shown the bullying chairman of Ironside studying an unexpurgated edition of '*Mein Kampf*'.

If, at one level, Greenleaf is England, a second correspondence is equally striking. The Greenleaf Brewery is like Ealing Studios:

'This small production centre was little known at the time. It somehow had the air of a family business, set on the village green of the queen of the London suburbs . . . The administrative block which faced the green looked like a country cottage and was separated from the studios by a neat little rose garden.'

This was Monja Danischewsky's impression of Ealing when Balcon appointed him head of publicity at the studio in 1938. In Balcon's own autobiography, his move from MGM to Ealing reads very much in Greenleaf/Ironside terms, with Louis B. Mayer as an autocratic Ironside, surrounded by a similar bunch of yes-men, from whom he escapes with relief 'to . . . the happiest and most rewarding period of my working life: to work in the little house near the studio entrance where my office was a small pine-panelled room leading onto a suburban garden, complete with beehive, for one of my colleagues was a keen apiarist . . .'

Like the Brewery, Ealing was physically small and happy to keep its operations to this scale: it would normally make between four and seven features a year. The 'benevolent paternalism' which characterised Greenleaf was equally found in Balcon's running of Ealing. Insiders and visitors alike remarked upon Ealing's 'family' atmosphere. On the walls was the slogan, 'The Studio with the Team Spirit'. For the film-makers whom Balcon employed, job satisfaction and security commonly made up for the modesty of the pay; the symbol of the Ealing system became the Round Table at which, every week, producers, writers and directors consulted freely together. The values acknowledged were those of quality and craftsmanship. Finally, it does not seem fortuitous that the Greenleaf firm should be a brewery. No-one's reminiscences of Ealing fail to mention the amount of convivial drinking that went on there.

Of course, at the time of *Cheer Boys Cheer*, this lay largely in the future: the Ealing identity, system and atmosphere had yet to be consolidated. But Greenleaf is prophetic of the way it would go.

Balcon's Ealing lasted for twenty years. In a business notorious for size and instability, for a rapid turnover of money, ideas and people, Ealing succeeded in keeping itself small and stable. Balcon fought a long campaign against the Ironside of the British industry, Rank, before accepting (like Greenleaf) a 'marriage' favourable to Ealing: the company was left free to go on making films entirely on its own terms, while Rank gave financial backing and a guarantee to release all the films as first features in Rank cinemas. This deal was made in 1944 and carried Ealing through the unstable postwar decade without the need for any structural change. At the heart of the British industry there remained, character-ised by its cottage in a garden on a village green, this anomalous 'family business'.

In 1955, the deal with Rank ended, and the studios at Ealing were sold. However, Balcon made a new deal with MGM and continued to make Ealing films in a section of their British studios at Borehamwood. The last was completed in 1958. In all, Balcon's name is on nearly a hundred Ealing features made in these twenty years. For most of this time, his staff remained substantially the same. The film-making team was built up in the early stages of the war, and many of its members stayed on with the company until it ceased operation. Both the broad policy and the operation of the studio remained the same over the whole period.

The result was a set of films expressing a tight continuity over a period of twenty years. They form a body of work that is unique—and I am not using the word carelessly. Not that a twenty-year continuity is in itself unheard of: the *Carry On* series has already lasted nearly that long, and the careers of many individual directors have gone on for much longer, as have the operations of some large studios. Ealing merges, pulls together, all these kinds of continuity. The films are not all made to a uniform pattern like the *Carry On* series: less than a third of them, despite the stereotype of Ealing, are even comedies. They are not the product of one man: Balcon never directed a foot of film himself, and part of his system was to let people follow through their own projects within a broadly agreed programme. A possible comparison is with some of the Holly-wood studios at times when their output bore a consistent and recognisable imprint, in form and content alike—perhaps Warner or Columbia in the 'thirties. Ealing remains distinctive, first, for the particular way the collaborative system operated, giving the films a consistent communal viewpoint but not an inflexible one, and, second, for the role which it played in British culture.

When the studio was sold in 1955, Balcon wrote the inscription for a plaque erected there: 'Here during a quarter of a century many films were made pro-jecting Britain and the British character.' It was not an afterthought. Balcon also records in his autobiography:

'Early in 1939 I put my thoughts on paper in the form of a memorandum which might have been called "How to put film to work in the national interest in wartime", and sent it to the proper quarter.'

Although at that time 'its impact on Whitehall was nil', Balcon went ahead at Ealing on his own account and waited for official thinking to catch up with him. Early in 1945 in a trade magazine, he looked ahead to the requirements of the postwar world: 'Clearly the need is great for a projection of the true Briton to the rest of the world.' And again his postwar work at Ealing was in line with this policy.

Another concept Balcon uses is that of reflection. Films can, if they choose, have the power of reflecting reality, and his films aimed to reflect the events and moods of those twenty years. It is a concept which criticism often takes up: films reflect their times (Raymond Durgnat's book on postwar British cinema is called 'A Mirror for England'). Projection, reflection: both are deceptively neutral-looking words describing optical processes by which a given image is made available to perception. The film camera itself operates in a mechanical way, recording what it is pointed at. It would be easy to slip into saying that, given Ealing's intentions, the films can be taken to reflect and project some kind of universal truth about the England of the time: a truth which is there, and which they express. But as Norman Longmate has observed, protesting against the historian who relies on Dickens for *factual* evidence about Victorian life, fiction departs from fact: that is its nature. Even the recording faculty of the camera may capture only superficial aspects of a period—buildings, style of dress, and so on. However, the concepts of projection and reflection can still be useful. The films at least project their makers' picture of Britain and the British character. And the status of the cinema as a mass medium (more so then than now: cinema admissions reached their peak in the immediate postwar years) means that films, if they gain any success, will do so by reflecting *back* to a wide audience something of itself, whether conscious or not: a mood, conflict, need, aspiration of some kind, put into dramatic form. To this extent, they stand as 'evidence', if nothing else (taking it a stage back, in the case of an unsuccessful film) as evidence of what the producers *thought* would mean something to the audience or of what meant something to the producers themselves. But at Ealing, the instinct of Balcon and his colleagues for gauging the feelings of an audience—or, it may be, the coincidence of their feelings with those of that audience—was reliable enough to keep the studio buoyant into the 'fifties; indeed, to be regarded by this time as something of a national institution.

But in what sense 'national'? What impression can one form of the Ealing team and the Ealing audience? In an essay on the Festival of Britain, Michael Frayn makes a distinction between two elements in our social and cultural life which he calls the Herbivore and the Carnivore.

'Festival Britain was the Britain of the radical middle-classes—the do-gooders; the readers of the News Chronicle, The Guardian and The Observer; the signers of petitions; the backbone of the BBC. In short, the Herbivores, or gentle ruminants . . .'

By 1951, the brasher values of the Carnivores—typified in the Daily Express as against the News Chronicle, in the incoming Conservative as against the outgoing Labour governments—were taking over. Here is another of Frayn's lists:

'The Festival was the last, and virtually the posthumous, work of the Herbivore Britain of the B.B.C. News, the Crown Film Unit, the sweet ration, the Ealing Comedies, Uncle Mac, Sylvia Peters . . . all the great fixed stars by which my childhood was navigated.'

The mention of Ealing is apt: 1951 is its last really buoyant year. After *The Lavender Hill Mob* and *The Man in the White Suit,* both released in the course of it, all the remaining comedies have a decadent or backward-looking character.

'For a decade, sanctioned by the exigencies of war and its aftermath, the Herbivores had dominated the scene'—the perspective in which Frayn places the events of 1951 answers to the time-span of Ealing: it is precisely this decade during which the studio flourishes in responding to, and making films about, 'the exigencies of war and its aftermath'. Ealing is indeed a part of this loose 'Herbivore' consensus (the very term like an echo of 'Greenleaf') which Frayn evokes, moulded by the same forces, then stranded and broken up in the 'fifties by the same forces, including its own resistance to change.

Talking to John Ellis, Balcon characterised the Ealing 'creative elite':

'By and large we were a group of liberal-minded, like-minded people . . . we were middle-class people brought up with middle-class backgrounds and rather conventional educations . . . We voted Labour for the first time after the war: this was our mild revolution.'

Compare Frayn on the Festival:

'There was almost no-one of working-class background concerned in planning the Festival, and nothing about the result to suggest that the working-classes were anything more than the lovably human but essentially inert objects of benevolent administration.'

A fair evocation of the role they occupy in many Ealing films. And here, finally, is Frayn on Sir Gerald Barry, the Festival's Director-General·

'The tone of the Festival was not unlike the tone of the News Chronicle, which he had edited for eleven years—philanthropic, kindly, whimsical, cosy, optimistic, middlebrow . . .'

Again there is the familiar time-span stretching back to the start of the war. And the adjectives are exactly those which occur in people's generalisations about Ealing.

Ealing, then, is the voice of a certain consensus: one voice among many. But the films of Balcon's Ealing are documents of a different order to the files of Barry's News Chronicle. They provide the most enduring and complex testimony to these values—complex because expressed and discussed in dramatic terms, and by individuals whose sensibilities, within their common background,

Reflecting postwar Britain? The bomb-site of Passport to Pimlico: *communal feeding, communal benevolence.*

varied widely. There is another factor, already touched on: the relation between the stories told on the screen and the experience of the studio itself.

Greenleaf, England, Ealing: the three were almost interchangeable, and this structure of parallels was sustained over the years. Of course, plenty of films were made elsewhere about communities in action, communities which may plainly stand for England, especially England at war. Good wartime examples, ones to return to, are the Noel Coward and David Lean film *In Which We Serve* and Asquith's significantly titled *Demi-Paradise*. They are made by groups of film-makers operating in the conventional hierarchic way: a 'team', admittedly, but not a community. Ealing makes films about community and co-operation—the central themes of the cinema of the 'forties, and not only of the cinema—from the inside. This doesn't make their films better, but it gives a special intensity to their evocation and analysis.

Two examples among many can illustrate what I mean. *Cage of Gold* is a drama made at Ealing in 1950. The heroine (Jean Simmons) is torn between two suitors: a dashing ex-RAF officer, who is involved in grandiose business schemes after the war, and a serious young doctor. In turn, the doctor has to make his choice of career: between taking on his father's practice in Battersea, within the new National Health Service, and joining a smart private practice in Harley Street. The person who keeps pressing on him the partnership in Harley Street is referred to as Dr Saville. One of his National Health Service colleagues is a Dr Mackendrick: 'I watched Mackendrick operate today. Wonderful job he made of it.' This not very common name belonged to one of Ealing's leading young directors, Alexander Mackendrick. And Victor Saville was a long-time associate of Balcon, who took over from him as head of MGM production in Britain and then became a powerful figure in Hollywood.

Clearly the names represent a private joke inside Ealing which general audiences would not recognise: what is significant is that the joke can be formulated in these terms, with names that fit so well. There were repeated attempts from the late 'forties to lure people away from Ealing, not least Mackendrick; he finally went to America in 1956 to make *Sweet Smell of Success*. They had to choose, like the doctor, between loyalty and roots on the one hand and prosperity and glamour on the other. In both cases, a sense of *duty* is called strongly into play. For the doctor: towards his father, the practice, and the new Health Service. For the film-maker: towards Balcon, the studio, and the 'responsible' side of the film industry to which Ealing belonged—the strength of this pressure at Ealing is well attested.

The doctor chooses the family practice, and the girl chooses him. They settle down modestly in an old, dark house, with his father and their child, reconciled to family solidarity and socially responsible work. All kinds of undercurrent operate in the film, forcing up into the heroine's consciousness an awareness of what this cosy kind of dispensation is repressing. These are very revealing and will be worth exploring in context; the point to stress here is the solidity of the basic correspondence. I don't mean that this film or any other is to be seen as a *film à clef*, one with a private message to yield up about what life was like in the studio, and that it is not fully understandable without that key. But this 'Ealing' dimension is still important. The film dramatises questions of ambition and security, austerity and glamour, co-operation and competition, which were vividly present both in British society as a whole at this time, five years after the war, and in the small society of Ealing.

Jean Simmons in an early scene of Cage of Gold, *caught between the doctor (James Donald) and her own painting of the airman (David Farrar).*

It is open to any company of the time to make films about these issues, or about the NHS in particular. But film-makers don't usually lead very modest or self-denying lives. They have already chosen glamour rather than a steady job: they don't commonly travel by bus or use the National Health Service if they can avoid it. It is precisely because it is still *living* the conflicts of *Cage of Gold* that Ealing is so topically drawn to them and expresses them with such evident empathy. The detail of the doctors' names here is a chance confirmation of the parallel, but it is one deeply inscribed into a series of films from *Cheer Boys Cheer* in 1939 to *Davy* in 1957.

Davy (Harry Secombe) is a comedian in a music hall act, the Mad Morgans, along with his uncle, sister, and brother-in-law. Between shows in a London suburb, he goes for an audition as a singer at Covent Garden, and is offered a job. But can he let down the family by leaving their act?

The film starts and ends with an extended performance of this rather tatty family act, set within a music hall tradition which it must already have been apparent was dying. Most of the time in between is spent in family arguments in the dressing room. Davy's querulous old uncle is played by George Relph, who was Archie Rice's father in the original production of John Osborne's play 'The Entertainer'. The music hall of 'The Entertainer' is an overt image for the England of its time; *Davy* offers a close parallel, with its family structure and with the attempt, in the act, to spin out a nostalgic communal gaiety which can

11

now only seem artificial and desperate. Davy has, of course, choked back his ambitions and slipped back into the family:
'I think we should all stick together, don't you? All families should stick together. Everything will be just the same then.'

The difference between the two works is one of viewpoint and distance. The impetus of Osborne's play is clearly a sense of what England amounts to in the late 'fifties, after Suez, which is a constant point of reference. *Davy* lacks this explicit dimension. Its impetus, deliberate or not, is the plight of Ealing, struggling to hold together after the move of their headquarters to Borehamwood. 'All families should stick together.' Michael Relph (director) and Basil Dearden (producer) have been with Balcon (executive producer) since before the war. George Relph, the actor, is the director's own father, and several others in the cast are Ealing veterans. The writer is William Rose, who will soon leave for Hollywood as his main Ealing collaborator, Mackendrick, has already done. The Ealing operation will cease after only three more films, but within the film the continuation of the act is asserted, the chance to go on to something new rejected. In fact, there isn't any discrepancy felt between the fate of the act and that of the studio—the act is so clearly doomed, the choice on Davy's part so clearly a quixotic one. Indeed, the act seems to have doomed itself by refusing any change, by insisting so rigidly on loyalty: in the uncle's words, 'You don't desert a family act, it's just not the thing to do.' Without imposing too facile an identification, one can surely hear Balcon's voice behind lines like this. He had committed Ealing to go on making films of the same type, with the same team, rather than make any adaptation to changing times and a changing industry.

Osborne, then, writes about a national stagnation and decay which Ealing partakes of, expresses from within: 'The Entertainer' and *Davy* are perfectly complementary, equally expressive of their time. This is not to be patronising about Ealing. It is the natural end of a twenty year cycle in which it has remained true to itself, consistent in its relation to a certain national culture. The exhaustion of this culture, of the Music Hall act in *Davy*, of Ealing itself, are bound up together. Appropriately, *Davy* is one of Ealing's dullest films on any level. At the end of the 'fifties, Ealing is making films about stagnation and weariness in a style that partakes of those qualities. By the same token, in its earlier days, Ealing expressed more dynamic moods in a fresher style. It is time to return to the beginning.

INTO THE WAR

'The movies seem almost unaffected by the war, i.e. in technique and subject-matter. They go on and on with the same treacly rubbish, and when they do touch on politics they are years behind the popular press and decades behind the average book.'

(George Orwell, writing in April 1941)

Orwell never discusses individual films, and one doesn't know what he has seen, but at first sight his comment seems valid. The film business, like many institutions, was slow in making what seems in retrospect a worthy response to the war, just as it had been timid in dealing with the great issues of the 'thirties. Orwell's complaint is like that of Balcon, who had been one of the busiest producers of the pre-war years: 'Hardly a film of the period reflects the agony of those times.'

Most of the British war films which are now remembered date from 1942 or later. This is true of Ealing, and the date corresponds to an important stage in Balcon's operations there. One set of directors had worked for him in the short term, from 1938; now a new set was taking over. Gradually supplemented, this would form the nucleus of his directing team for 15 years. It looks as though it had taken Balcon until around 1942 to pick and train a team which could respond to Britain's war experience with the type of inspirational feature most appropriate to it—films like *The Foreman Went to France, Nine Men*, and *San Demetrio London*, which embody classic British qualities of team spirit and good-humoured doggedness.

But this is an over-simplification: it is not that there was a certain type of worthy film waiting to be made which Ealing eventually reached the point of being able to produce. Rather, these mid-war films mark a decisive point in a process of change at many levels: in the official conduct of the war, in the place found for the commercial cinema within this, in the whole war experience of the nation—as well as in the workings of Ealing itself. Nor does change at Ealing merely happen to coincide with these national developments: it is closely bound up with them and is part of them. The broad congruency between the Ealing community and the 'national community' is already operating: both come together in time of war. To look at the films in sequence is to be forced to cut through the familiar sentimentalities about the 'timeless sense of unity' of the nation at war and to consider the genesis of this feeling and the obstacles it had to overcome.

We need to look at the early films in a spirit other than George Orwell's. The remarks quoted at the head of the chapter reveal a surprisingly narrow approach

Left: Harry Secombe as Davy. *Music Hall act, Covent Garden audition.*

to the cinema. Indeed, it is curious that (while evidently going to the cinema himself) Orwell should never engage seriously with its products, even on the level at which he discusses comic papers or comic postcards. Perhaps this is because he can't work out where the cinema stands, between these artefacts for mass consumption and the self-expression of an individual through the written word. Films rarely deal as directly with 'politics' as do books or the press: their response to the times, their reflection of and on events, is generally of a different order. A more useful text here will be Orwell's own famous evocation of England in 'The Lion and the Unicorn' (1942):

'England . . . is a family in which the young are generally thwarted and most of the power is in the hands of irresponsible uncles and bedridden aunts. Still, it is a family. It has its private language and its common memories, and at the approach of an enemy it closes its ranks.'

Irresponsible uncles and bedridden aunts: immediately this evokes some of the dominant figures of British cinema. Alistair Sim, A. E. Matthews, James Robertson Justice; Margaret Rutherford, Joyce Grenfell, and those little old ladies who exert their castrating powers over so many films, most memorably Ealing's *The Ladykillers* (1955).

The other parts of the formula, too, are well illustrated over the years. It makes a particularly apt text for what the British cinema does during the war—especially Ealing, which plays such a central and sustained role within that cinema.

Inheriting Dean's contract with him, Balcon made five George Formby comedies in quick succession. (I use the word 'made' as a convenient shorthand: it will cover varying degrees of involvement on Balcon's part. On the Formby films, this involvement was evidently small). The rest of his pre-war films at Ealing—in fact, all the first twelve non-Formby films—were directed by three men: Walter Forde, Robert Stevenson, and Penrose Tennyson. Then, abruptly, others took over. Soon, Formby went elsewhere. The permanent Ealing 'team' began to emerge. It would be wrong, however, to present the early films simply as the Before stage in a Before and After transformation.

The Formby comedies represent a tradition which links Balcon's Ealing with Dean's and survives their star's departure. Like the Gracie Fields films, which were also made by Dean, they have a different feel from later Ealing comedy, much more vulgar (in a way that can be bracing to return to, after a surfeit of the later films), but there is a continuity in the values of the small community which they celebrate: like the Greenleaf community of *Cheer Boys Cheer*, they depict, in Orwell's description, a family with a private language. At the time, Ealing did not turn its back on 'low' music hall forms of comedy, as Balcon brought in both Will Hay and Tommy Trinder and made a succession of films with them.

Forde, Stevenson and Tennyson were also hired by Balcon; they were all long-term associates who worked in close partnership with him. The departure of the first two may retrospectively seem appropriate, as it left the way clear for more committed successors of 'purer' Ealing stock with their careers still waiting to be shaped—of Ealing's post-1940 group of directors, only Cavalcanti had made features before coming to Ealing. Forde had already had a career in America, and soon returned there; Stevenson, a pacifist, went to Hollywood at the start of the war. But Tennyson, a protegé of Balcon's, would certainly have played a leading role in Ealing's development had he lived. Instead, he was called up and died in a plane crash in 1941.

Of the dozen films the three made between them, only one, Tennyson's *Convoy*, is a straight war film; few of them reflect in any direct way 'the agony of the time'; several are based on theatre originals in a way that few Ealing films would be in later years. Some have worn badly, especially among Forde's; but he also made *Cheer Boys Cheer*, and the twelve films amount to a vivid picture of the England which Orwell described: 'a family in which the young are generally thwarted and most of the power is in the hands of irresponsible uncles and bedridden aunts'—in fact, of old men more than ladies. In film after film, young people, for the most part predictably colourless ones, are frustrated by employers and fathers who are at best selfish, at worse vicious. This goes some way beyond the conventional drama of the generation gap.

Obviously, a sinister authority figure in a film of the late 'thirties can stand for Nazism. Early 1939 saw the release of Ealing's *Four Just Men*, not the first film to be based on the book by Edgar Wallace. Reviews of the time recognised the adaptation as being angled to 'hit Britain's current mood of defensive defiance' and present the nation as the 'defier of dictators'. As we have seen, *Cheer Boys Cheer* operates in the same way, with the Ironside boss explicitly presented as a Nazi sympathiser. Yet he remains English, boss of an English

Traitors in high places, victims of The Four Just Men. *Alan Napier, Basil Sydney.*

firm, father of an English son. It is a significant ambiguity, making the film more complex than it might seem. We can't just take the easy way out of reading Ironside as Germany, Greenleaf as England. Nazism is related to certain forms of class and money power, of monopoly capitalism, which are shown operating in the very English industry of brewing. So far from failing to 'reflect the times', then, this whimsical comedy dramatises one of the key issues: the question of how to mobilise opposition to the dictators of the 'thirties when so many political and business leaders in our own society appeared unable, because of their place in that society and their whole system of values, to express such an opposition whole-heartedly—witness the official attitude to the Spanish Civil War and the length of time it took for the concept of 'premature' anti-Fascism to be abandoned. It is interesting that Orwell, who had fought in that war, makes the central concern of his journalism early in World War II how to fight the war properly, given the nature of the governing class. Meanwhile pictures like *Cheer Boys Cheer* can refer to these issues in a way that is no less expressive for being oblique.

Robert Stevenson's Ealing films offer a very bitter picture of the ruling class. Clive Brook in *The Ware Case* is a spendthrift baronet whose aristocratic grace allows him literally to get away with murder, charming alike the jury and the crowds who line the street to cheer him. He is a 'museum piece' who only ceases to be an obstacle in the path of the film's young people by sacrificing himself at the end—nothing in his life becomes him like leaving it. One thinks of the country's elected, and hereditary, leaders of the time: Clive Brook has the right arrogance and expects the right kind of deference. *The Ware Case* is stiff and stagebound, as if made by its main character as his own obituary; the new generation is weak, paralysed. Much more powerful is Stevenson's next film, *A Young Man's Fancy* (1939).

It is set in 1870. The young lovers visit Paris and are trapped there by the advance of the Prussian army. But the topical anti-German associations have small weight beside the conflict of generations in London. Aristocracy, recapitulating centuries of British history, plans a merger with business wealth: the hero's

Left: Clive Brook with Glen Alyn in The Ware Case. *Right: Griffith Jones and Anna Lee as the lovers in* A Young Man's Fancy.

parents give a party to announce his engagement to the daughter of a brewer. But the young aristocrat rebels and finds a working-class girl. They run off, have their Paris adventures, but return: it seems that parental choice will prevail after all. As in *The Ware Case*, it comes down in the end to the aristocrat himself. Braving his wife's rage, he turns the son away from the church door and back to true love.

Though this film also has its stagey and conventional aspects, it is admirably sharp where it matters, in its analysis of class and family conflicts. The hero to his imposed fiancée, coldly, not joking:

'You remind me of my mother.'

'You needn't pay me compliments.'

'I wasn't.'

At the end of their time in Paris, the lovers wonder how they will survive a return to the realities of home. While he insists 'I'll never change my mind,' she recalls the details of the life they have shared, which will come to seem 'so far away': 'Oh, let's enjoy this minute before it goes. It's slipping away so fast. It's behind us already, it's gone, it's gone . . .'

Already at the words 'so fast', images crowd in and force the lovers' faces off the screen in a long dissolve into rails, station names, images of England, then a reception committee which swallows them up. The whole passage of which this is the climax has a romantic concentration, a delirium, which belongs to a British poetic tradition but has been very rare indeed in British films—unlike American ones. One of the few films which do offer any kind of parallel is *The Faithful Heart*, which Stevenson wrote in 1932; Victor Saville directed it for a Balcon company. It seems likely that Stevenson's Hollywood career, latterly for Disney, would reward attention, and it is interesting to speculate on what might have resulted if he had stayed longer at Ealing. Far from pulling the film out of shape, the romanticism of *A Young Man's Fancy* gives the class analysis its dynamism. It is a quality which Ealing will not recapture. Indeed, losing it seems a natural part of the process of maturing into the solid, reliable, Ealing which we know and love, or detest, or both. A phrase which has haunted me in working on this book is Ernest Bevin's remark that the British people (during the Ealing years) suffered from a 'poverty of desire': it reverberates on so many levels, from social to sexual, and the films—not only Ealing's—offer so many illustrations of it. Desire, the intensity of feeling caught in *A Young Man's Fancy*, is habitually damped down into a more muted and resigned sense of loss: the romantic mode of *Brief Encounter*.

I need hardly say that this is a profound cultural issue to which a study of Ealing has to keep returning. 'Poverty of desire' comes to form an inevitable accompaniment to—no, it is deeper than that: constituent of—the notions of social responsibility and community which the British cinema, in the war years and after, so assiduously reflects and promotes. The first Ealing films which seriously explore these notions are directed by Penrose Tennyson.

If it is tempting to speculate about Stevenson, it is still more so about Tennyson, whose career, with that of Michael Reeves, is the great might-have-been of British cinema. Both men died while still in their twenties, after making three feature films, the last of which was a big commercial success (*Convoy, Witchfinder General*). Behind the very different character of their works lies a commitment to the cinema of a kind that has been rare in Britain, especially from those who (unlike, say, Hitchcock) have a background of public school, family wealth, and

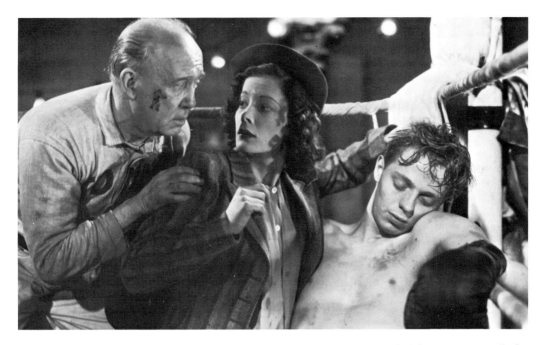

Honesty under pressure in the fight game. James Hanley tended between rounds by his 'good angel' (Jill Furse) and his trainer, in There Ain't No Justice.

access to 'high' culture. Of course, their early death has something to do with their appeal: the reputation of the similarly precocious Anthony Asquith would stand higher than it does had he made no film after the age of 30. Tennyson was the great-grandson of Lord Alfred; like Reeves, he by-passed university (though he was briefly at Oxford) in order to go directly into films. Where Reeves, in the 'sixties, would address himself to Donald Siegel in Hollywood, Tennyson became a protegé of Balcon and worked as assistant to Hitchcock on *The Man who Knew too Much* and *The Thirty-Nine Steps*. He went with Balcon to MGM and then to Ealing, where at 26 he was immediately given the chance to direct.

Here the Reeves comparison can end: each set of films belongs closely to its own time. In fact, the British horror film tradition to which Reeves belongs is in such strong contrast to all Ealing stood for that one can make a link of a negative character. It is striking how close the coincidence is between the decline of Ealing and the rise of Hammer, with both taking place from the mid-'fifties to 1958, the year which sees both the release of *Dracula* and the end of Ealing production. Hammer's films are like the explosion of forces which have been rigidly repressed in the post-war years. Reeves, though working for others, comes in the wake of Hammer's revolution, making films which are certainly not characterised by restraint. Tennyson is involved in the beginning of the Ealing tradition, the most influential director in laying the foundation for what it became.

His three films exactly span the outbreak of war. The second, *Proud Valley*, was half way through shooting on the day war was declared and had its ending changed for patriotic reasons. The third, *Convoy*, was the studio's first war film.

The first of the three, *There Ain't No Justice*, is a modest second feature. Its very modesty, as a small film by a new director aiming at quality on a budget little higher than that of a 'quota quickie', is a significant Ealing ploy. The opening title states a commitment, and hints at the closeness of film-maker to hero:

'This film is dedicated to the small-time boxer, who has for too long been at the mercy of both managers and public. If it in any way helps those who are struggling to improve his lot, we shall be more than happy.'

The villain of the piece combines the roles of manager and promoter. Like the aristocrats of the two Stevenson films (and like the theatre manager of a third, *Return to Yesterday*), he is an authority figure who ruthlessly blocks the hero's aspirations, using the familiar routines of fight-fixing. The introductory title also implies a sinister role for the public. In the film, there is little sense of this, except insofar as people go to watch boxing at all; but the words don't say boxing should be abolished, only that life should be made better for the individual boxer. The audience is even active, at the end, on behalf of the hero, Tommy. But having won his fight and foiled the manager, Tommy abandons the game and returns to a steady job in his own community.

It is hard, then, to see what impetus the film can give to 'improving the lot' of the boxer: it seems rather to encourage him to get out of what is a dirty business run by crooks, and back into a less ambitious and more rooted community. The London neighbourhood is presented with real warmth: we first see it, and meet Tommy's family, at a local dance which culminates in 'Knees Up Mother Brown'. The father is a pigeon-fancier and runs a pony and cart business. The film sets this working-class community against the world of the impresario, the dancehall against a modern milkbar (also with a hard manager), the homely local girl against a sexy blonde provided by the promoter. At the end, as Tommy renounces boxing and kisses the right girl, the 'Knees Up' tune returns again on the soundtrack. It is a pleasant, predictable resolution, implying the rejection of a whole 'commercial' world in favour of these community values; and the tension thus created with the film's overt aim is characteristic of early Ealing. Broadly: as a committed patriotic enterprise, it believes in individual integrity and community loyalty and would like not only to create a studio, but to show a society, which can run by these values. But society doesn't in fact seem to do so, and it requires too big an effort of will to depict it as doing so. *Cheer Boys Cheer,* where the Greenleaf values conquer the Ironside ones, is essentially a fantasy, to which *There Ain't no Justice* is the more realistic counterpart. Both are in effect retreats (in no dishonourable sense) into communities which are restricted, cut off, like the regional ones of the Formby and Fields films that were so strong a feature of the immediate studio background.

The Proud Valley is a film on a quite different scale of resources, ambition and substance. Its community is a mining one, in South Wales, which is joined by a migrant black worker. He, and through him the audience, are caught up in the life of this society: work, home life, the choir.

The name of the character, played by Paul Robeson, has great resonance: it is David Goliath. The strength of the underdog—but you can take it two ways, and the tension between the two is central to Ealing. A weak sense: the underdog is strong in his own values, the little man is the salt of the earth. Or, the strong sense: the underdog can prevail. He can impose his will, communicate his values to the rest of society. But how can the film dramatise this, given the conflict of interests between masters and men?

An underground explosion closes the pit, killing, among others, Mr Parry, choirmaster and head of the family with whom David lives. The owners are remote, in London, and communicate only by letter. They welcome the excuse this disaster gives them to keep the place closed indefinitely. The community starts to fall apart, and the exploiters within it to declare themselves. All the familiar warm rituals of this kind of picture—massed choirs, family high teas, anxious pithead gatherings—are linked to economic realities. A year later, people are picking lumps from the slagheaps. Any sentimental solidarity has dropped away, leaving a bedrock of what is genuine.

In the original version of the script, what happens now is that the nucleus of the unemployed miners defy the owners by opening up the pit and working it themselves. This is certainly the logic of the picture, if the 'David Goliath' idea is to have any strength. Not surprisingly, Ealing ran into problems. No mining company would give location facilities. What caused Ealing to rethink the end of the film was, it seems, not this opposition but the approach of the war. Studio shooting began on 23rd August 1939, the day of the Nazi/Soviet pact and eleven days before war was finally declared. Looking back, Balcon writes of the planned ending:

'This was obviously neither tactful nor helpful propaganda when the country was at war, especially since in real life the miners had given a lead by reacting vigorously to the national call for greater production.'

In the film's terms, this seems a little off the point, the question rather being one of how the *owners* will respond. In fact, the film resolves its dilemma honourably and powerfully, not by the dropping of grievances which Balcon's words might imply. Instead of opening up the pit themselves, the men march to London and shame the owners into doing it for them. One of this deputation spells out the message:

'Coal in wartime is as much a part of national defence as guns or anything else—so why not let us take our chance down the pit?'

Proud Valley, then, becomes the first in the Ealing cycle of war-effort films which dramatise the contribution that a section of the nation, military or civilian, can make to the whole. From these and other people's films of England at war, we take away a composite image of national unity: officers and men, employers and workers pulling together for the communal good. But this was a type of film which had to be evolved; it didn't exist at the outbreak of the war any more than did the reality to which it referred. Even the accounts of the war years which insist most strongly that this feeling of national unity was more than a myth stress that it was not static or timeless but a function of specific forces early in the war. Thus A. J. P. Taylor refers to the middle years of the war as 'a brief period when the English people felt that they were a truly democratic community,' and the stress is as much on the brevity as on the feeling itself. Before this, he has spoken of 'The Government moving into war backwards with their eyes tightly closed,' and noted the internal divisions in, particularly, the coal industry. *Proud Valley* registers both the extent of the divisions and the will for change.

When the deputation set off for London, the whole village gathers to see them off with banners and singing. It is a moving expression of community feeling, directed solidly against the owners. To keep going on the march, they raise money by singing as they go—which recalls the title and spirit of the most celebrated of the Gracie Fields films, set in Lancashire during the Depression, *Sing as We Go*. As it approaches London, their march is intercut with a succession of newspaper placards announcing Hitler's actions. Before our eyes, we see

Paul Robeson as David Goliath, welcomed into the mining community of The Proud Valley; *with Rachel Thomas as Mrs Parry, Edward Chapman as Parry.*

hostility towards the owners being displaced on to Germany. Which summarises what in 1939 had to be done. This community spirit—the resilience of tightly knit societies, which Ealing is in touch with, partly through the continuity from the Fields and Formby comedies of the 'thirties—is there, an asset if ways can be found of exploiting it. But these were still early days. *Proud Valley* is too honest to present the co-operation of masters and men as anything beyond a necessity which has to be worked for. Things don't suddenly dissolve into sweetness and light, with everyone marching forward together. The same small group of men bear the brunt of the new effort in the mines, and the film ends with David sacrificing his life to save his fellow workers in a new accident.

The film's strength is that its sense of community—a concept that so easily lapses into staleness—is real and unidealised. A repeated device is to involve us with a group of people, absorbed together, then to have them startled, broken into by a 'voice off' which comes from outside the group, from offscreen. When David first arrives at the village, the choir is rehearsing. We stay with the rehearsal, indoors, up to the point when the bass part is cued and the voice of Paul Robeson is heard from offscreen, below in the street. It is a stirring set piece, the first thing which anyone who has seen the film recalls; it is also a sequence which balances two images: the group as exclusive (the shock his voice causes, the resentment some feel against the intruder), and the group as inclusive—a force for growth, not complacency—as shown in the harmony of David's contribution, the way in which (mainly through Parry, the choirmaster) he comes to be absorbed. This tension is the main structural principle of *Proud Valley* and underlies the whole of the Ealing output over the years.

Towards the end, we are with the mine-owners as they sit around the boardroom table, discussing in a detached way whether they ought to try opening up

Officers on the bridge in Convoy: *Clive Brook as the Captain, flanked by John Clements (left) and Stewart Granger.*

any pits. Now it is their turn to be interrupted by an offscreen voice, the deputation's answer: Yes. The device again dramatises not only their separateness, but also the potential unity which the film goes on, very tentatively, to show in action.

It was around this time that Balcon was himself knocking on official doors to try to get support for Ealing's way of helping the war effort. The words of the men's spokesman in *Proud Valley* need only slight adaptation in order to paraphrase Balcon's case: 'Films in wartime are as much a part of national defence as guns or anything else—so why not let us take our chance in the cinema?'

Early in the war, an official policy was to try closing down studios and cinemas altogether, partly because of their vulnerability to bombing. Second thoughts acknowledged that the psychological value of continued film-going outweighed the dangers and that there might actually be something in the idea that British films could be designed to serve a patriotic function. All the same, there was a sharp and inevitable decline in the number of studios active and of films produced. Ealing, which was already a compact studio, kept up its output and quickly acquired a semi-official status, turning out shorts for the Ministry of Information and other service and government departments. More importantly, it began making war features: one plus a war-based comedy in 1940 (*Sailors Three*, with Tommy Trinder outwitting a shipload of Germans), four plus two comedies in 1941 (its total feature production in that year). Apart from the comedies, the war features were made in consultation with official bodies. The first, *Convoy*, followed discussion with the Ministry of Information, and Tennyson prepared for it by taking part in operations at sea; the titles carry a long list of official credits in the style that would become familiar. At the same time, it was only partly an official project: it was made by Ealing people, in their way, with their money, as a commercial enterprise, and it became the most successful British film of its year. Other companies were making official shorts and individual war-effort pictures. Ealing's distinctiveness was in committing itself to a sustained programme and building up a permanent team of film-makers for the purpose.

Convoy, naturally, takes up the themes of unity and co-operation from the end of *Proud Valley*. Just as naturally, it can't yet dramatise them with complete conviction; it is a film split down the middle in an eloquent way. The co-operation is both between ships in the convoy, and between officers and men in a particular ship, on which class and personal differences are shelved in facing an enemy. Made in the early months of 1940, *Convoy* fits the Orwell idea of England as a family which 'has its own private language and its common memories, and at the approach of an enemy it closes its ranks.'

The private language. A seaman herding people on a lifeboat, however urgent the crisis, will call out 'Any more for the Skylark?' Another, loading a shell, writes on it 'To Goebbels with love'. Wounded men are offered 'a nice cup of tea'. Common memories: a merchant navy captain and the wife of a naval officer join in reciting Nelson's prayer from the Eve of Trafalgar. Then, the closing of ranks. All hostility is directed towards the Germans, specimens of whom are presented as objects for contempt. There are impressive moments of shipboard ritual and of collaboration between units, enacting the co-operative theme.

'Closing of ranks', however, can remain only the vaguest of metaphors: the hierarchy of ranks both in the ship and the society it represents is still steep. The hauteur of the officer class, laid bare in Ealing's pre-war films, can't suddenly be wished away, especially when the Captain is played, with his habitual presence, by Clive Brook, the aristocrat of *The Ware Case*. The other star among the officers is John Clements.

One way of following the shifts in Ealing production is through actors, in spite of the lack of respect with which many actors felt their craft was treated there— or perhaps because of this lack of respect. The main dissatisfaction was that they were typecast, and not stretched. Though few of them seem to have been admitted to the core of the Ealing community, several were under contract in the days before the link with the Rank Organisation, which had its own long list of contract players; a certain 'stock company' is always in evidence. Only occasionally—Alec Guinness in the postwar films—is an actor encouraged to vary roles creatively. Typecasting is the norm. Thus, the recurrence of an actor indicates a consistent factor in the Ealing world of the time.

During the war, John Clements was in four Ealing films. The central wartime development can be traced in some detail through the move from him as officer-class protagonist to Ralph Michael, who appeared in six wartime films from 1943. Ralph Michael made films before and has done since, but he will not be as widely recognised as Clements; part of the significance of the change is that he is less of a star (although his face may be familiar from recent television work, as well as from his Ealing films such as *Dead of Night*).

Clements is a star with a strong theatrical presence. In his Ealing films, he is at once rebel and leader, a dashing individualist and a ladykiller. At the start of *Convoy*, he arrives for his new posting in a limousine, kisses a girlfriend goodbye, and reports to the captain. Beneath their startled formal exchanges, a previous acquaintance is evident; we learn that Clements went off with the Captain's wife and then failed to do the decent thing by her. In the course of the film, he is put under arrest for insubordination. Released for action, he redeems himself by going down to the engine room to keep the ship afloat at the expense of his own life. Intercut with this story is the arrival on board of the lady in question. Tennyson undercuts some of the melodrama through the good humour of the actress's performance—it turns out that she left him, not the other way round—but the plot remains a theatrical contrivance, and the performance of Clements, like that of Clive Brook, underlines this. The emphasis given to it conflicts with the obvious wish to show the ship as a genuine community, with the men as something more than deferential cogs in the machine. Equally, the melodrama of the ending is at odds with the sobriety of the film's project to show, in strategic terms, a determined holding operation rather than an inspirational victory.

Ships with Wings was directed a year later by Sergei Nolbandov, who had worked on all three Tennyson scripts. John Clements is again a dashing young officer; during Fleet Air Arm training before the war, he has disgraced himself, for the sake of a woman, and has been dismissed the service. When the action comes, he contrives to reach his old ship in a crisis and to take up a plane for her. The climax has him not only intercepting a bomber bound for this ship, but flying his plane and the bomber, locked together, into a massive enemy dam. Single-handed, he has achieved the ship's mission for it when all seemed lost. The two senior officers who have trained him, dismissed him, and then accepted him back, speak his epitaph:

'I knew he wouldn't come back.'

'I think he'd have preferred it that way.'

It is not only in retrospect that all this seems amazingly dated. Churchill, by then Prime Minister, had a preview, and gave Ealing a severe fright by threatening to delay or even cancel its release—as Balcon recalls—'on the grounds that it would cause "alarm and despondency", as the climax of the film was something of a disaster for the Fleet Air Arm.' It is a disaster which turns at the last minute to triumph; what could well inspire despondency (though Churchill

Left and opposite: Ships with Wings—*John Clements with Ann Todd; model work for the final action: the lower orders in* Convoy, *Edward Chapman, Edward Rigby.*

allowed the film's release, after arbitration) is the wildly romantic way in which the triumph is achieved, plus the lack of anything in the film for general audiences to associate with. Clements, his girl-friends, his slangy young fellow-officers and their stiff superiors play out a drama whose stagey contrivance, like that of the numerous model shots, is only heightened by the urgency of the subject matter. Life with Ralph Michael will not be like this.

So what is Ealing doing, releasing a film like this at the end of 1941? Roger Manvell, in his book on 'Films and the Second World War', can't bring himself to believe the chronology of it and reverses the actual order of production: he presents *Convoy* as evidence of Ealing's growing maturity, a move away from the melodramatic pattern which had proved a failure in *Ships with Wings*. It is a warning against trying to fit every film into too neat a pattern of development. Blind alleys were followed; individuals worked in different ways. But we can still make sense of what happened without splitting Ealing's war production into fragments and contradicting the picture of it as a coherent joint enterprise.

The early films, on the eve of the war, have shown a sharply divided society. To fight a war, society has to change, and Tennyson's films show it changing. Whether we say they reflect this, or prophesy it, or will it, they show it very precisely: they enact it. In *There Ain't No Justice*, the hero retires from society at large into a close local community; in *Proud Valley,* the split is forcibly and precariously healed at the last moment, so that the community's energies can feed into the national effort; the ship of *Convoy* illustrates this unity in action. But the problem with urgent calls for national unity is that they habitually mean uniting behind a particular established leadership. Here, it is the same officer class whose decadence by now we know all about. Tennyson makes a brave try at incorporating them within a unified structure that can have some appeal, but he is weighed down by the actors and the dramatic modes of the 'thirties and has in effect to take a step back to advocating unity behind the *men* of the 'thirties. The impasse of the film clearly relates to a national one: the men of the 'thirties

were still clinging to power. The film belongs inescapably to the stage in the war marked by the notorious official poster:

> Your Courage
> Your Cheerfulness
> Your Resolution
> Will Bring Us Victory

The distinction between leaders and led is inscribed into the syntax, as it is into the dramatic syntax of *Convoy* and *Ships with Wings*. The latter, and later, film, acts as a *reductio ad absurdum* of this desire for unity, showing that if there is no deeper structural change, it means simply accepting *these* officers, these conventions of behaviour (as of drama)—the whole package which in the earlier films has been perceived as moribund. All the embarrassing elements in *Convoy* are doubled: the heroics are more unlikely, the men more deferential, the enemy more caricatured.

By the time of its release, things had changed too much, both outside the studio and inside, for it to be seen as anything but anachronistic. One can't separate the content of *Ships with Wings*—the picture it offers of England at war—from its dramatic form and the orientation of those who made it. The whole effort is a theatrical one, belonging to the West End theatre and to a national cinema which had never decisively broken with it: this tradition encompasses its acting style, its dramatic conventions, its class assumptions and its implicit audience. It is the Ealing film which best fits George Perry's account of the path the mainstream British cinema chose for itself after the coming of sound, an account which—all particular exceptions granted—can hardly be challenged as a general reading:

'The British cinema [by the mid-'thirties] had become a middle-class institution; it was the "cultured" West End accent that was heard and it was the *mores* of the county drawing-room that were being observed. In Middlesborough and Smethwick they opted for the classless accents of America, just as they preferred the slicker pace and the glossier technique. It was a time of misery, poverty and unemployment for the working classes on both sides of the Atlantic. Most British films failed absolutely to sense the mood of the audience and equated it with the same people who paid fifteen shillings for a stalls seat in Shaftesbury Avenue.'

Despite Tennyson's first two films, Ealing had not yet freed itself from this tradition. The war did not transform things altogether; it by no means killed the popularity of American imports, nor did it totally change British films and film actors, but it enforced more than a token change of stance and a widening of the implicit (and actual) audience.

The question of theatrical influence should not be over-simplified: the careers of many film-makers (e.g. Arthur Penn, Ingmar Bergman, Orson Welles), as of innumerable actors, remind us that cinematically there is nothing inherently disabling in theatre experience—it is a question of what kind of theatre, and of state of mind. Given the state of British theatre and cinema in the 'thirties, it was an important move on Balcon's part to look where he did for his four most important directorial recruits of the war years: Cavalcanti and Harry Watt came from the documentary film movement, while Robert Hamer and Charles Frend had both worked as editors for Alfred Hitchcock, the English director least imprisoned by Shaftesbury Avenue conventions.

Contrasting styles of leadership in the briefing sessions of The Big Blockade. *Leslie Banks, listening; Robert Morley, orating.*

The first war film after *Ships with Wings*—and the first film from Ealing's new intake—is *The Big Blockade*, which was directed by Frend and produced by Cavalcanti. Dramatising the work of the Ministry of Economic Warfare, it is more closely linked to actuality than its predecessor, incorporating facts and figures and politicians' speeches. The fictional material, though, is almost as bombastic as before. The Germans are presented with relish as bullies and cringing cowards, through lengthy caricatures by such heavy actors as Robert Morley and Alfred Drayton. The British are cool and resourceful. The first serviceman we meet, preparing to go out on a bombing raid, asks his companion, 'What's the beer like in Hanover, cock?' The first civilian embodies, in an incognito exchange with a boasting Nazi, the qualities specified for him in the script: 'His unassuming manner conceals a well-developed sense of humour.' Again Orwell's 'private language' is asserting itself, but this British understatement is still being overstated, both in the performances and in a construction which takes the stiff upper lip quality and the strength it represents very much for granted: we need only rely upon it in order to smash these cowardly Germans.

Except in one Will Hay film, *The Goose Steps Out*, and in a lesser way *Under-cover* (set in Yugoslavia, the one film to be directed by Nolbandov after *Ships with Wings*), there will be no more caricature of the Germans. The simple displacement of all hostility on to *them* is not adequate. It is replaced by a respect for their power and resource, and a concomitant overhauling of the structures and assumptions of our own side.

Next of Kin was a commercial feature, developed from a War Office commission, on the urgent subject of security. It represents the underside of those British qualities of insouciance and understatement: amateurism and complacency.

'I've always thought if I wanted a nice cushy job I'd come to England as a German spy,' the security officer warns the army unit to which he is sent at the start of the film. Abundantly bearing him out, *Next of Kin* remains extremely disquieting in the way it works on its audience to show the dangers behind the familiar, laziness bound up with niceness (the gentlemanly way officers refrain from questioning too insistently men whom we know to be spies); it even allows us to become involved with the spies' projects and see these from their viewpoint. At the end, a raid on France is successful in spite of heavy casualties which result from security leaks—they give the film its cryptic title. But the main spy remains free. In the final shot, we see him in a railway carriage listening to the careless talk of two new officer types, played by the familiar duo of Basil Radford and Naunton Wayne. The film ends with the same title that began it: 'The story is imaginary, but the lesson it teaches is real and vital.' The casting of Radford and Wayne could be taken as defusing the urgency of the message, accustomed as we are to smile indulgently at them. Instead, it works to wipe the smiles off our faces, to make us look more rigorously at what our acceptance of certain stereo-typed images of Britishness may involve us in.

Although Churchill was again worried about certain aspects of the film and delayed its release, it turned out to be a big success with service and general audiences alike. Lord Alanbrooke told its director, Thorold Dickinson, that he believed it would save 50,000 lives.

Dickinson had worked at the studio in Basil Dean's time, but was not one of the Ealing team. The film was a one-off commission, for which he was specially seconded from the Army, and it was only gradually raised in status from a training film into a commercial feature. Dickinson himself protests against classing it with the rest of Ealing's output, but while its separate status is undeniable, it still belongs in any account of Ealing in wartime. The whole operation illustrates the link between the high-level conduct of the war and Ealing, the

Integration of comedians Will Hay and Tommy Trinder into Ealing's war effort. Right: Hay as an English spy in Germany in The Goose Steps Out, *with Peter Ustinov. The Foreman Went to France:* Clifford Evans as the Welsh foreman with (left) Gordon Jackson and Trinder, and (opposite) Constance Cummings and French refugees from the German advance.

studio on which official bodies most relied for inspirational films, both direct and indirect. Once commissioned, *Next of Kin* was worked on by Ealing people, including writers, and Balcon and his board committed Ealing money to it. Above all, its immediate success as both propaganda and entertainment taught important lessons about the kind of film needed at this stage in the war, lessons that would be incorporated into Ealing's own programme of films. The emphasis was already shifting away from the anachronistic *Ships with Wings* model, and *Next of Kin*, made at Ealing, even though by a visiting film-maker, reinforced and helped to define this shift.

Its production overlapped at the studio with *The Foreman Went to France*. In this film, too, the threat is as much from English complacency and amateurism in the early stages of the war as from enemy operations. The foreman, resolved to go to France to rescue his company's plant from a factory in the path of the German advance, is nearly held back by red tape and the lack of urgency felt by his superiors. When he does go, his own amateurishness continually gets in the way. His group finally reaches a small French port, just ahead of the Germans. A boat is about to leave for England, carrying peasants and their bundles of possessions; only at the expense of these bundles can the machinery be taken on board. The captain gives the passengers a free vote, and they vote for the machinery. The end thus celebrates democracy and Anglo-French solidarity, while the foreman's own group unites a Welshman (himself), a Scot, a Cockney, and an American girl. This solidarity does not include officers—the officer class impinges mainly in the form of bureaucrats, quislings and spies; the constant danger is the complacency which makes the solidarity vulnerable to spying or to the enemy's resource. The most dramatic reversal in the film comes when an impeccably British officer in France, whose friendly help the group welcomes unquestioningly, turns out to be a spy for the enemy. It is an incident which is writ large in the next Ealing war film, *Went the Day Well?*, which was shot in the spring of 1942.

Went the Day Well? *The German commander entertained by the Lady of the Manor, with the Vicar and his daughter. Valerie Taylor, Basil Sydney, Marie Lohr, C. V. France. Opposite: German adjutant (David Farrar), English traitor (Leslie Banks).*

Again, a seductive community: an English village in wartime, so cut off by its leafy lanes that the visit of one car is a real event. Squire, vicar, lady of the manor, at the head of a hierarchy of people who all know their place, right down to the local poacher; for protection, the Home Guard. An Army platoon appears unexpectedly on a secret exercise and is accommodated in the village. Clues build up which undermine the soldiers' credibility: we, and gradually the villagers, discover that they are Germans who have been parachuted in by night. They take over the village, but in the end word is got through to the outside world and the tables are turned.

Referring to the film in an interview/article on its director, Cavalcanti, in Sight and Sound, Elizabeth Sussex puts most weight on the ruthlessness with which the villagers avenge themselves on the Germans at the end: 'It is devastating to see the cold-blooded revenge they now wreak on the men they had initially entertained as guests in the vicarage, the manor-house and elsewhere according to their station.' and, quoting Cavalcanti himself: 'People of the kindest character, such as the people in that small English village, as soon as war touches them, become absolutely monsters.'

This seems a perverse way of placing the emphasis: Mrs Sussex makes it sound like a lapse in hospitality, but the guests turn out to be ruthless enemy troops, and the revenge comes across less as cold-blooded violence than as an urgent, belated act of self-preservation. Cavalcanti's talk, thirty years later, of the film's 'deeply pacifist nature' is at odds with the way it works. It is no more pacifist than *Straw Dogs*, which is no denigration of it; it belongs with its Ealing predecessors as a parable for the early war years, a vivid warning against complacency. The villagers are slow in putting together the clues to the soldiers'

identity, slow in taking their chances to get an appeal for help through to the outside world. Enormous frustration is built up through scenes like that in which the switchboard operator goes on gossiping and thus delays answering a warning call until the Germans have had time to block that means of communication. Most bitter of all is an incident during the time the main body of the villagers are being held prisoner in the church. The vicar heroically contrives to ring the bells as an alarm signal, for which his captors at once shoot him dead. Cut to the local Home Guard members, at whom the signal is directed. They are outside the village on an exercise; they hear the bells, but then decide they can't have done so after all, on the grounds that this would be the signal that enemy parachutists have landed, and what they are on now is only an exercise. So they do nothing, the villagers remain captive, and the Home Guard men are duly ambushed and shot down on their way home. The coldness with which this execution in an idyllic country lane is done and shown is more chilling than any of the action at the climax.

Taking a long view, the film might be exploited in a pacifist cause, but in the short term it unequivocally urges alert and robust self-defence. It continuously undermines the seductiveness of cosy English façades, easy-going English qualities: to be easy-going can in war be criminally negligent. Don't be lulled by church bells, or English-looking faces. Be prepared. And don't defer automatically to well-spoken officers. The commander of the infiltrators talks his way smoothly into the confidence of the community and its natural leaders, although he does not need to do so with the squire, who is a quisling. Until a very late stage, the villagers defer blindly to him, unable to imagine that he could be suspect.

The casting of the two leaders, who combine against the villagers, is artful. Basil Sydney and Leslie Banks were the two high naval officers whose pomposity helped to make *Ships with Wings* so alienating. Here, Sydney plays the occupying leader and Banks the treacherous squire. It is like an exorcising of the kind of 'thirties leadership they represent (its reactionary quality underlined by the fact that Banks's most celebrated role of that decade was as *Sanders of the River*). In contrast, the village is saved by the efforts of an unconsidered boy (the Cockney actor, Harry Fowler) and the local poacher (Edward Rigby, veteran of innumerable working-class cameos), who contrive between them to get the message of warning through to the world outside.

At the climax, the defenders of the village gather confidently at the big house. Everything now seems to be settled; they barricade themselves in, waiting for reinforcements to arrive. Yet the Squire, amazingly, is still free. He assures them that the Germans can't possibly approach via the front of the house, and in any case he will keep watch: let them protect the back. Alone on the ground floor, he waits as arranged to open the windows. Upstairs, we get this image: on the left, the defenders cheerfully move into place, where the Squire told them to. On the right, the Vicar's daughter faces away from them, thinking back on the suspicions she has repressed. As in a trance, she says nothing, but starts to descend the stairs, screwing herself up to the act of shooting him dead. As he falls in front of her, a use of slow motion rare for the time conveys the strength of the taboo that she has broken. She's far from being an 'absolute monster'; yet Cavalcanti's comment is, in a way, borne out by the simple heroics that shortly go on upstairs, as villagers compete in picking off Germans. The balance of these two elements is very disturbing, and the whole scene, with the house functioning

German and English violence in Went the Day Well? *Opposite : James Donald threatens the villagers. Above : Valerie Taylor about to eliminate the traitor.*

diagrammatically as a map of 'England' under attack, is one of the most intense in all British war films.

These three films, *Next of Kin, The Foreman Went to France* and *Went the Day Well?*, work as a loose trilogy. Though the climax of all is action, they are mainly battles of wits. The threat of an enemy who may be all around enforces resource and alertness, and penalises complacency and amateurism. The next three Ealing war films also belong together.

These show more positive action, belonging to a more confident phase of the war when the fear of invasion had receded and the essential lessons (of the first years, the first films) been learned. Close-knit teams perform specific jobs. In *The Bells Go Down*, it is firefighting, in *Nine Men,* a holding operation by a small patrol in Africa, in *San Demetrio London,* the salvage of a Merchant Navy tanker by its crew. The Germans are now simply 'out there', scarcely seen and subjected to no ridicule: a soldier in *Nine Men* remarks of some Italians that 'there might even be a Jerry among them, they're fighting so well.'

What the films essentially do is to dramatise the internal workings of the group in a crisis. They are the most satisfying of the Ealing war films because they communicate, without straining after it, a real sense of the spirit to which A. J. P. Taylor referred ('the brief period during which the English people felt themselves to be a truly democratic community'). There is no Leslie Banks or Clive Brook in command in these films, nor anyone like them. Such officer-type actors as are evident operate simply as part of the team (Philip Friend in *The Bells Go Down*). The Spanish Civil War is no longer unmentionable: characters in *Bells* and *Nine Men* speak of having fought with the International Brigade, and the continuity between that war and the fight they are involved in now is

The Bells Go Down: *newlywed (Philip Friend), greyhound enthusiast (Tommy Trinder), criminal (Mervyn Johns), International Brigade veteran (Billy Hartnell).*

taken for granted. Then, as in *The Foreman Went to France,* we leave behind the West End and Home Counties accents of *Convoy* and *Ships with Wings.* In both *Bells* and *Nine Men,* leadership is exercised by robust Scots, respectively Finlay Currie and Jack Lambert.

These small groups of men operating in small corners of the war obviously have hierarchies stretching above them. But they are offered without affectation as representative of the nation as a whole. *The Bells Go Down* opens with the voice of a narrator:

'In the East End they say London isn't a town, it's a group of villages. This is the story of one of those villages, a community bounded by a few streets with its own market place, its church, its shops, its police station, its fire brigade.'

One 'village' stands for a city, a nation, of interlocking communities, just as a small detachment of firefighters stands for a nationwide service. For the final scene, the camera is on a small group standing in a bombed church: a baby is being christened Tommy, in memory of one of its father's comrades (Tommy Trinder) who has died heroically. As the vicar speaks, the camera cranes up and back from the church, merging the group visually into the bustling crowds of the city; and from here we go straight to the End title, superimposed on the Union Jack motif which Ealing was still using as an identifying symbol ('A British Picture Made and Recorded at Ealing Studios'). An identity is powerfully asserted: these individuals, the crowd, London, Britain.

Of course to assert this identity is not necessarily to communicate it successfully. But all three films, despite local bits of clumsiness (for example in the Trinder section of *Bells*), manage to do so and provide powerful *images* for the nation at war, images so satisfying that we will keep looking back to them, in a sense be imprisoned by them. I don't mean that these particular films have been widely remembered—they deserve to be more so. But they contribute to, and draw on, a 'bank' of imagery expressing the way the war was and is seen.

Their power comes from a combination of situation, people, and mood. Situation: firefighting in the Blitz (as in Humphrey Jennings's near-contemporary *Fires Were Started*), a drifting boat, a beleaguered patrol—three groups under pressure. The genuine 'Western' feeling of the patrol film, *Nine Men,* is a measure of the pregnancy of the historical moment, since British films have so rarely been able to achieve the concentrated meaning and the national dimension that are virtually built in to the Western form proper. The people: a wide spread of regions and class, with no-one patronised. The mood: a balance between good humour and professionalism, with the Britishness of the humour stopped from going flabby and complacent by the pressing awareness of danger.

All three films were shown during 1943, *San Demetrio* not until December. In the next two years, few films on war subjects would be made at Ealing or elsewhere: the crisis was passing, the drive to victory beginning, and the centres of interest shifting. *San Demetrio* stands as the culmination of Ealing's war programme, the ideal fulfilment of Balcon's policy, of which it is useful to have his own statement (from his autobiography):

'The aim in making films during the war was easy enough to state but more difficult to achieve. It was, first and foremost, to make a good film, a film that people would want to see, and at the same time to make it honest and truthful and to carry a message, or an example, which would be good propaganda for morale and for the war effort. I think *San Demetrio London* was an outstanding example of a film that amply fulfilled all those requirements. The story came from the news. San Demetrio was an oil tanker which was practically cut in half in mid-Atlantic and heroically brought home by its stricken crew.'

Jack Lambert (foreground) in the improvised desert fortress of Nine Men.

Some of the San Demetrio's *crew Robert Beatty as the American (right), Frederick Piper as the bo'sun (next to him), Gordon Jackson (left, background).*

It represents a characteristic fusion of entertainment and propaganda, fact and invention; a fusion of effort between crew members and—one of them (like the oil itself) being American—between America and England. Also, between colleagues: it was a work of collaboration between two of the men brought to Ealing by Balcon, Robert Hamer and Charles Frend. Although Hamer is credited only as joint writer and as producer, he directed much of the film when Frend fell ill.

An introductory title stresses the factual basis of the story and acknowledges the help of one of the real-life officers. But its achievement is to forge fact into myth: the story becomes a myth of Britain's war experience.

The ship is bringing its oil back from America when the convoy to which it belongs is attacked. The leading ship, with six-inch guns, ploughs gallantly ahead straight at the eleven-inch guns of the Germans and is blown to pieces. The San Demetrio itself is badly hit; the crew abandons it. We stay with one of the lifeboats as the men drift and row for two days, hoping to be picked up. When they do sight a ship, it turns out to be the San Demetrio, still burning, but sound; the impact of this discovery is like a fairy-tale unmasking. The men board the ship and eventually succeed in bringing it home.

The story would work in political cartoon terms, with the ship labelled 'Britain': the failure of the gallant head-on encounter with superior strength, the extreme crisis, the sea miracle (like Dunkirk), the second chance, and the dogged, resourceful way the men go about taking it in spite of being left with 'no charts, no compass'. Though this is wisely never made explicit, the ship is the ship of state.

So, in their own terms, were those of *Convoy* and *Ships with Wings*: it is a measure of how Ealing's image of the nation at war has changed. Through the challenge to the German guns, *San Demetrio* recapitulates the kind of romantic heroism which *Ships with Wings* glorified, and shows the futility of relying on it; other leadership and other qualities are needed to do the work of bringing the ship to port. Being on a different lifeboat, the captain is not one of those who return to the San Demetrio. The senior officer among this group (Ralph Michael) accepts his formal authority, but modestly, without imposing it. The crew is democracy in action. They take the two major decisions by vote, first to risk boarding the smoking tanker, then to sail it to England rather than—at less risk—back to America. The bo'sun's part in the discussion is characteristic:

'I look at it this way. We set out to take this petrol to England, and we've got it half way already. Doesn't seem much sense in turning it round and taking it back again.'

Stolid British understatement, easy to parody. But the very fact that the tone is so familiar, hovering so close to the edge of cliché, suggests that it does refer to a profound national characteristic. Its matter-of-factness is, surely, the obverse side of the officer stereotype which enshrines the effortless superiority of the amateur. 'His unassuming manner conceals a well-developed sense of humour'— the Leslie Banks character in *The Big Blockade* belongs to the same charismatic line as Leslie Howard in his own (non-Ealing) *Pimpernel Smith*, released in 1941. Pimpernel Smith: as with David Goliath in *Proud Valley* the name here says it all. Smith, the effete, dreamy Professor of Greek, wandering with apparent naivety through Europe on the eve of the war, is really the resourceful Pimpernel, undermining various German schemes. The film is insidiously gratifying, showing us how we can trust this romantic 'amateur' image, of which Howard is the perfect embodiment, because deep down it is strong. This is the image that in the course of the war is progressively tested and found wanting, in ways I have touched on in terms of Ealing. It represents something too deep-rooted, though, for it to be easy to reject altogether—what would be left? There is a touch of *Pimpernel Smith* in an early scene of *San Demetrio*, when an American signs on for the return journey across the Atlantic. Before sailing, he tells his bar companions what he thinks of England (and of English beer) and what he will do to the bo'sun when he meets him. The man next to him, who happens to be the bo'sun, and a beer connoisseur, responds with good humour, saving up his revelation, and the quiet gratification it opens up for him and for us, until later. He is the same man who articulates the case for taking the petrol on to England, and it is to him that the middle-aged stoker replies when he is seen to be too ill to go on rowing: 'It's all right, bo'sun, I'd rather finish my spell.' In short, the distinctive and attractive quality of Pimpernel Smith—a heroism that is unexpected, unostentatious and ready to defer its gratifications—is now embodied in the crew, scaled down and rethought in terms of a 'people's war'. Looked at another way, a whole set of lower-order stereotypes have been redeemed, given life and meaning, in two ways. Structurally, by giving them a strong context: testing the men's traditional cheerful stoicism in a decisive role where they are more than just deferential support for the men who count. And (related to this) by casting: Frederick Piper, who plays the bo'sun, is one of several actors who join Ealing during the war to form a strong, unpatronised, working-class stock company. Piper, here, is from Kent, and Gordon Jackson from Glasgow. Both have already been in *Nine Men*, and Jackson was the Scot of *The Foreman Went to France*. The presence of these and other characters and actors from Scotland, Wales and identified English regions is a reminder of the real concern in these mid-war Ealing films (as at times later) to create inclusive images of *Britain*. This should be remembered even when one slips into referring to Ealing's picture of 'England', as it is hard not to occasionally—just as Orwell wrote of England, not Britain, as being a family with a private language and common memories that closes its ranks at the approach of an enemy. In *San Demetrio*, it is very definitely Britain that is so identified.

Because this closing of ranks now means something substantial, the shared language and memories which the film quietly celebrates are given extra meaning. They cease to be bits of local colour at the edge of the films, embodied by cameo players. Even the 'nice cup of tea' cliche is redeemed, almost reinvented, when the Chief Engineer takes the risk of lighting a fire, despite the petrol fumes, to make tea for the men who have been working in intense cold for several days. And the scenes of nostalgic evocation belong with those in the wartime films of Humphrey Jennings: the singing of 'I Belong to Glasgow' as the stoker lies on his deathbed, and the London memories:

'Wednesday. Early closing. Wednesday when I'm home the missus shuts up shop—got a little newsagent's and tobacconist's—and we go off to the pictures. When we come out we go and have one—Ooh, what wouldn't I give to be having a pint in the old Elephant now!'

The ending is at first sight curious. The men, having put out the fires, repaired the engines, and brought the ship to harbour by their own efforts, find themselves awarded salvage money, £14,000 of it. The final scene is in court, with a judge confirming the award. It is a surprise to find this stress on personal rewards for a wartime action: was it perhaps put into the film with some embarrassment, simply because it had happened in reality? But it works at a profounder level.

It is clear that the thought of reward has not occurred to any of the crew. By the time they enter harbour, we know that the reward legally depends on their not accepting help from tugboats to bring them in, but neither they, nor the tugboats offering the help, know this. When they refuse help, it is not for mercenary reasons but as a final assertion of communal pride, voiced by the Ralph Michael character: 'We've come more than a thousand miles on our own. I think we can manage the rest.' The reward is for *not* seeking reward, and for the qualities of pride and initiative that inspired the journey home; again, it follows the logic of myth.

There is also the fact that the film-makers were being paid, and the studio was making a profit from its wartime operations. It is hard not to be conscious of such an analogy in reflecting on the final scene. As the judge sums up and congratulates the men, the camera moves over their faces—the faces of Ealing actors. The actors, like the men they portray, the film crew, like the ship's crew, are rewarded with cash for a work of patriotism, and are justified. The last words belong to the judge, as the camera rests on the faces of Ralph Michael and his colleagues:

'I would not like to leave this case without thanking everybody concerned for having given me the best working day of my life in listening to the very modest recital of some gallant gentlemen concerning a memorable achievement.'

'The very modest recital' is the phrase the judge applies to the crew's own account in court of their exploit, an account which of course we do not hear directly, having witnessed the events already through the film's action. The phrase applies equally well to the narrative: it has been 'a very modest recital'. The style of the film is at one with that of the protagonists and based on a comparable teamwork. At every level, *San Demetrio* is the consummation of Ealing's war effort: making films which were accounted as useful as the petrol salvaged in this film and, looking back further, as the coal in *The Proud Valley*.

THE TEAM

During Balcon's twenty years with Ealing, 1938–58, no fewer than 60% of the feature films were directed by six men:

Charles Crichton
Basil Dearden
Charles Frend
Robert Hamer
Alexander Mackendrick
Harry Watt

All but one of the six (Mackendrick) were at Ealing by 1942. All stayed for at least seven years; they were there together in the early 'fifties, they made most of the Ealing comedies between them, and four of them were still with Balcon when he moved to the MGM studio in 1956 for the last cluster of films to bear the Ealing trademark. Even the two who had left by then, Hamer and Mackendrick, were to make films with Balcon soon after Ealing folded, films one can describe as quasi-Ealing: *The Scapegoat*, and *Sammy Going South*. None of the six, then, simply passes through Ealing: it is a home and a continuing identity for them: it was here that they became directors, apart from Harry Watt (the oldest of the six), who had made documentaries for the GPO and then Crown film units, culminating in *Target for Tonight*.

Left: Mervyn Johns as the ailing stoker of San Demetrio London, *in the long sequence shot in the studio tank. Right: some warm food at last—the bo'sun (Frederick Piper), Pollard (Walter FitzGerald), Hawkins (Ralph Michael).*

Subdividing further: of 30 Ealing films up to and including *San Demetrio London*, this group between them directed six, or 20%. Of the 65 that follow, the figure is 52, or 80%. The turning-point, the 'takeover' of Ealing by this group of directors, comes exactly with the trio of films I have just dealt with.

The Bells Go Down is Dearden's first solo credit after co-directing two comedies with Will Hay. *Nine Men* is not only the Ealing debut of its director, Harry Watt, but Crichton's first film as a producer. *San Demetrio* is Hamer's first film after promotion from editor: he functions as producer, co-writer and (uncredited) co-director. Although its main director, Charles Frend, had made two features before this—*The Big Blockade* and *The Foreman Went to France*—both were shot under the strong guidance of the experienced Cavalcanti, Ealing's midwife or nurse figure, of whom Monja Danischewsky wrote in the characteristic family language of Ealing: 'If Mick [Balcon] was the father figure, Cavalcanti was the Nanny who brought us up.'

In this trio of films, Ealing grows up, settles: the apprentices graduate. Four recruits, all in their early or mid-thirties, have been launched as directors, and a fifth is about to join them: when *San Demetrio* is released, Crichton is already at work directing *For Those in Peril*. Hamer gets his first official credit as a director in 1945, with the release of the omnibus film *Dead of Night*. (The sixth member of the group, Mackendrick, will join Ealing in 1946.)

All this gives weight to the analogy, which I have underlined in *San Demetrio*, between national team and studio team: the same trio of films does mark, on different sides of the camera, the forging of a studio identity and of a national image, both of which will endure. If Britain has notoriously tended to hark back to those early war years (lasting from the time these films refer to—Dunkirk, the Blitz, Britain alone—to the time of their release), both explicitly and implicitly, both as a source of strength and as a means of evading present reality —I am writing this during Labour's campaign for the succession to Harold Wilson, with candidates from all sections of the party invoking the wartime spirit of community—then Ealing was ideally placed, or fated, whichever way you see it, conditioned by its *own* history, to express this tendency most eloquently, to reinforce it by providing images in the wartime spirit for the rest of us. Balcon had brought his team together *for* a mission of patriotic film-making, they emerged at the right time to fulfil it, and were in turn conditioned by the experience of it; they were kept together, in the same wartime formation, to continue to express and come to terms with this conditioning in their films.

Dearden was already at Ealing in Basil Dean's time, having first worked with him in the theatre. Frend, Hamer and Crichton had worked elsewhere in the industry, as editors. Frend was employed by Balcon both at Gainsborough and at MGM. Watt, and briefly Hamer, had worked with the Government-sponsored GPO Film Unit, which became the Crown Film Unit early in the war; they came to Ealing in the wake of Cavalcanti, who had become the senior member of that unit after John Grierson's departure. The most recent experience of both Mackendrick and Henry Cornelius—a recruit of 1944, who surprised Balcon by leaving him after only one film as director—had likewise been in wartime documentary, and they belonged to the same age-group. All seven were born between 1906 and 1913.

This gathering of people from commercial and documentary backgrounds, to forge what would become a distinctive Ealing identity and style, seems to have been a considered policy on Balcon's part:

'I felt of course . . . that the type of film we'd been making in the past would not do, either in war conditions or in the future, and that is why I was eager to get Cav into the studio. I felt sure, to use these ugly words, some cross-fertilisation of our respective experiences, something different, would emerge—and indeed it did.'   (from an interview in 1975 with Elizabeth Sussex)

This is not the place for a history of the Crown Unit and its predecessors, but it is important to note that in the 'thirties the term documentary (Grierson's definition: the creative treatment of actuality) had not yet acquired all its grey, safe, official connotations. The Unit stood not only for socially 'relevant' subjects, shot on real locations, but also for formal experiment: it attracted young enthusiasts, ready to work for modest wages, and functioned by teamwork and informal apprenticeship rather than by strict division of labour. It contrasted with the main body of the commercial industry in all these respects and in one overriding one, its Britishness. By definition, it was engaged in exploring and promoting British institutions. The first sponsor of the Unit, founded in 1929 as the Empire Marketing Board Film Unit, was the Secretary of that Board, Sir Stephen Tallents, whose pamphlet of 1932, advocating a dynamic policy of propaganda in which film would have an important role, was entitled 'The Projection of England'. This of course looks ahead to Balcon's own later formulations ('projecting Britain and the British character'), and it helps to explain what the 'thirties documentary tradition contributed to Ealing. To see why Balcon was attracted by it, we need to look back to his own experiences.

The 'thirties were a decade of unstable internationalism for British films, characterised by the pursuit of foreign markets, and the use of American and European personnel on both sides of the camera. The home audience was felt to be too small to produce enough profit on its own, a prophecy that was self-fulfilling, since it went with a failure to work at developing the type of indigenous cinema which could have a genuine popular appeal.

Balcon was one of those who did try to build up a valid tradition of British film-making, notably with Alfred Hitchcock, but in the mid-'thirties he had been increasingly caught up in this internationalism, with dispiriting results: 'The policy of using American artists had not paid off and the attack on the American market again fizzled out.' And after his two years as MGM production head in Britain: 'My hope of making Anglo-American films for the world market, blending the best from both sides, was dust and ashes.' It was at this point that he felt the need to run for cover, to go back to making unashamedly British films, with a British team, in a situation unlike that at MGM, one where he could work on a modest human scale.

And Ealing was available. The place itself: this is the third in the trio of influences that come together to create the Ealing we know. Balcon, the documentary tradition, and the studio taken over from Basil Dean. It was appropriate not only for the modesty of its physical size and location. Although Dean, in his seven years there, had rented the place out to a variety of international companies, his own production programme had a determinedly national bias. Like Balcon, he had reacted against an unhappy experience of American collaboration (with RKO, in the early 'thirties). His most profitable films were the series of comedies with Gracie Fields and George Formby, and he gave Carol Reed the chance to direct small, indigenous dramas. In spite of low morale caused by financial crisis, it was more than an empty shell that Balcon took over.

There was a distinct tradition and atmosphere; the famous slogans on the Ealing walls—'Co-operation', 'The Studio with the Team Spirit'—were put there by Dean, and when Balcon wrote the now familiar inscription for the commemorative plaque, he set the time span to cover Dean's period in control as well as his own: 'Here during *a quarter of a century* many films were made projecting Britain and the British character.'

All this Britishness became increasingly welcome with the approach of a war in which Britain was to find itself standing alone and under pressure. Balcon was in the classic position of the right man in the right place at the right time: given these original co-ordinates of time and space, the emergence of the institution that was Ealing follows on naturally, or at least so it seems in retrospect. He and the documentarists were natural allies. Their experience was in reconciling the creativity of individuals with accountability to public bodies, Balcon's in mediating with another public, at the box office. Both disciplines were indispensable and interacted; as important an influence as Cavalcanti, from the other side of the tracks, was the less celebrated Angus Macphail, a long-time colleague of Balcon's who would stay at Ealing as story editor until 1949 and have his name on some two dozen scripts in his own right. The merging of commercial and documentary traditions which took place in the first years can't be reduced to a standard form of compromise between commerce and art; it was a marriage of two partners predisposed to one another.

To sum up. The studio at Ealing, the documentary movement, Balcon himself: each of them already stands in 1938 for a modest, independent form of *British* cinema, and all favour teamwork. It is the coming together of these three currents, at precisely the time when an authentic national cinema is being called for—in order to encourage, and interpret to itself, Britain at war—that creates the Ealing identity, the Ealing system, and the Ealing style.

There is scope, I believe, for a small shelf of books on Ealing to include not only other readings of the films themselves, but an account of the studio 'sociology' that would be of interest both in itself and in providing data for real analysis of the relation of production system to filmed product. To some extent this has already been done, both in Lindsay Anderson's book describing the studio operation at a particular moment (1951) and in John Ellis's wider-ranging analysis for Screen magazine (1975). What my own account of Ealing is consciously leaving out, or rather taking for granted, can be summed up in a single name: that of Hal Mason, the man on whose importance everyone who worked at Ealing is agreed. To quote Balcon, 'his name appeared on every film made and deservedly so, as the whole organisation and physical control of the films came under his charge'—every film made, that is, after he was recruited to Ealing, like so many others, in the early years of the war. The graduation of better known names through a set of 'creative' jobs had its parallel in that of Mason through organisational ones to that of General Manager and Production Supervisor. Even in this rôle, his screen credit is unobtrusive, sharing the

Ealing's music-hall tradition. From the top: Gracie Fields leading a stall-holders' campaign against supermarket pressures in the pre-Balcon Look up and Laugh *(1935); George Formby in* Let George Do It, *with Phyllis Calvert; Claude Hulbert and Will Hay in* My Learned Friend; *Tommy Trinder and Stanley Holloway in* Champagne Charlie.

frame with others, but he was present at the regular Round Table meetings which brought together Ealing's 'creative élite' for discussion of projects, and in the photograph of this which posterity sees, in Balcon's Autobiography, he sits at Balcon's own right hand. That seems an important symbol of the real nature of Ealing, acknowledging the indivisibility of the creative and practical sides of the enterprise.

To survive, Greenleaf, however picturesque and liberal on the surface, has to be not less but more efficient than Ironside. Ealing proved itself not just the cosiest but the most efficient studio of its time. It was altogether rare for a film to over-run its schedule, thanks to the work of Mason and *his* team in planning the production work and controlling it when in progress, as well as to the priority which this work was given within the studio system.

At least in its heyday, Ealing achieved a harmony that seemed almost too good to be true. Cosiness, with efficiency; freedom, under control. Balcon himself was dominant, but not overbearing. People would let off steam at his expense in the Red Lion, across the road, when work ended; but they came back next day. Conversely, when a writer, T.E.B. Clarke, was assigned to research *Pool of London*, and went off at a tangent to sketch a comedy idea, Balcon 'blew his top'; yet he was careful to look at the idea. The result: *The Lavender Hill Mob*. For writers, directors and producers, a strong framework was created within which they could follow up their own ideas, a system which made possible the very low reliance which Ealing placed on adaptations from other media. Others besides Clarke could persuade Balcon to let them go off in unexpected directions. His door was always open. Danischewsky knocked on it one day as a dissatisfied publicity manager and came out a producer. Hamer was allowed, albeit after argument, to follow the downbeat East End drama of *It Always Rains on Sunday* with the exuberant black comedy of *Kind Hearts and Coronets*. Harry Watt, typed as a documentarist, was allowed to try a musical (*Fiddlers Three*) and Charles Frend, typed with equally good cause as a sober realist, was given three chances to fulfil his wish to make a comedy. Of course, this freedom was strictly limited, both in how it was used (each project going through the normal Ealing processing) and in who it was granted to: the group of people whom Balcon had picked out because he trusted their potential.

Of this select group, the main directors converged, in the early years, from the diverse backgrounds which have been mentioned above. Dearden from Ealing, Watt from the GPO Unit, Frend from working with Balcon, whom he had already impressed as being 'a man with his roots firmly planted in the soil of this country . . . the ideal man to deal with any subject concerned with the traditional English values.' Hamer and Crichton come from editing feature films, Mackendrick and Cornelius, at a later date, from documentary work, all of them at an early enough stage in their careers to take the imprint of Ealing. The rest of the staff constitute a similar mix. More important than charting the actual previous experience of everyone in the studio is an understanding of the kind of 'career structure' which operated. Balcon's policy was to pick or retain people who seemed right for Ealing and offer them continuity of employment and the chance to graduate from specialised jobs.

This happened rapidly with the Six, as we can call the main six directors who emerged—more rapidly than if the war had not removed others from the scene, whether directly by conscription (like Tennyson) or indirectly. (The hazards of conscription, in fact, helped to shape the Ealing system of continuity, since the guarantee of long-term employment made it easier to gain exemption from call-up for a given worker). Less rapidly, it happened to others. Thus, Monja Danischewsky, whose reminiscences of Ealing are such a vivid and useful document, came to Ealing in 1938 as publicity manager, had his first script credit in 1943, and his first producer credit in 1949. Sidney Cole came in 1942 as an experienced editor who had also made films on the Republican side in Spain and been active in the film workers' union, the ACT; he moved from editor to producer in 1944, and also did some writing and (in 1949) directing, staying until 1952. Seth Holt, an actor, joined the editing staff in 1944, became a senior editor in 1949, a producer in 1954, and a director in 1958 (*Nowhere to Go*). Michael Relph moved from art director (1942) to writer/producer (1946) to director (*Davy*, 1957). And so on. Of course, the principle is nothing new: isn't the classic way of rising to the top in the film industry to start as tea-boy and work up? What is peculiar to Ealing is the extremely close, almost closed, nature of the system; the fact that it all comes together during the war is all-important in forging it—in a fire of patriotism, as it were—and making the loyalties so strong: loyalty both of staff to studio and of studio to staff.

It was not only that five of the Six were directing at Ealing during the war, and went on into the 'fifties: the 'new' directors of the 'fifties tended to be men who, like Holt and Relph, had been at Ealing continuously from the war years, and the same applies to the 'new' producers—indeed, almost every Ealing film was produced by a pair of men (Balcon and one other, who might have either Producer or Associate Producer for his official title) forming part of the wartime solidarity. Writers were less constant, but there is one of them whose career is similar to that of the Six and whose part in creating the postwar image of Ealing is as great as anyone's: T. E. B. Clarke, who came to Ealing in 1943 and stayed with the company until the end.

A scene from Charles Crichton's Painted Boats *(1945), centred on the life of canal people, one of the Ealing features with a strong documentary element.*

Balcon took pride in the fact that, once he had got the system going, pro-
motions were normally made from within the staff. All the people mentioned in
the last three paragraphs, Cornelius apart, stayed for ten years or more. After
1942 only three people came in as directors from outside Ealing, to make one
film each. At times, one almost has the feeling that the system in operation is
that of 'Buggins's turn'; at least, that is the obvious danger. (Why else did it take
the extremely talented Seth Holt so long to be given a chance as director?) In
'Making a Film', which annotates the making of *Secret People*, a project brought
to Ealing by Thorold Dickinson in 1951, Lindsay Anderson quotes Balcon's
welcome to the outsider as 'a stranger bride in a family tending to inbreeding'.

The norm, the Ealing code, is nicely indicated in Balcon's own account of an
incident that took place soon afterwards. Henry Cornelius had moved on from
writing and producing to direct *Passport to Pimlico*, but then left Ealing to work
independently. A few years later, he brought Balcon the outline of *Genevieve*
with a request to be allowed to make it at Ealing. Balcon writes that he 'knew at
once that it could not miss' (and it was indeed to become a spectacular financial
success)—but:

'Our own schedule of films was arranged and if I took Corny back it would mean
displacing another director, an idea which would not have proved popular for
good and valid reasons. Although Corny was immensely popular with his ex-
colleagues at Ealing, he had left of his own volition and, by the way, it was very
rare for anyone to leave Ealing.'

That beautifully deadpan 'by the way' is eloquent of the values of Balcon and
Ealing. In the event, *Genevieve* was made at Pinewood, for Rank—partly, let it
be said, through Balcon's own influence as a member of the Rank board.

The Six could have been seven, had Cornelius not strayed from the fold. But
this doesn't mean the others were uniformly conformist, or made up a homo-
geneous, interchangeable group. We tend to label films as 'Ealing' or 'Ealing
comedy' without feeling the need to classify them any further, and this seems to
make sense, at least superficially, given Ealing's strong corporate identity. People
will do this even if they are accustomed to identify films, including British and
American ones, by their 'authors', which usually means directors. This raises
important questions of method in dealing with the films Ealing makes as it goes
forward from the crossroads of *San Demetrio London*.

If one envisages the whole block of Ealing production set out on one sheet of
paper, the 1938 titles at the top, 1958 at the bottom, there are two main ways of
reading it: horizontally (line by line, year by year) or vertically, slicing it into a
number of strips which represent the work of individuals (*see* Appendix). Hitherto
I have been combining the two in a fairly loose way, but with a bias towards the
line-by-line method because of the studio's single-minded concentration on the
war and the quick turnover of film-makers. But production now, after *San Demetrio*, starts to broaden out and individuals to build up substantial bodies of work.

The main directors, the Six, fall easily into two groups of three:
a) Crichton, Dearden, Frend.
These three stay at least 15 years and between them direct 43 films, close to half
of the entire Ealing total from 1938. They are continuously active on a wide
range of projects without establishing any immediately identifiable consistency
of theme or style.

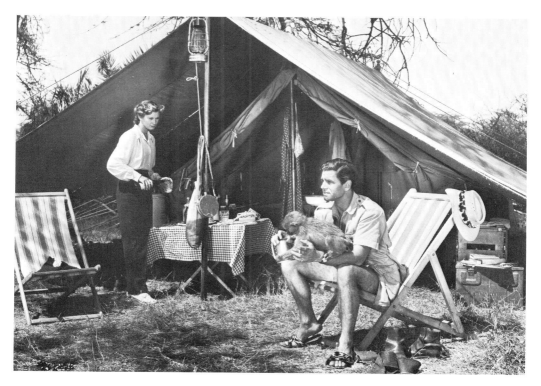

Dinah Sheridan and Anthony Steel in Harry Watt's Where No Vultures Fly, *one of the most profitable films Ealing ever made.*

b) Hamer, Mackendrick, Watt.

These are less prolific—only 17 films in all—and more selective in their projects. Although, as I have shown, none would cut himself off from Balcon definitively, they all grew restless. Watt's Ealing films were mostly made abroad, three in Australia, two in Africa: he also went for a time into television. Mackendrick, another Scot, was drawn to Scotland (*Whisky Galore, The Maggie*) and then right away from Ealing to America; Hamer, a Francophile whose intellect is commonly treated with awe in Ealing reminiscences, tended towards France, where four of his non-Ealing films would be set.

These three, as might be predicted, have a much clearer signature on their work than the first group. In terms of his projects and personality, Watt is the most evident individualist at Ealing, the nearest approach in the British cinema to the great Hollywood 'adventurer', Howard Hawks: if *Nine Men* is like a desert Western, *The Overlanders* (Australian cattle drive) has affinities with Hawks's *Red River* and *Where No Vultures Fly* (African game preservation) with his *Hatari!* His are the most robust of Ealing films, and *Nine Men* contains what seems to be the only Ealing dirty joke. At a less obvious, more masked level of structure and style, the films of Hamer and of Mackendrick exhibit as strong a personal continuity as those of any of their British contemporaries, like Lean and Powell, who were working in more independent set-ups, not *for* a company like Ealing but with small companies (Cineguild, the Archers) operating around them. It is in Hamer and Mackendrick's work that one quite plainly finds the best of the mature Ealing. The films of each, at Ealing and outside, are clearly susceptible to, and reward, the kind of treatment known clumsily as *auteur* analysis (from the French word for author), which isolates the body of films made by an individual and explores them as belonging to him in the same way that a novel belongs to its writer.

It is a tempting approach, but I don't want to take it too far, since to detach the best Ealing films from the rest of Ealing may be to do violence both to the films and to one's view of the studio as a whole. Hamer and Mackendrick belonged to Ealing: it nursed them and forms the context within and against which their individuality defines itself. Their work both contributes to and comments on Ealing and its values, and we need to see them in continuous relation to this context. The mainstream of Ealing production down the years, represented by Crichton, Dearden, Frend, and the writer T. E. B. Clarke, does not deserve to be relegated to the background as a mere foil for the brighter talents—these men made some considerable films, their work is not anonymous, and it is essentially this main stream which gives Ealing its fascination as a social and cultural phenomenon. Thus, Hamer's *It Always Rains on Sunday* (1947) is a more distinguished and personal work than Dearden's *The Blue Lamp* (1950), but I will be inclined to give *The Blue Lamp* more space rather than less.

England's football victory over Germany in the World Cup Final of 1966 served as an endorsement of Sir Alf Ramsey's team-building and cemented that particular team together in a strong unity, with national approval. Every time a side was selected in the next few years, one counted how many of those eleven were still in it.

At Ealing, the block of mid-war films are the equivalent of the tournament—the test, for the nation and the studio—with *San Demetrio* perhaps as the Final. After coming through the test, it seems right and natural for Balcon to keep his team together as long as possible. His protective (and reciprocated) loyalty to them is like Ramsey's to his players.

The comparison is not frivolous. Football teams, like films—at least while they have a central role in a national culture, as films hardly do in Britain today— are perceived as *representing* a nation: they respond to the pressures of a mass following, and can 'speak for England'. Sir Michael and Sir Alfred embody similar values, like teamwork, loyalty, puritanism, a valuing of craftsmanship and reliability over flair, a certain insularity. By virtue of this, one might locate them within a typically British tradition; beyond this, there is the pattern of what follows initial achievement. Nice as it was to win the World Cup, it could be felt quite soon as a drag on the English game: not only the individual players but the team's style, philosophy and direction had put themselves above criticism, or at least were well able to resist it, so that it became difficult to contemplate any fresh start—the memories of the great test were too vivid and the values rewarded then by victory had become ingrained and inflexible.

Balcon faces similar problems in his determination to preserve a continuity, both of team and of values, from the decisive mid-war films. Even in the 'fifties, he considers no radical change of scale, style or personnel, despite all pressures, for instance from television. Like Ramsey, he finds himself stranded in a changing world: Ramsey is sacked, Ealing folds up. You could say that this is no more than a natural rhythm of change, the ups and downs of human affairs. But it takes a particularly British form: if the fond memories and tested values are specifically ones of teamwork and loyalty, it is all the harder to contemplate real and perhaps painful change. How to honour past achievement and respect continuity, while avoiding stagnation? This is a problem familiar to us in wider fields than sport and art, and it is one that Ealing increasingly has to confront, both in its own organisation and within its films. However, this is to anticipate. Ealing's crisis will not loom up for a decade after *San Demetrio*. Between come the Ealing comedies, and even they are still some way off.

Two more Harry Watt stills: from The Overlanders *and* Where No Vultures Fly.

OUR MILD REVOLUTION

'It was difficult to realise in a time of national inspiration and unity that this inspiration and unity would ever fade.'

(A. J. P. Taylor)

One might expect that the end of the war in 1945 would mark a main turning-point in Ealing production. The obvious neat headings would be Prewar/ Wartime/The Postwar Years. Then perhaps Into the 'Fifties. In fact, the divisions work differently: in terms of release dates, the effective groupings are 1) up to 1941, 2) 1942–43, 3) 1944–48. Two pivotal films are *Ships with Wings* and *San Demetrio*, and the next of this order is *Passport to Pimlico*, released early in 1949.

From 1940 to *San Demetrio*, almost all the films dealt, directly or indirectly, with the fighting of the war; the emphasis then changes. War films do not stop entirely, but are isolated and fairly marginal. Likewise, comedies were made at Ealing before *Passport to Pimlico*, including one, *Hue and Cry*, which is an Ealing comedy by any definition. But *Hue and Cry*, released at the start of 1947, has no successor for two years, being just one among a wide range of films which Ealing turns out in the years before and after the Armistice. Until *San Demetrio*, one can say that Ealing was broadly identified with the war film, and after *Passport to Pimlico* with a distinctive form of comedy. In the five years between, there was no such easy identity, and the 21 features of this period cover a greater range than before or since.

This diversity does not indicate any break-up in the cohesion of the studio's operation—far from it—but a natural widening of horizons. The crisis of the war having passed or at least shifted to more distant locations, attention turns to what happens afterwards, specifically to ways of learning from the experiences of the war, consolidating its social changes, carrying over the discovery of unity and solidarity into the postwar world. I know of no better expression of this impulse than the words which J. B. Priestley gives to one of the newly-demobbed soldiers in his 1945 novel 'Men in Three Suits':

'We don't want the same kind of men looking after our affairs as pre-war. We act as if we've learnt something. We don't keep shouting "That's mine—clear off!" We don't try to make our little corner safe—and to hell with anybody else! We don't talk about liberty when what we really mean is a chance to fleece the public. We don't go back on all we said when the country was in danger. We stop trying for some easy money. We do an honest job of work for the community for what the community thinks we're worth. We stop being lazy, stupid and callous . . . Instead of guessing and grabbing, we plan. Instead of competing, we co-operate.'

(quoted by Arthur Marwick in 'Britain in the Century of Total War')

It is the mood which helped to elect and motivate the first postwar Government. To relate Ealing to this is not to take refuge in the idea that the studio was merely in some intangible way 'in touch' with this mood; it is more precise. I have already quoted Balcon's characterisation of himself and his colleagues as people who 'voted Labour for the first time after the war; that was our mild revolution.' And one can't overstress the way that the summation of Priestley's message—instead of competing, we co-operate—describes Ealing's system of working. To quote Danischewsky again: 'The various projects were not regarded as competitive; so we read each other's scripts and kicked in with our suggestions and contributions to all the films.'

Making a successful film did not earn any extra reward for individuals, nor did failure bring penalties. Nor, except to the extent that any film can be seen as competing with others for the public's money (a doubtful concept anyway), was Ealing competing with other film-makers, its object being essentially to keep going in a modest, self-sustaining way. In its sanctuary combining responsibility to the public with freedom from short-term market forces, Ealing would become the perfect example of a particular kind of postwar experiment in collective benevolence. Everything in the Priestley paragraph applies. No easy money. No exploitation of the public in the name of liberty—one of the first things the comedy writer T.E.B. Clarke was taught when he went there in 1943 was that 'one can get no satisfaction out of a laugh wrung from the mindless.' No going back on what was said in the crisis, i.e. on the implications of the films that culminate in *San Demetrio*.

Priestley's words date from 1945, but in the summer of 1942 he had already written a play dramatising the same issues, 'They Came to a City'.

'I was fortunate in this play in finding a dramatic formula that enabled me to express, in dramatic form, the hopes and fears and sharp differences of opinion about the postwar world of various sections of the British people. This made it a topical play that nevertheless was not a war play.'

(from his introduction to the published script)

The play was staged in 1943 and filmed by Ealing a year later, early in 1944, with Basil Dearden directing. It is highly instructive.

The city is Walt Whitman's 'Dream City of Friends', a just society in action—or a Welfare State ideal. Nine civilians, representing a full range of classes and attitudes, are magically plucked out of their everyday surroundings and assembled outside the gates of this city, which soon open to let them in. Though we don't see the city, we get a succession of responses to it, as the nine decide whether to return to it for good. The first instinct of the better-off—aristocrat, plutocrat and bourgeois alike, carefully delineated—is to reject its system of caring and co-operating. But Raymond Durgnat is badly wrong in reporting, in 'A Mirror for England', that the nine *all* turn their back on it and that this marks a repudiation by them and by the film of 'a colourless uniformity'. It's not clear whether he has seen the film and remembers it wrongly, or has been betrayed by secondary sources, but that ending would be quite alien to the kind of idealism which was released, or focused, during the war, and for which Priestley and Ealing alike speak very sincerely. In fact, two of the nine commit themselves whole-heartedly to the city, and three others resist their longing to follow them, only in order to go back and communicate the vision of the city to others in the old world, our world. Morally, then, it is five out of nine.

Sally Ann Howes as the schoolgirl who hopes to re-unite her estranged parents (Valerie White as the mother) in Halfway House.

Nine men in the desert, nine civilians brought to the city: the story is like a recapitulation of the main thread of Ealing's war films, with their microcosms of the nation. The kind of arrogance based on money and class that clogged up the pre-war and early-war films is directly challenged: if it won't adapt to a new dispensation, it will find itself stranded by history. The city itself is akin to the communities that Ealing showed operating in a unified and co-operative way during the war, an extension of those communities into peacetime. The affinity of Priestley with Ealing is clear; he had already done some work there both for Dean (as a scriptwriter for Gracie Fields) and for Balcon (the story for *The Foreman Went to France*), and the sustained role he made for himself during the war, for instance through his 'Postscript' broadcasts, as a radical/conservative, popular, middlebrow voice, is comparable with that of the studio. Even before *They Came to a City*, Dearden had directed, from another writer's play, *Halfway House*, which assembles people from diverse backgrounds to play out similar issues.

Given, then, the aptness of the marriage of theme and studio in *They Came to a City*, why should the film be the dismal experience that it is—arid, abstract, statuesquely posed and declaimed (all of which applies equally to *Halfway House*)? It can't all be blamed on the director: none of Dearden's other Ealing films is as bad as these two; his output already includes *The Bells Go Down*. More plausible is the hypothesis that Ealing's form of cinema, like its whole mentality, is a profoundly empirical and naturalistic one, at home with people, not ideas, with the solidly realistic, not the abstract or stylised. It cannot make the leap into showing, or summoning up, the dream city, but needs to base itself on what is known and familiar. I don't believe that this is merely a platitude, something that is true of the whole 'concrete' medium of cinema itself, or of all British culture: it manifestly does not apply to the films of Michael Powell. No, Ealing's style of cinema—at least that of its mainstream—is bound up with the type of character and community which it celebrates: quiet, friendly, feet solidly on the ground.

It is anomalous to find such an ideal projected in an abstract, high-flown manner. The anomaly is pointed by the casting of the hero. The champion of the city and its values is played by John Clements, and the film as a whole is in his declamatory style—the same style that was so wrong in the early war films. The exception is a prologue and epilogue that were not part of the original play, nor indeed of the first conception of the film as indicated in its script: it looks as though the scenes imposed themselves as a necessity in the course of the project's development at Ealing. In them, Priestley himself talks with a soldier and his girlfriend who are sitting together on a hillside, above the chimneys of an industrial city. The soldier is Ralph Michael. The contrast between the two actors and what they represent could not be more clearly laid out: Clements is the metaphorical soldier fighting the good fight for the dream city, Michael the real, unglamorised soldier preparing to make a life in the real city. Michael is passive, Clements active, but it is Michael's qualities, and social being, that Ealing has shown itself at home with, and it is on these, and with these, that it has to build.

In the Spring of 1941 Louis de Rochemont, director of the American news-film series *March of Time*, wrote in Sight and Sound:

'We Americans are an excessively violent people and when we get confused and irritated we are likely to sock someone on the jaw. We don't much care who it is. The nearest person, mostly. This is a definite *catharsis* for us, and we feel better after it. And we like to see others acting in the way that we consider normal. The films which come from England have given Americans little emotional support in this respect. We have seen all types and conditions of men, and men smiling amid inconceivable ruins. We have seen them do 'thumbs up'. We have heard them sing. And we feel, more and more, that if we were in the same boat we would not feel that way about it at all. And since we are beginning to climb into the same boat with you, we wish you would act a little more the way we would.'

It is easy to dismiss this as crude and arrogant and to point to the singular lack of response: the British only became more 'British'. The Robert Beatty character in *San Demetrio* does literally climb into the same boat and is slowly taken over, absorbed into the life style which de Rochemont finds so alien; the film is a triumphant retreat into, and celebration of, all those dogged qualities. Conversely, the style de Rochemont calls for has its British representative in John Clements. In *Ships with Wings* (in production at the time of the article's publication), he finds a German making advances to a girlfriend of his and does, indeed, sock him on the jaw, time after time, telling this 'filthy Hun' exactly what he thinks of him. And the whole action of the climax at sea is *catharsis* on a grand scale. But as an inspiration for the British at war, this climax and this character were so plainly wrong that they were ridiculed out of existence—hence the transformation in Ealing films. There is a parallel in the story of the great Danish director Carl Dreyer, who was invited to make the documentary *North Sea* for the GPO Unit in the 'thirties. Cavalcanti recounts a detail from the script that resulted: 'When these tough Scottish fishermen see the rescuing trawler, he had them bursting into tears. Can you imagine that?' No, nor did it occur in the film as eventually made by Harry Watt. Stoicism and restraint, the *containing* of violence and personal emotion, are a part of the image of Britishness which is inexorably consolidated and is embodied in the crew of the *San Demetrio* and its senior officer.

This doesn't mean we can complacently dismiss the feeling behind de Rochemont's remarks, or their long-term implications. That impulse to 'sock someone on the jaw' has been expressed in images not only of unthinking violence *ad nauseam,* but ones like, to pick examples a third of a century apart, 1) Gary Cooper, in *Mr Deeds Goes to Town* (Frank Capra, 1936), punching the obstructionist lawyer on the jaw, in court, at the end of the case that has vindicated him and 2) Sissy Spacek, the innocent of *Prime Cut* (Michael Ritchie, 1972), brought face to face with the orphanage/brothel keeper who has raised and oppressed her, and punching *her* on the jaw. These are images of violence, at once personal and symbolic, the climax of their films; they punish the villains and assert a morality; they are undeniably satisfying to audiences; we can't, if we dislike these moments, detach and will them away because they are too integral to the drive of the films as a whole, the drive of their stories and characters, and the onward drive of the images. In more measured and respectable terms, the critic Thomas Elsaesser is, I feel, restating the same basic point as de Rochemont when he writes in 1969 of Hollywood's rigorous application of the *pleasure principle*:

'There is a central energy at the heart of any good Hollywood film which seeks to live itself out as completely as possible . . . There is always a central dynamic drive—the pursuit, the quest, the trek, the boundless desire to arrive, to get to the top, to get rich, to make it.'

Here the contrast with British cinema is only implicit but we need to pursue it. Have British films in general any equivalent of these Hollywood characteristics? Or do they need to have? If not, what real gratifications can they offer their audiences? The mid-'forties are a good stage at which to consider these questions: cinema admissions, like the nation's pride in itself and its films, are at a high point, and the British cinema is ready to face outwards and grow, both thematically and commercially.

Ralph Michael's first Ealing appearance is in a brief pub scene in *The Bells Go Down,* as one of the soldiers who has returned from Dunkirk. He embodies the post-Dunkirk mood of dogged resistance for the long haul. He has two more service roles, in *San Demetrio* and then in *For Those in Peril* as a young officer assigned to Air-Sea Rescue: after initial resentment because he wants 'real' action, he becomes a solid professional. In *They Came to a City,* it is he who is going to inherit the future—along with his girl. But we don't really think of him as a lover; indeed, this is a main part of the contrast with the flamboyant Clements and of his greater authenticity. His persona is modest and unpassionate, though we can envisage him settling down to a sedate married life. For a screen hero, this is somewhat limited.

Leaving aside the prisoner-of-war camp drama *The Captive Heart*, he has two civilian roles which probe rather deeper. In *Johnny Frenchman* (1945), he is a fisherman in Cornwall, well-spoken and engaged to a local beauty. The girl is called Sue, and he has a boat, Girl Sue, which seems to interest him more keenly. She is slightly worried that he hasn't shown any passion in wooing her but has preferred a jokey relationship doing things like 'putting pilchards down her back'. A Frenchman enters the story and carries her off after a protracted drama contrasting his own honest sexuality with Ralph Michael's inhibited, disappointed decency. This is only one of a number of threads in the film and is presented with no great intensity, but it is remarkable how the Englishman 'sleepwalks' through the action, his smile scarcely changing; displacing his personal feelings into his fishing and then (offscreen) his naval service, accepting at the end his role as a sporting loser.

It is hard to discern any clear attitude on the film's part to the wetness and immaturity of this character, but a devastating payoff comes in the Ealing film that immediately follows it, *Dead of Night*. This omnibus film of the supernatural is possibly, after the comedies, the Ealing film most frequently revived and remembered, and it remains one of the key films of the whole output, most notably for the section directed by Robert Hamer. Four directors collaborated on the film; the short episode made by Hamer tells the story of a complacent,

The narrative framework of Dead of Night. *Characters tell their stories successively to the visiting architect, Craig. Anthony Baird, Googie Withers, Roland Culver, Mervyn Johns as Craig, Frederick Valk, Sally Ann Howes, Mary Merrall.*

Googie Withers, Ralph Michael and (opposite) gift in Dead of Night.

comfortably-off couple about to be married. The girl is Googie Withers, the man Ralph Michael. She gives him a present, an antique mirror. Looking at it in his room, he progressively comes to see in it not reflections, but inexplicable visions of an alien time and place which drive him to the edge of insanity.

There is nothing arbitrary about this haunting. The man's life is presented as one of pure surface, his relation to his fiancée and to his work (accountancy) appearing equally shallow. The mirror visions are an assertion, forcing their way up as though from his unconscious, of all that he represses: the dark of the mirror world looks out at his white modern apartment, its mystery and its receding perspective confront his flat, ordered life. The stages by which it comes to dominate him are plotted skilfully and with a Hitchcockian logic (compare the attacks of *The Birds,* punishing complacency). They start from the engaged pair's self-satisfied pose before the mirror: 'a handsome couple'. Later he tells her 'The trouble's not in the mirror, it's in my mind,' but the doctor finds nothing wrong. How does he overcome these psychic attacks? By confronting them squarely, describing them to her, trusting her: it is the image of their hands, and wills, joined in determination that dispels them.

So they marry. But their social world remains the same, and they will turn back from this glimpse of a depth in their relationship into their accustomed lightness and smartness. The visions return with new violence, and the man's incipient madness takes the form of intense sexual jealousy.

The wife gets an explanation from the dealer who sold her the mirror: it 'witnessed' a murder and suicide in the 1830s and has stayed shut away ever since. Far from explaining it *away,* this intensifies the fable's meaning. The owner was a handsome man in the prime of life who was confined to bed after an accident and, going mad, killed his wife and himself. In the dealer's words, 'the effect of such constraint on a man of his enormous energy became more than his mind could endure.' In effect, Ralph Michael, with his repression of his own 'energy', is *assimilated* to this figure: it is he, after all, who is open to the vision and sees it, while his wife, until the final moments of the story, does not.

The ending is extremely ambivalent. It is by her sudden insight and strength that she saves him from re-enacting the violence stored in the mirror world and in himself: she struggles with him and smashes the mirror. But the effect is to restore the *status quo*, this time definitively. He no longer remembers the nightmare, and they are free to go back to being a charming young couple, which is what they presumably will do. It is like a lobotomy.

In writing about this Ralph Michael character across a range of films, I of course mean to imply no identity between character and actor: when I asked him about his experience being under contract to Ealing, Mr Michael spoke of his unhappiness at being restricted to such limited and limiting roles. They can reasonably be looked on as a single composite one: the accountant of *Dead of Night* is, essentially, the officer of *San Demetrio*, demobbed and tested in a new context. The test opens up appalling conflicts and inadequacies. But Ealing shuts the door on them, smashes the mirror. It will not enter the dark world, the Lawrentian 'otherness', again; it accepts instead, to use the terms articulated within the film itself, *constraint* on *energy*, meaning sexuality and violence. In British cinema these will, to change metaphors, form a current running underground, surfacing only intermittently, for instance in the line of lusty Gainsborough productions of the 'forties (Margaret Lockwood as *The Wicked Lady*) and in the films of Michael Powell. Such work finds itself commonly written off as being in bad taste, a reaction which seems to indicate with equal frequency an

embarrassment on the part of the films in dealing with such subject-matter and on the part of the critics in dealing with films that are *not* embarrassed by it: the latter applies more to Powell, the reception of whose films by English critics forms nearly as interesting a study as the films themselves. Increasingly, in a kind of reversal of Gresham's Law, 'good taste' drives out bad, and rules absolutely in the early 'fifties, leaving sex and violence—the very phrase still retains its scandalous overtones—so repressed and deplored, so unintegrated, that they deviously force their way up again like the *Dead of Night* visions—most spectacularly in the explosion of British horror films, a cycle to which Powell contributes with the most execrated film of his career, *Peeping Tom*.

In 1969, Roger Manvell contrived to write a survey of 'New Cinema in Britain'—in effect of the whole of post-war British cinema—without making any reference at all to the *Carry On* series and granting the horror cycle a single, disdainful footnote. Whatever one's estimate of the achievement of these series, I don't think that such a selective perception of the field, selecting for respectability, is critically defensible. The popular impact of the series indicates that they offered satisfactions which other British films had ceased to: at their strongest, in the late 'fifties, they were outlets for forces which mainstream British cinema had increasingly rejected as vulgar or shocking. (One can see the new 'adult' cinema of around 1960 as a more conventional attempt to achieve an integration). Our understanding of both currents in British cinema gains if we see them in relation, if we make the link between, for instance, a) those stereotypes of 'fifties films, the juvenile lead for whom 'bloodless' is the best adjective and the demure young lady so regularly framed by a window, looking and waiting for—something, and b) the one who comes, Dracula. The great merit of David Pirie's book 'A Heritage of Horror' is that it makes such connections, basing its detailed account of the horror cycle on a reading of the wider British cinema tradition out of which this emerged. In establishing the same perspective in reverse, I don't want to be over-insistent, setting Dracula at the shoulder of every nice young couple and hearing in the background of every Ealing comedy a *Carry On* snigger. But we can't look back to the heyday of Ealing without asking questions about what it leaves out: even the simplest nostalgic viewing asks such questions implicitly. Ealing became typed as the safe, responsible, U-certificate British cinema *par excellence*. Balcon told Francis Koval in 1951 (for a Sight and Sound feature linked to the Festival of Britain):

'None of us would ever suggest any subject, whatever its box-office potential, if it were socially objectionable or doubtful. We want to achieve box-office success, of course, but we consider it our primary task to make pictures worthy of that name.'

Even the full context does not make it easy to say *what* name he is referring to at the end, but the sincerity of the statement is incontestable. Richard Winnington, writing in 1948 about the influence on Hollywood of the Un-American Activities Committee, allowed himself a sardonic aside on the contrasting way things work this side of the Atlantic, 'where a spectral un-British Activities Committee spontaneously inhabits and inhibits the minds of writers and directors.' In the nicest possible way, Balcon constituted himself permanent Chairman.

All this is not intended to pre-empt analysis of Ealing by characterising all its films in advance; it is a necessary perspective for looking not only at the successive stages of the company's post-war production, but also at the conflicts which still arose within Ealing and within certain of its films. And it emphasises the crucial importance of the mirror story in *Dead of Night,* one which David Pirie singles out as a rare 'pre-echo' of the Hammer films of a decade later.

'When a disaster comes, the English instinct is to do what can be done first, and to postpone the feeling as long as possible. Hence they are splendid at emergencies. No doubt they are brave—but bravery is partly an affair of the nerves, and the English nervous system is well equipped for meeting a physical emergency. It acts promptly and feels slowly.'

E. M. Forster wrote this in 1920: it could have been the 'forties, so well does it fit the war and its aftermath, and the Ralph Michael character, capable in a crisis but slow to feel, perhaps the more capable precisely because of being so slow to feel. In the same essay, 'Notes on the English Character', comes Forster's well-known description of English middle-class youths going out from their schools 'with well-developed bodies, fairly-developed minds, and undeveloped hearts . . . An undeveloped heart—not a cold one. The difference is important . . . for it is not that the Englishman can't feel. It is that he is afraid to feel.'

Within this essay, indeed within these few lines, Forster makes a shift from the public school product to 'the Englishman' in general, on the assumption that the values of this class are culturally dominant. They certainly dominate the Ealing product as they did the Ealing 'creative elite' (Balcon's term), most of whom had a background of public school and/or Oxbridge. Within the films' lower ranks, the 'vulgar', potentially subversive energies of, in their varying degrees, George Formby, Will Hay and Tommy Trinder—and, going further back, Gracie Fields—gave way progressively to the more conformist image of actors like Jack Warner, Stanley Holloway and Sid James. It was Richard Winnington, again, who coined the word 'Huggettry' in disparagement of the cosy picture of working-class life given in the post-war series of films about the Huggett family: Jack Warner, Kathleen Harrison, and children. They are not Ealing films, but Warner will be an important figure there in comparable roles, albeit with more tone to them.

The Huggetts and their contemporaries at Ealing and elsewhere illustrate the apparent paradox stated by Anthony Howard: that the first post-war years, following on the upheavals of the war and the landslide victory of Labour in 1945, bring 'the greatest restoration of traditional social values since 1660.' Of course, this is an immensely complex issue whose roots go far back into English history, but simply within the war films, it is revealing to trace the complementary 'scaling down' of the officer class (the shift from Clements to Michael) and the scaling *up* of the working class, giving it greater respect and responsibility: in *San Demetrio* the gap in authority and in style between officers and the rest—between Ralph Michael and the bo'sun, Frederick Piper—is not large. Nationally, there was a comparable *rapprochement,* symbolised and fostered by the power given to Ernest Bevin in the war cabinet. This sort of development, and the major shift in power that followed in 1945, can be interpreted in two broad ways: as radical change or as incorporation. The working class triumphant or the working class tamed, brought within the traditional structures and values of government. In the long run, the access of a man like Bevin to power, though it seems a radical break with what Martin Green has described (in 'A Mirror for

Anglo-Saxons') as 'our paralysed and paralysing hegemony of gentlemanliness,' scarcely undermines it, since it creates no new structures and embodies compatible values of patriotism, fair play, and restraint—as one would expect, given that powerful experience of *unity* in the war years.

Again, this is to anticipate. But again, it supports my sense that the *Dead of Night* fable, like Forster's 'Notes on the English [public school] Character', has a wider application than it might at first seem to: it plays out (alas) the tensions of a whole culture, not simply of the particular night-clubbing class to which its protagonists belong.

The date given in that film to the events inside the mirror, the 1830s, places the man's inner conflict as a 19th-century inheritance. By another route from Forster's—the analysis of Victorian attitudes to sexuality—Steven Marcus arrives at a comparable national character sketch:

'I am not suggesting simply that repression of sexuality took place, although repression was certainly part of a more complex process. What happened was that a general restructuring of the personality occurred, and what emerged at the end was a character which was more armoured and more rigidified, a character capable of sustained executive action, yet also a character less spontaneous, less openly sexual—and probably sexually thwarted. This is the character which the modern middle class has inherited and that everyone is miserable about, and it is not open to doubt that a loss of tragic magnitude was entailed in the change.'

(from 'The Other Victorians')

'Capable of sustained executive action': as in Forster, there is a suggestion of sublimation. Forster's list, in his essay, of 'national characteristics' includes, along with 'solidity, caution, integrity, lack of imagination, hypocrisy', that of 'efficiency'. The really interesting question about the Ralph Michael character—and it is he, remember, whom Priestley left on the hillside, ready to inherit the City below—is just *what* he is capable of after the war. Which corresponds to asking what Ealing is capable of.

In the week of January 1945 in which shooting began on *Dead of Night*, Balcon wrote a powerful article for a trade magazine looking ahead to the scale of national 'projection' for which the film industry should now gear itself. Expressed in a rhetoric which, as its author is the first to point out, has dated to the point of embarrassment, it crystallises a mood of the time in an illuminating way:

'Never, in any period of its history, has the prestige of this country, in the eyes of the rest of the world, mattered so much as it does now . . .

'Clearly the need is great for a projection of the true Briton to the rest of the world. The man in the street in New York, Moscow, Paris, Brussels and Rome must know something more of our country than the immediate foreign policy of its present Government.

'For it is characteristic of Britain that while its Governments and policies can be altered at the will of the people, the people and the background which has shaped them remain . . . The world, in short, must be presented with a complete picture of Britain and not with enlarged fragments from the canvas: Britain as a leader in Social Reform in the defeat of social injustices and a champion of civil liberties; Britain as a patron and parent of great writing, painting and music; Britain as a questing explorer, adventurer and trader; Britain as the home of great industry and craftsmanship; Britain as a mighty military power standing alone and undaunted against terrifying aggression. We do not set ourselves up as a master race if we remind the world that Britain has this background; we merely seek a place of recognition among nations who have too long been presented only with the debit side of our account.'

A major way of gaining such recognition is, of course, by making films, and a later paragraph adapts this vision into a more sober blueprint for a film programme:

'Every shade of opinion should be represented, and the scope of the films should go far beyond the purview of the Government documentary. Fiction films which portray contemporary life in Britain in different sections of our society, films with an outdoor background of the British scene, screen adaptations of our literary classics, films reflecting the postwar aspirations not of governments or parties, but of individuals—these are the films that America, Russia and the Continent of Europe should be seeing now and at the first opportunity.'

Even though a slight shift is evident between the two passages, relaxing the overtly nationalistic stress, the tone remains confident and aggressive. It is a bold programme for a cinema which is to be both popular and true to its national identity, and it goes without saying that there is an important role in this for Ealing. The opportunity before it is to build upon the studio identity and the national solidarity, both forged during the war, to create strong, outward-looking dramas: to look both back and ahead to greatness.

Now jump eleven years to the words with which Balcon sums up the Ealing tradition in 1956, as he prepares to move his operations into a corner of the MGM Studios at Elstree:

'There we shall go on making dramas with a documentary background and comedies about ordinary people with the stray eccentric among them—films about day-dreamers, mild anarchists, little men who long to kick the boss in the teeth.'

It is an amazing contraction of purpose. What has happened in the meantime? It is a profound question not only for Ealing but for postwar British culture. In the event, Ealing simply could not sustain the energy needed to translate that first fine, careless rapture of 1945 into successful forms. To put it schematically: having smashed the mirror in *Dead of Night*, it couldn't, and its characters couldn't, sublimate those darker energies into imposing social and public achievement. Ealing's vision contracts as Britain's vision contracts.

Yet it was paradoxically the extent of this failure that kept Ealing successful for so long: it recognised its limitations early and made a virtue of them. There was never any danger of Ealing contributing to the damage done in the early postwar years by such inflated patriotic enterprises as *Caesar and Cleopatra, London Town* and *Bonnie Prince Charlie,* aimed at great expense and with small success (financial or critical) at the international market. Basil Wright has summarised in 'The Long View' the crucial 'conflict between two schools of thought' at this time:

'The first, represented by J. Arthur Rank and to a degree by Korda, stood for high budget productions aimed at breaking into the world, and especially the American, market. The other, led by Michael Balcon, held that British production would remain economically viable only if costs were kept low enough to be recovered from the home market alone. This was of course the principle on

Françoise Rosay as the leader of the Breton fishing community in Johnny Frenchman, *giving comfort to English soldiers. At her elbow, Alfie Bass.*

which Hollywood had always worked, the only difference being that *its* home
market was vast and that it had also built up a near monopoly as far as the world
was concerned. Balcon's proposition therefore postulated films of a modest
nature.'

In this, as Wright points out, there is a double irony. 1) Balcon was himself on
the Rank board, and it was Rank that provided the guarantees of finance and
distribution which enabled Ealing to put this policy into operation, enabled it,
in turn, to demonstrate, on Rank's own doorstep and to its advantage, the good
sense of the policy. 2) Ealing's films had a more sustained success abroad than
anyone else's. This was not achieved by incorporating 'international' stars,
themes, or production values. While many studios expanded the scale of their
operations in a 'gold rush' spirit, Ealing maintained the economy and the spirit
of its wartime production. While others dealt in superlatives, Ealing in a typical
deadpan style took as its slogan 'The Studio for Good British Films'.

This suggests a third irony. Balcon was committed to making 'films of a
modest nature' even while he was talking (e.g. in the January 1945 piece) in
terms of ambitious patriotic themes. The two aims may have seemed to be compatible but in the long, or not very long, run they were not. It was the *same*
deeply-rooted instincts which led Ealing to reject the Rank/Korda policy for the
industry and to scale down the pretensions of the films themselves. And when
Europe and America showed interest in the pictures, it was not a response to the

type of straight 'projection' which Balcon had envisaged ('a complete picture of Britain . . . Britain as a questing explorer . . . contemporary life . . . postwar aspirations'). The response was almost exclusively to the Ealing comedies, from 1949 onwards.

In the meantime, where others failed by over-reaching themselves, Ealing failed (in its ambition to turn out 'important' pictures) by being true to itself, by thinking small even when it was ostensibly aiming high. Thus it lost neither its financial stability, nor its soul. Lacking either of these, it could not have made the comedies.

In looking at Ealing's post-war films, we get the impression of an animal emerging from its burrow, blinking in the sunlight, making a few excursions without ever cutting itself off from its base, then scuttling back again into the familiar warm atmosphere of home.

The 21 films between *San Demetrio* and *Passport to Pimlico* carry out many of the suggestions made by Balcon in 1945. A Dickens adaptation, in *Nicholas Nickleby*. British heroism: *Scott of the Antarctic*. The British countryside: *The Loves of Joanna Godden*, shot on location in Kent. Several stories of contemporary life and problems, such as *Frieda* and *It Always Rains on Sunday*. At the same time, this is the only period during which Ealing films are frequently set in the past, in what comes over as an exploration of a cultural heritage rather than as any kind of escapism. Seven of the 21 are period films, set in the early years of the century or before, and this does not count *Dead of Night* or the comedy *Fiddlers Three*, both of which reach back from present to past by means of the supernatural. There is also an element of internationalism. *Johnny Frenchman* and *Against the Wind* are about British collaboration with, respectively, a Breton fishing community and Belgian resistance workers; the heroine

A Cornish village disguised as Brittany for Johnny Frenchman.

More Ealing internationalism. Above: The Overlanders. *Opposite:* Against the Wind, *with Simone Signoret and Jack Warner as Belgian and Irish members of a wartime spy mission. Below: diggers fight colonial troops in* Eureka Stockade.

of *Frieda* is a German girl, the hero of *The Captive Heart* a Czech prisoner-of-war, both in English communities. European players are generally cast where appropriate: Françoise Rosay, Mai Zetterling, Simone Signoret, Paul Dupuis. And Harry Watt makes two films entirely in Australia, with Australian casts.

Many of these films are interesting and could be written about at some length, though I will be concentrating on only a few. Overall, they form a series that seems to reach out in all directions but always to pull *back*, within the perspective of here and now. This can work in a strong or a weak sense. It is a common and fruitful device to allow contemporary meanings to emerge from material remote in time and space: in the cinema, this is classically exemplified in the Western.

We see this 'strong' effect in *The Overlanders*, itself a quasi-Western, looking back to an epic wartime cattle-drive across Australia. In the course of it, one of the men gives the leader of the drive (Chips Rafferty) a prospectus for the Northern Territory Exploitation Company which he intends to promote after the end of the war. Rafferty surprises him by arguing passionately against private development of the North: let's not make the mistakes we did in the South. 'It's a national job, too big for little people like you.' Clearly this reflects, and would be felt to at the time, a commitment on the part of the film as of its hero to the public ownership policies of the Labour government: it is the spirit of *They Came to a City* given much more satisfying realisation because it emerges

From Saraband for Dead Lovers, *Ealing's first film in colour. Flora Robson and Stewart Granger; Joan Greenwood and Jill Balcon (daughter of Sir Michael).*

so strongly and logically out of the spirit of the enterprise at hand. But *The Overlanders* is unique in recapturing in its fresh context the dynamic of the mid-war films.

Contrast the 'weak' contemporary perspective in *Saraband for Dead Lovers*, set in 18th century Hanover. In a passage that recalls the reference to England in 'Hamlet', Koenigsmark tells Princess Dorothea about his visit to England:
'The whole nation's mad, but the sanest lunatics in the world.'
'What kind of madness?'
'A peculiar sense of what matters. Do you know what has really changed England's history in the last fifty years? The Civil War? The Bill of Rights? Habeas Corpus? Not a bit of it. It was Nell Gwynn, the first cup of tea, and the wart on Oliver Cromwell's nose.'
This whimsical national identification marks the sort of thing into which solemn projects—like *Saraband* itself—are liable to relapse. In effect, it is a deflation of Balcon's ringing declaration of intent. Though the message is seldom as explicit, the tone is a common one: Ealing films *want* to settle back into modesty and good humour and self-deprecation. None of the attempts to explore substantial new genres of film, as in *Saraband* and *Nicholas Nickleby*, quite comes off, and the one film of this period which does turn out to create a new genre is a modest comedy which no-one at the studio seems to have seen at the time as a portent: *Hue and Cry*. It is the writer of that, T. E. B. Clarke, who settles Ealing definitively on its new but 'natural' course with *Passport to Pimlico* and then *The Blue Lamp*.

But before that course imposes itself, I want to look more closely at three films which fight out the conflict of these years between ambition and limitation: *Frieda* and *It Always Rains on Sunday* (both 1947) and *Scott of the Antarctic* (1948).

Googie Withers played the wife in the Hamer story in *Dead of Night*, and she has the main part in his two subsequent features, both of which rework the same structure as *Dead of Night* on a more realistic plane: they bring a suppressed dimension of passion to the surface.

The family dining-room in Pink String and Sealing Wax. *Mervyn Johns and Mary Merrall as the parents, Sally Ann Howes and Jean Ireland as their daughters.*

In *Pink String and Sealing Wax*, set in Victorian Brighton, Gordon Jackson plays a respectable young man training to join his father as a chemist. The title refers to the way the chemist ties up his customers' parcels; it sums up the correct formality of life in the shop and at home, and of the father's views. The film offers a paradigm of repressive Victorian family life: a rigid father, weak mother (played by the same actress as Mrs Nickleby), and protected children. The son has his attempts at amorous assignations stamped upon. In defiance, he goes to a public house and finds himself in a totally new world, as it were a mirror world, of drink and lust, at the centre of which is the landlord's wife, Pearl (Miss Withers). She infatuates him. The core of a convoluted plot is that the son is caught up in a nightmare sequence of events and ends up accused of acting as Pearl's accomplice in the murder of her husband.

The film starts and ends with the father, initially rigid and repressive, but finally relaxing. We see this relaxation in one shot only, the last of the film, after the intrigue has been sorted out: the father is shown smiling in a photograph of the family group at the wedding of the son to the eligible young lady whom he was originally courting from afar.

It is a story of this man being humanised; but the happy ending is very equivocal. Like *Dead of Night*, the film has conjured up a world of violence and sexuality with which the respectable characters simply can't come to terms. Even when she is exploiting the son and plotting to kill her own husband, we can't see Pearl as evil; her warmth and tenderness are too convincing. Trapped in a dull marriage and job, she is too big and too passionate a character for her *milieu*, and for the film. The resolution has exactly the same resonance as *Dead of Night*. Pearl, her guilt betrayed, throws herself into the sea. Like the breaking of the mirror, this releases the young bridegroom for a conventional happy end. We know nothing about the bride, who has not been seen, and we are shown the new, smiling, united family only in the final still. We are free to make up our own minds about the quality of life that is in prospect, and thus what kind of resolution this actually marks. Not that the question seems important for very long: the film's main effort seems to go into the elegant period reconstruction, and the conflict is little more than a sketch, realised with nothing like the intensity of Hamer's next film.

The definitive Googie Withers role is in *It Always Rains on Sunday*. In effect, it merges two separate strands from the earlier film. Rose Sandigate is the repressive head of her East End family, bullying her husband, George, and their children, in the manner of the father in *Pink String*. At the same time, the sexuality which threatens the family's cohesion is her own.

Sunday morning, rain, the News of the World. Rose is making up her face when George, from their bed, reads out an item about the escape of a Dartmoor prisoner, Tommy Swann. Startled, she looks in the mirror and summons up her memories: meeting Tommy a decade before, having a brief idyll with him, then hearing of his arrest. Back in the present, George asks her what's for breakfast and she tells him 'Haddock'.

Succinctly, in word and image, the structural core of the film is thus set out, opposing dreams and drab reality, passion and family routine. Not only does the 'other' dimension rise up through the mirror, Hamer even cuts from the bedroom mirror to a second mirror shot: of Rose younger, blonde rather than dark, seeing in the mirror of the pub where she was a barmaid the face of Tommy as he walks in and meets her for the first time. Tommy was a 'dream' interlude even then, and she is at two removes from it now.

The *Dead of Night* structure is followed very closely. The 'mirror' world comes closer, and takes over: Tommy reaches London, and hides out in Rose's house. He represents both a more real life and a threat to her stability. She longs to relive her memories and go away with him, but his return turns out to be

It Always Rains on Sunday. *Opposite: Robert Hamer (foreground right) directing Googie Withers and John McCallum, as Rose and Tommy. Above: Rose at home, with her husband George (Edward Chapman) and step-daughter Doris (Patricia Plunkett).*

purely destructive: he wants only to use her. So the pattern is followed. Violence, destruction of the threat, an 'exorcism' of the energies that it represents. An ambivalent happy ending, with the family brought together. In a hospital bed after trying to kill herself, Rose speaks gently with George and tells him about her past relations with Tommy (before she met George); then she asks if their son is all right.

Such has been her hardness at home that this marks as strong a reversal as the last shot of *Pink String*. It is a moving, understated ending, and we can't regret that she has been humanised towards her family, nor that she has escaped from the clutches and the memory of Tommy, now that we have seen him. It is open to one to argue, as at the end of the earlier film, that the resolution marks some form of integration, that the warmth which Rose has been unhealthily reserving for Tommy can now flow towards her husband and into her daily life. It is more convincing, I think, to take from it a sense of renunciation, resignation, make the best of it, haddock for breakfast.

In these three films, Hamer shows people trapped in situations where their family and community and daily life have already had passion (and the word is meant to have wide connotations) drained out of them: it forces its way back, but in distorted and destructive forms, and there is no alternative but to stamp it out. Hamer is the Ealing director most aware of the loss, and he makes us feel it acutely, especially in *It Always Rains on Sunday* and the performance of Googie Withers. One feels his frame of reference is similar to that of Steven Marcus, reflecting on the inheritance of a character 'more armoured and more rigidified . . . less spontaneous, less openly sexual', and coming to terms with it, while agreeing that 'a loss of tragic magnitude was entailed in the change.'

The enduring strength of the film is the way it exploits its story to compress the conflict of Rose's life and soul into concrete dramatic images. Tommy first hides out in the wartime Anderson shelter in the Sandigates' back yard. Going out surreptitiously to see him, Rose is interrupted by her cheerful neighbour (Edie Martin) leaning out of her window to gossip about what they are giving their families for Sunday lunch, and has to reply in kind. The scene enacts very directly the way the closeness of the community puts pressure on the private emotional life and forces it underground. The whole film works on this level, expounding, like *Wild Strawberries*, the inner story of a life through the images of an 'unnaturally' eventful day. Rose soon manages to smuggle Tommy up into the bedroom. For most of the day, we have, upstairs, the physical embodiment of the romance which she clearly does not experience with George; downstairs is the routine of Sunday with the family. The tension between the two is oppressive and builds up in Rose to near-hysteria, yet the family notices nothing much out of the ordinary . . . what we see, then, is a dramatic intensification of the conflict which Rose was already experiencing from day to day, a conflict which is, finally, brought out into the open.

At the end of the film, then, Rose is socialised. She accepts the loss of her private dreams and goes back to her family and the street in the East End. From one point of view, the clutter of intersecting lives and cameo performances in this teeming East End environment is a distraction from the main drama of the film, and one wishes that the adaptation of Arthur la Bern's undistinguished novel had not been so faithful to this feature of it. But it exists as a context for Rose, and as an alternative—for her and for Ealing. She will restrict her horizons and submerge herself into the good neighbourliness which we are aware of all around her (at least as a standard, though not everyone is shown to live up to it—hence the sub-plots). Ealing in turn will soon cease to deal with such strong personal conflicts as hers, and revert to the community and to themes of social action. This is the last of the six films Miss Withers made at Ealing: an early Formby comedy, *They Came to a City*, these three with Hamer, and *The Loves of Joanna Godden*, where she played an independent-minded farmer. She leaves a gap which is not filled; to gauge the change that takes place in Ealing's presentation of women, compare her roles and what she makes of them with those of Moira Lister, who effectively takes over from her as the studio's representative of feminine sexuality and ambition. (There is also, fortunately, Joan Greenwood, whose roles include Sibella in Hamer's next film, *Kind Hearts and Coronets*.)

Rose has two step-daughters. One (Susan Shaw) is flighty, sexy, and resentful of home; she is involved with a married man. The other (Patricia Plunkett) is quiet and helpful; she is shyly courting a young mechanic. They are blonde and brunette respectively, like Rose's past and present. The contrast is like a morality play, and there is no doubt which one fits the mores of the community: Patricia Plunkett's performance is one of the best things in the film, and the working out of the story, sub-plots included, vindicates her as it vindicates Rose's socialisation. Put together these developments, the close-knit character of family and community, and the presence of Jack Warner as the policeman who leads the pursuit of Tommy, and you get a strong premonition of the type of films Ealing will soon be making—though Hamer will not be their director.

More from It Always Rains on Sunday *(Susan Shaw as Vi, Jack Warner in his first police role); and, right, Googie Withers as* Joanna Godden.

Jack Warner as a policeman means, of course, George Dixon in *The Blue Lamp*, directed by Basil Dearden, and released early in 1950. If Hamer is the Ealing director most concerned with the psychology of the individual, Dearden's line is social responsibility, which gives to the two men's early films something of a complementary relationship. Hamer soon drifted away from Ealing; Dearden became the most prolific of the Ealing Six, and it is well known that he was readier than anyone else to pick up and realise any project that was on offer rather than waiting for one that specially appealed to him; it seems possible, then, to consider his work as constituting an Ealing norm or baseline. Not as *the* norm: the lines of interaction are more complex, as I hope will appear.

The first four features that Dearden directed, collaborations apart, are:

The Bells Go Down (released 1943)
Halfway House (1944)
They Came to a City (1944)
The Captive Heart (1946)

All of these bring together large groups of people from diverse backgrounds and set them to co-operate: in firefighting, then in two 'abstract' communities, then in a prisoner-of-war camp. No individual roles are dominant; the main psychological tension comes with the redemption of individuals, as they see the light and come to work by the group's values. In *The Bells Go Down* and *The Captive Heart*, small-time criminals show themselves to be public-spirited in a crisis. The equivalent in *They Came to a City* is the conversion of a hitherto mean-spirited bank manager to the city's social values. *Halfway House* is a mosaic of such stories. A disparate group of civilians converge independently on the House of the title, a small Welsh hotel which (unknown to them) was burnt to the ground a year ago but is magically there when they start to arrive. They spend a day there together, interact, and talk to the God-like proprietor; before the illusion is revealed to them, they experience a change of heart which sorts out their problems, each a form of anti-social behaviour. A black marketeer repents, an estranged couple are brought together for the sake of their child, and so on. As the film ends with the re-enactment of the burning, the ghost proprietor sums up the experience to his guests in a speech of great import:

'Soon it will be as if you had never come at all—or if you remember, it will be as you remember a forgotten snatch of song. It will be a picture before your eyes, gone before you realise it is there, or an echo in the hidden place of your mind. But you *have* been here, and your lives will prove the reality of the faded dream. The world is what you make it, for your lives make up the world—and it is a good world . . .'

This is addressed, one infers, not only to the group of characters but to the cinema audience. We come to the cinema as disparate individuals each with our own problems, and see unreal pictures, dreams; the memory fades, but we can retain the lesson. There seems no doubt that we can take this as an articulation of Ealing's somewhat simplistic conscious view of the cinema and how it operates in society (as in Balcon's repudiation, above, of any subject that might be 'socially objectionable or doubtful') and, related to this, as an articulation of Ealing's view of society itself. Dearden's films insistently *generalise* their moral lessons. In the first place, these lessons point the individual towards the community. This community is shown in action, or at least evoked. In turn, this community is presented as part of a wider society involving all of us—and

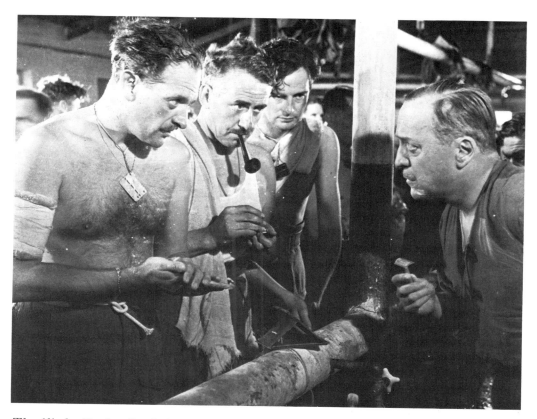

The 'little England' of the p.o.w. camp in The Captive Heart, *Basil Dearden's first commercial success. Guy Middleton (left) with three regular Ealing actors of the 'forties: Jack Lambert, Derek Bond, and Basil Radford.*

encompassing England. It is Dearden who continues to give to the 'wartime' vision its most organised and explicit expression.

The culminating visual rhetoric of *The Bells Go Down*—the camera linking individuals to neighbourhood to London to Britain—has a close equivalent in the final shot of *Halfway House*. As the hotel proprietor finishes his last speech, the camera pulls up and back from the burning building to look down over the whole countryside. Coming at the end of a film so static, even primitive, in style, theatrically posed and declaimed, the movement is eloquent. 'Your lives make up the world': the camera insists on these generalisations, refers us outward.

The Captive Heart creates a little England in its prisoner of war camp in Europe. The structure of the group—the way they all draw together, sorting out their individual problems in the 'mosaic' fashion of *Halfway House*—is reinforced in an elaborate sequence of one character's letter home. As he reads out his account of camp life, the camera puts together images of it. Various individual and communal activities including games, gardening, arts and crafts, a picture of the King being stuck on a wall, and the receipt from England of letters and parcels which, he writes, 'keep our bodies and our faith alive. And this is true not only of us here in our little wire-enclosed cinder-patch, but also of the scores of other camps, great sprawling towns of twenty thousand men, or hamlets of a few hundred: each a little piece of England.'

All the detail in these four films is held together within this earnest grasp of a total society, of England (Dearden also directed *Saraband for Dead Lovers*, which can't resist its little aside about the quirkiness of English life). But the 'towns and hamlets' of this England are, so far, artificial communities, brought into being by war or by the theatrical devices of a dramatist. What happens when people go back into the 'real' England of peacetime?

Dearden's first film to deal directly with this transition to post-war life is *Frieda*, made between *The Captive Heart* and *Saraband*. A wounded English officer—called Bob, like many Ealing heroes, and played by David Farrar— brings home his bride during the last months of the war: she is a German-born nurse, Frieda, who has saved his life. Sitting in the train with her, he tells her about his home, and Dearden dissolves from his face into small-town images which combine with the words to make a typically affectionate little sequence:

'It's a pleasant, peaceful spot—at least it used to be. Tucked away in the south. They're kindly, good-natured people, most of them—easy-going. Nothing to be frightened of in Denfield, nothing at all. It's quite an ordinary town. Like any town in England. Most of the families have lived there for donkey's years. Ours has . . .'

. . . and this makes the transition into their arrival.

'Would you want your son to marry a German woman?' asked the posters. Frieda is gentle, charming and anti-Nazi; she saved Bob's life at the risk of her own, but the family and community take time to accept her. Bob's brother was killed in the war; his sister, a new Labour MP of 1945 whose campaign we follow, opposes 'softness' to the Germans and is hostile, as is a schoolmaster colleague of Bob's, a veteran of Dunkirk.

On the surface, the film is a fairly straightforward social-problem drama (like those made by Dearden and Relph after Ealing came to an end—*Victim*, *Sapphire*, etc) showing prejudice being broken down: showing an essentially 'kindly, good-natured' community, whose strength is its closeness, opening up to admit a

Frieda. *Above: Bob (David Farrar) and his German bride (Mai Zetterling) arriving home. Opposite: with war memorial, and waiting for the newsreel film.*

blameless outsider. When Frieda attempts suicide, even the MP's sister comes round, and the sister-in-law (widow of the dead brother) points the moral to her: 'You were wrong . . . You can't treat human beings as though they were less than human without becoming less than human yourself.'

It is a development like that in *Johnny Frenchman* (1945, directed by Frend) where the early hostility between Cornish and Breton fishing communities— 'English and French weren't never meant to mix'—gives way to inter-marriage and the affirmation by the same speaker that 'we are all just people.' Or, to cite the title of the short made at Ealing in 1946 by Ivor Montagu, *Man, One Family.* It is the logical extension of Ealing's vision of a benevolent community.

But in *Frieda,* all kinds of conflict seem to be seething just below the rational humanist surface, particularly in Bob himself. If ostensibly he may register just as the hero overcoming misunderstanding, he is also a version of that archetype one can't help returning to, the Ralph Michael character of *Dead of Night.* What seem to be problems outside him are in reality projections of his own conflicts and repressions. Like the Ralph Michael of *Johnny Frenchman* (another 'Bob'), he sleepwalks through the film. His treatment of Frieda is unconsciously sadistic. Indeed, he is not very far from the common type of 'forties protagonist represented by Cary Grant in *Suspicion,* Anton Walbrook in *Gaslight,* and Charles Boyer in the remake of that film and in other roles: the charmer who may or may not be 'killing' his own wife. Witness Bob's actions in exposing her to this family and to this community while the war is on, with no smoothing of her way; in arranging for separate bedrooms (they have been through a marriage ceremony in Europe, but he wants a second one in England, and to take his time about it); in leaving his teaching job because of the gossip, an act guaranteed to double her guilt feelings; in bringing her 'accidentally' into a series of awkward situations, for instance to a public place where his sister is making an anti-German speech, and to a cinema showing concentration-camp newsreels. The moment he does tell her that he loves her, and kisses her, her brother abruptly appears on the doorstep and turns out to be a fervent Nazi who accuses her of having been one too. Irresistibly, he comes over as a figure conjured up by Bob himself, and his own feverish acceptance of the accusations—'I wish she were dead'—as a way out from his own conflicts and fears. His fear of growing up, away from his own family, his own town, his own school where he has returned to teach; his fear of women; and his fear of thinking. He seems never to have dared to think about the question of Frieda's relation to Nazism, any more than has the community, which swings between blind prejudice and blind sentimentality.

The melodrama of the climax is a release in that it at last plays out the masked emotions of the story in a full-blooded way. Bob fights the brother, is openly cruel to Frieda and finally rescues her from suicide by drowning; the image of him bearing her body in his arms, back to the house in moonlight, has a quality of 'romantic agony' which evokes the horror genre. But this is only momentary. As in *Dead of Night,* there is little sense that the hero will have learned from his nightmare, or that the lessons of the experience can be integrated into his personality, and the film ends with the drawing of the cosy humanist moral.

Though *Frieda* was a financial success, it seems to close many doors for Ealing. As in the Hamer films, though with less control and awareness of what is going on, there is a *suppression* of a dark world: a reluctance not only to look levelly at Nazism and what it represents, but to go behind the bland exterior of the hero and his community and actually investigate their passions and their conflicts. It makes us ask seriously what kind of adult hero, or heroine, Ealing can encompass, and whether there is any dynamic in this community that can reach outwards and forwards.

Ealing and Dearden are here failing to resolve a dilemma posed by the very success of the war effort and the war films. It will be useful at this stage to look back briefly to that central trio of *The Bells Go Down, Nine Men,* and *San Demetrio London.*

Their images of triumphant wartime solidarity make, on the face of it, good blueprints for future development. But they have a seductive element of nostalgia built in to them—already built in, at the time they were first seen. *Bells* celebrates the work of the London Fire Brigade, one of the network of regional organisations which had already, early in the war, been consolidated into a National Fire Service for pressing reasons of efficiency. The story of *Nine Men* is narrated in flashback by the Scottish sergeant, talking to a platoon of new conscripts: the story of the few who stood alone is to inspire the many. *San Demetrio* was made after America's entry into the war, but the events which it shows came before, and this creates a profound ambivalence of feeling. In a sense, the later stage is forecast and welcomed within the film through the presence on board of the initially cynical American played by Robert Beatty: his gradual absorption into the crew, accepting and being accepted, enacts the theme of Anglo-American co-operation. However, he is only one individual American, and he ends up by being, in effect, converted into a Briton. The main drive of the film is an enjoyment and endorsement of the spirit of going it alone, sealed by the refusal of the tugs' help: 'We've come more than a thousand miles on our own. I reckon we can manage the rest.'

In theory, this is the spirit which, at the time the film is released, can be carried forward into the wider alliances which have been established—and into the future. The same goes for the other two films. Let the spirit of the small independent group inspire the large organisation. But however sincerely this aspiration is conveyed, it remains an aspiration: it is in these (now outdated) small structures and clear-cut heroic actions that the films' emotions are in fact invested. Along with others, Ealing tails off its production of war films once this stage has passed. In part, this simply reflects a universal principle of what makes interesting drama, but for Ealing, as for England, the problem goes deeper than this, conditioning the insistent double movement of its subsequent films: outwards, to generalise, to envisage large units all knit together by warmth and solidarity, and inwards, back into the comfortable original unit which is *there* and to which one tangibly belongs.

The war films, not unnaturally, give subordinate roles to women, or omit them altogether. They submerge their heroes within a team and show close-knit communities drawing on traditional strengths. After the war, the range is widened, and the films deal with 'the aspiration of individuals' (Balcon), with relationships between men and women, and with larger communities: we have already seen some of the problems this brings, when the individual is detached from his service role and from the all-male group.

One solution is to put the group back together again.

'Balcon has never made a film which paid any real attention to sex. His favourite productions—*The Captive Heart, Scott of the Antarctic, The Cruel Sea*—deal exclusively with men at work, men engrossed in a crisis, men who communicate with their women mainly by post-card. A wry smile, a pat on the head, and off into the unknown: such is Ealing's approximation to sexual contact.'

Kenneth Tynan wrote this in 1955. The comment is witty and not unfair, but two reservations need to be made. First, it is a view after the event. Not all Ealing films and Ealing directors accepted this image without a struggle. Second, these three titles do not represent a dominant Ealing genre: Ealing had little share in the post-war cycle of British films nostalgically recreating the comradeship of war and of the p.o.w. camp. Its approach became less direct.

Until *Dunkirk* (1958), Ealing's only straight war film after 1945 is *The Cruel Sea* (1953). The director both of that and of *Scott* is Charles Frend. Of the Ealing regulars, he is the man most occupied with themes of heroism and ambition, often within a naval context. It was he who directed *San Demetrio*, and his subsequent films keep trying to recreate the spirit of that film and of its historical moment.

Scott of the Antarctic is important as the Ealing film which best reflects the ambition (Balcon, 1945) to present 'Britain as a questing explorer and adventurer'; indeed it is the only such film. It was a major project, committing resources and talents (extensive locations, colour, a Vaughan Williams score) to a story of British heroism. It became one of the first Royal Performance films, and the terms in which the Sunday Dispatch received it were not untypical:

'Such a film as *Scott* is welcome at a time when other races speak disparagingly of our "crumbling Empire" and our "lack of spirit". It should make those who have listened too closely to such talk believe afresh that ours is the finest breed of men on this earth. And so it is.'

Yet it is the story of a failure. Given the choice of subject, this is inevitable. What is more significant is the way the failure is presented. Scott's team is beaten to the South Pole by the rival Norwegian expedition and then fails to survive the return journey. Both failures result from an outlook which is essentially amateurish: Scott is shown making crucial decisions of selection and planning in an arbitrary or sentimental way. Nevertheless, one has no sense that the film 'detects' him in this, concerned as it is to present him with due reverence as a British hero. The film itself, one could say, is amateurish in failing to sort out a clear attitude to Scott and his team. Typical is its treatment of Pilot Officer Evans (played by James Robertson Justice). Just before the final five selected by Scott leave their colleagues for the final lap of the journey to the Pole, Evans cuts his finger quite badly. But he quickly hides it, saying nothing, and no kind of medical check is held. Inevitably the injury comes to handicap him, and thus the entire group. But he, too, is presented as heroic: his unprofessionalism, and Scott's, counts for nothing beside the pluck of his repeated insistence that 'It's nothing'. He dies gallantly during the journey back from the Pole, and the team never recovers.

All this could be presented with conscious irony, but the film seems to lack this dimension entirely. It is a strange, dreamy, elegiac film, often a moving one (compare the account by Jeffrey Richards in 'Visions of Yesterday' which locates it in 'the Cinema of Empire'), precisely because the film is so close to its pro-

John Mills as Scott of the Antarctic, *with James Robertson Justice and (opposite) in a scene closely modelled on a photograph of Scott himself.*

tagonists, in their boyishness, their stolid, cheerful empiricism—and in their attitude to women, which is well evoked in the passage from Tynan. The film loyally charts the fate of the expedition, re-enacting but not analysing its failure. Towards the end, passages from Scott's diary are given in voice-over narration: 'Amongst ourselves we are unendingly cheerful, but what each man feels in his heart I can only guess.'

This is the code of the expedition and the film alike: a tact which avoids intruding into 'personal' feeling and is equally reluctant to bring tensions to the surface. When a mistake by Oates holds the team up for an hour, Evans is irritated and tells Scott, 'Can't trust myself to speak, Sir'. Scott replies 'Well don't then, Taff,' and he doesn't. At no stage has anyone seriously argued with Scott. The respect for team spirit, avoiding 'unpleasant' tension, has meant—fatally— the sacrifice also of the tension that is creative.

This relates clearly to the repressions of *Frieda*. There is in both films a sense that to go behind the mask, to release inhibitions, is to open up a terrifying abyss. Like *Frieda*, *Scott* closes doors. Ealing is not equipped for heroic stories: at least, there is a limit to the mileage that can be got out of this sort of gallant failure and this stiff-upper-lip hero. The amateurism diagnosed in the early cluster of war films reasserts itself and is seen to be deeply ingrained in the British tradition.

T.E.B. CLARKE

It is easy after the event to make patterns appear too neat: certain kinds of film, like *Frieda* and *Scott of the Antarctic,* proved to be dead ends, so Ealing turned to other kinds. The actuality was less clear-cut, with projects overlapping all the time. *Passport to Pimlico* had finished shooting before *Scott* was released, and although *Passport, Whisky Galore* and *Kind Hearts and Coronets* were all in production simultaneously, they were, by all accounts, three quite separate projects which happened to come to fruition together, rather than a calculated attempt to create a new style of 'Ealing comedy'.

Nevertheless, this is how they were received. Though he had already been at the studio for ten years before making them, it is these films and a few successors which Balcon takes as being the quintessential Ealing material, a judgment which public opinion has confirmed.

The three comedies in this cluster are very distinct, in some ways as distinct as three comedies from the same studio team could possibly be from one another. This diversity, though rarely acknowledged, is the strength of Ealing comedy, a genre which several people 'invented' at the same time in their own ways: it was an authentic response to certain forces in post-war Britain as experienced at Ealing.

Frieda, Scott and *It Always Rains on Sunday,* in their various ways, indicated paths which Ealing found it difficult to follow; they help to explain why Balcon's plans to make ambitious outward-looking films could not be convincingly sustained. In Bevin's phrase, they and their characters are inhibited by a 'poverty of desire'; in Forster's phrase, they are 'afraid to feel'. They end in failure, or at least loss of drive, like others among the post-war films—*Saraband for Dead Lovers,* or *Joanna Godden,* or *Another Shore,* a gentle comedy in which a young man dreaming of escape to a South Sea island is deflected at the last moment into a conventional marriage (to Moira Lister). The need is to prevent this pattern being merely drab, to find appropriate *forms* which can stop this drain of energy, or at least accommodate the loss in an interesting way. The breakthrough is into fantasy: fantasy which deals with postwar Britain and works through the basic issues which will by now be familiar.

Passport to Pimlico is set in a close-knit London 'village' community, like that of *The Bells Go Down.* The difference is that the war is now over. This brings a sense of release but equally one of disquiet: what happens now? The Council debates what to do with the great bombsite which dominates the area. One of the shopkeepers, Pemberton (Stanley Holloway), has a plan to convert it into a playground for use by the community, but the majority want it to be sold for profitable development. It is explicitly a test case: can the wartime community spirit be preserved or must the hard-faced men and their principles take over? Pemberton is constantly harking back to the war, in which he was an Air-Raid Warden. His wife remarks early on that 'I think he misses that white helmet of his.'

As the Council prepares to vote on what to do with the site, a colleague tells Pemberton, 'We've got to face economic facts, Mr Pemberton. This borough is in no position just now to finance daydreams.' A daydream: is this all it is? It's the same issue, in essence, that Priestley put in *They Came to a City;* compare also the 'dream' of *Halfway House,* defined as such in its final words. Priestley tested out the idea of basing a community on a 'wartime' spirit of solidarity by using an overt theatrical contrivance. *Passport* does something similar within its more realistic conventions. (The link is strengthened by the presence in both films of Raymond Huntley, in near-identical roles of a bank manager converted from 'hawk' to 'dove', or in Michael Frayn's terms from carnivore to herbivore).

As the Council members watch from their window, some local boys playing on the site contrive to set off an unexploded bomb—one of the last such bombs surviving from the war. Everyone, surely, knows what happens next: the explosion reveals an underground cave containing treasure trove, together with documents which prove this area of London to be legally a part of Burgundy. The community, then, is independent of the State and has resources of its own. It can stay small and insulated, can go on being *itself* as it was in the war: after the explosion, the script tells us, Pemberton 'assumes his old blitz-time authority'. Daydreams can be financed after all.

This is only the start: what happens once this plot is set in motion is intricate and fascinating. All I want to stress at this point is the liberating nature of the basic device. Given the 'fantasy' premise, the story proceeds in a naturalistic style, in real or at least realistic settings. It creates a blend of fantasy and realism, and of wartime and postwar feeling—a blend which will impose itself as quintessentially Ealing. Within this framework, Ealing can play out at leisure the daydream of a benevolent community and can partly evade, partly confront in a more manageable form, those awkward 'postwar' issues, social and personal, with which it has hitherto been somewhat glumly trying to deal.

Passport to Pimlico was an original script by T. E. B. Clarke, whose credits illustrate the close connection between Ealing comedy and Ealing drama. He wrote *Hue and Cry* (released early 1947), but he had also worked on noncomedy scripts for Frend, Crichton and Dearden, including *Halfway House,* and he went on from *Passport to Pimlico* to write *The Blue Lamp,* based on Ted Willis's creation of PC George Dixon.

'Don't daydream in my time,' the school-leaver hero of *Hue and Cry* is told by his employer. But he does, and it comes true. As in *Passport,* this process brings alive a London community centred on a bombsite: a group of boys, coming together in solidarity against a gang of criminals. We know from Clarke's reminiscences that the germ of the film was an image discussed between him and the film's producer Henry Cornelius (later the director of *Passport*): a huge crowd of youths converging at the end of the story to trap the villains. And this is the liberating climax the film works up to. Telegraph boys and football teams, icecream sellers and choristers all rush in instinctively on the side of the good.

The end of *The Blue Lamp* is very similar. In fact, *The Blue Lamp* is closer to the T. E. B. Clarke comedies than those comedies are to *other* Ealing comedies. This is the main key to understanding the output of Ealing's second decade.

Both *Passport* and *The Blue Lamp* made an enormous impact and inaugurated new cycles of comedy and drama which embodied Ealing's adjustment to the post-war world. Clarke wrote five more comedies: *The Lavender Hill Mob, The Titfield Thunderbolt,* and three less celebrated ones. After *The Blue Lamp* he was less active outside comedy, but Basil Dearden directed many more films in this 'social drama' mould, including Clarke's own *The Rainbow Jacket* (1954).

This is where I would locate the mainstream of Ealing production after the war: the work of Clarke as writer, and of Dearden and Crichton as directors. (Crichton directed three of Clarke's four main comedies, the exception being *Passport to Pimlico*). Certain films by others operate outside this mainstream, subtly undermining its norms without ever breaking free of the Ealing framework to the extent of offending the expectations of a loyal audience. Among these films are the comedies directed by Alexander Mackendrick.

The only film on which the names of Clarke and Mackendrick appear together is, ironically, *The Blue Lamp*. Mackendrick's contribution was some additional dialogue. The significant collaboration is that of Dearden and Clarke. As we have seen, Dearden has persistently tried to grasp the reality of England as a unity, a family structure—local solidarity and mutual responsibility writ large. But this has remained a dramatic abstraction, an aspiration. Clarke provides an idiom and a structure to realise it in action. The solemnity of *They Came to a City, Halfway House* and *Frieda* gives way to a touch of fantasy. It is the idiom of *Hue and Cry* and *Passport to Pimlico;* and before returning to those comedies

Communal goodwill expressing itself in Hue and Cry.

The police station of The Blue Lamp: *P. C. Mitchell (James Hanley) brings in a missing person (Peggy Evans). Campbell Singer as the desk sergeant.*

in detail, I want to examine the significance of *The Blue Lamp,* and its relationship to them.

Not that *The Blue Lamp* is a comedy: George Dixon is killed halfway through the film, and the rest of it is a determined operation to avenge him. But, like the other Clarke scripts, the story rests on a 'daydream'—of universal benevolence—and a structure that expresses it. (Incidentally, let us correct once and for all the myth, propagated by Jack Warner and endlessly retailed, that Dixon's is a small part that ends after 20 minutes. In round figures, he is shot after 40 and dies after 45 minutes of an 80-minute film; he dominates the film physically up to his death and morally to the end. It is a plum role if ever there was one.)

The progress of the film is order shown, disrupted, restored: Dixon's work, his murder, the capture of his killer. Along with this goes the absorption of a recruit (PC Mitchell, played by James Hanley) into his new work. The film opens with a traditional image of police benevolence, Dixon giving directions in the street to a passer-by, and ends with Mitchell doing the same.

What Mitchell has been absorbed into is a family. First, a literal one: he finds lodgings with Dixon and his wife, and comes to fill the place of their son of the same age who was killed in the war. Second, a professional family: the close community of the police station in Paddington, characterised by convivial institutions—canteen, darts team, choir—and by bantering but loyal relationships within a hierarchy. Third, the nation as a family, which may have its tensions and rows but whose members share common standards and loyalties;

The pivotal scene of The Blue Lamp: *Peggy Evans with Dirk Bogarde at the doors of the cinema, just after he has shot P. C. Dixon.*

in a crisis, the police can call upon a general respect and will to co-operate. This sense of a national family is something fresher and more precise than the image of cosiness and moralising associated with Dixon in his later television days: it is built very profoundly into the structure of the film.

The main police case we follow at the start is that of a girl who has left home. A spoken commentary accompanies her walk through the West End; she and her two male associates (one of whom will shoot Dixon) are a postwar excrescence, delinquents, 'extreme cases' who 'lack the code, experience and self-discipline of the professional thief—this sets them as a class apart, all the more dangerous because of their immaturity.' Code, experience, self-discipline, maturity—strong words. They are exemplified in Dixon himself, but we are also shown an underworld which shares the same qualities and adheres to the same values as the police, making its own sort of modest living within a tolerant society. These fellow-professionals are shown in cheerful surroundings of their own, mainly billiard hall and greyhound track. They contemptuously refuse to help the three delinquents in setting up their robberies. And when Dixon is killed, they are as keen as anyone to avenge him.

Dixon is shot by Riley (Dirk Bogarde) when the second robbery goes wrong. Riley's mate (Patric Doonan) has already warned him not to be so trigger-happy: 'You want to take it easy. These things ain't pea-shooters, you know.' The sentiment, and the idiom of understatement, align this character with the code of the police and of the 'mature' underworld; his co-operation with Riley becomes increasingly reluctant. The girl, too, reacts against Riley, and he has to hold her by force. The case resolves itself into a confrontation with Riley alone.

As the investigation closes in on Riley, we see Dixon's former colleagues gathering in the canteen. Just as they are settling down to eat, the sergeant calls them all out on duty. They look up protestingly: 'What is it *this* time?' 'They're on to the bastard that shot George Dixon.' At once, in a reaction shot of the men, we see resolution hardening simultaneously on a group of faces. Cut from this to the local greyhound stadium and the crowd cheering. Juxtaposed like this, the cheer 'expresses' exultation at the prospect of catching the killer. It may at first seem a somewhat gratuitous rhetorical device, but we soon find this is not so.

The stadium is the place Riley has reached: he thinks he can lose himself within this anonymous crowd, within a recognised sub-criminal milieu (compare the status of the greyhound fraternity in *The Lavender Hill Mob*). The police now have to find this one man in a crowd of many thousands.

At the stadium, Mike, the film's senior underworld man, is presiding over a network of operations. His wariness with the police is transformed when he hears who it is they are seeking; he immediately puts his network into service to track Riley down. A montage of eager signals shows the bookies and their tic-tac men passing the word round the stadium. Riley is spotted, the message comes back in, Mike tells the police, and they close in.

Groups converge on Riley in the corridors below the stands. He tries the gates, but the authorities have locked them. He backs towards the track, but at that moment the meeting ends and the crowd spills out. He is physically caught up by this crowd and carried into the arms of the police.

It makes an extraordinary climax, an extraordinary vision. Police, stadium authorities, the 'underworld', the anonymous crowd, all unite to bring to justice a criminal who has transgressed the *code* referred to in the early commentary and expressed in action throughout the film. The conscious action of society: the montage of purposeful sign language which reaches out and pulls Riley in. The unconscious drive of society: the cheerful crowd spilling out at the end, the roars which were 'in fact' only cheering the excitement of a race but which the editing can without any sense of strain or sleight of hand place as cheers for the discovery of the criminal because this is so true to the spirit in which people, society, crowds, have been shown responding all along.

This is the 'daydream' of *The Blue Lamp*, not (as in the comedies) the following out of an initial plot device, but a way (which they have too, the ones written by Clarke, at least) of presenting people and their instincts and motivations. At the start we saw a barrow-boy protesting mildly at being moved on. During the search he comes up to PC Mitchell and asks:
'How's that copper doing? Not that I've got much use for coppers, mind, but I don't hold with having them shot, all the same.'
'That's very decent of you,' Mitchell replies.
Only two characters stand aloof from this shared code and shared idiom. One, of course, is Riley: violent, hysterical, irresponsible, and—a significant part of the package—sexy. (The way he handles his gun, when threatening the girl, announces that his violence and sexuality go together; the girl is rejecting both together, and renouncing her surrender to both impulses.) He is labelled from the start as a postwar phenomenon, disrupting the 'social contract' of the war years.

The other outsider appears only once. After Dixon's death, we see Mitchell stop a car for speeding. It is an expensive sports model, driven by a lady. She reacts bitterly:

'Haven't you anything better to do? One of your own men shot down in cold blood, and all you do is waste your time pestering the lives out of innocent respectable people. I'm not surprised all these murderers get away with it.'

She is played as unsympathetically as possible: she talks *at* him, her shrillness, arrogance and lack of humour clashing with the style of every other character in the film bar the delinquents. And she is, very pointedly, the film's one upper-class character. We may again think back here to the wartime films and to the way in which, for Ealing's vision of community to take shape, upper-class arrogance had to be exorcised. Here as in *They Came to a City*, the 'lady' opts out of the peacetime community, and the community is strong enough to let her do so, given the extent of the consensus which it can feel itself to encompass: as was said in the aftermath of the 1945 election, 'we are the masters now' (and that was said, moreover, by the lawyer and new Labour MP Hartley Shawcross, able —then—to use the word *we* in so inclusive a way). Not that it needs to be articulated. Mitchell's response to provocation—the lady doesn't of course know of his closeness to the dead man—is remarkable:

'I'm just warning you this time, madam, to drive more carefully in the future.'

The film refuses us the pleasure of putting her in her place. As so often in British cinema, the satisfaction comes precisely from the *refusal* of satisfaction, from the exercise of stoicism, restraint, secret knowledge. To earn his superiority to the lady, Mitchell has to refrain from expressing it and answering her in her

Home and work in The Blue Lamp. *Opposite: 'bantering but loyal relationships within a hierarchy'. Jack Warner, Bruce Seton, Hanley, Meredith Edwards and (standing) Clive Morton. Above: Warner and Gladys Henson.*

own terms. The values of the community and the film are defined positively in his response and negatively by the lady's behaviour. They include sympathy, humour, restraint, and the correct performance of a job. These are part of what he has learnt from George Dixon, at home and work—and from Mrs Dixon. The scene just described follows on from his visit to her to break the news of George's death, a visit which forms a *locus classicus* for Ealing, and British, emotion, and has to be described.

Dixon's death in hospital comes as a surprise since he seemed to be making a good recovery. The hunt for the gunman is even being played for comedy, as a pair of witnesses fail to agree on their story. Then one of the CID investigators takes a phone call: he listens, then says grimly to his colleague 'This is a murder case.'

At this point Mitchell returns to the station from exploring a lead and is asked to speak to a senior officer. This man assumes he knows of Dixon's death, but he doesn't. He takes it in with silent shock, staring ahead of him, away from the man's eyes (and away from the camera)—looking and reacting obliquely, just as the CID man spoke obliquely.

The reason for summoning Mitchell was to ask *him* to tell Mrs Dixon. He obediently goes along, with his superior. Mrs Dixon bustles in from the garden with a bunch of flowers: 'I want these to be the first things he sets eyes on, when he comes round.' Mitchell looks down at the floor, away from her: he can't 'face' telling her, and it is thus, once more, told obliquely: from this and from the senior man's presence she makes the inference, 'He's dead.' The latter explains that there was no time to get a message to her any other way, and she accepts this respectfully: 'No, sir.' She moves over to the sideboard with the flowers, saying 'I'd better put these in water'—moving *away*, displacing grief into activity. The camera pans left with her as she turns away from Mitchell to do this—then back with a small, unobtrusive movement as she falls on his shoulder and weeps.

I remember, before seeing *The Blue Lamp*, having known about this particular scene through a critic's scornful reference to it (which I haven't been able to track down for quotation) as the epitome of falsity, a crude and patronising stiff-upper-lip stereotype. But it's not like that at all. It is observed and organised very precisely, finding a balance between 'English' restraint and the unembarrassed expression of a grief that can't be contained: the scene does end on an image of weeping. In position and feeling alike, it is right at the centre of the film. I would go further and say that it is central to the twenty years of Ealing production, in the same double sense, and that the response of impatient irritation is not hard to understand. The scene has an obstinate 'weight' to it that is hard to discount, a representative quality which transcends the particular context (integrally though it belongs to that context) and makes it a definitive enactment of certain codes of behaviour and expression, which, whether we welcome this or not, are deeply rooted in our culture. Banal though it may seem, it is a scene on which I feel a compulsion to linger. Why? Because if challenged to grasp and illustrate, through particular moments in films, the core of 'Hollywood' and its gratifications, one is likely to fix on people like Bogart, Cagney, Gene Kelly, Grant and Hepburn, Gary Cooper, and on moments which seems to distil pregnant existential or historical issues. I don't think this is to romanticise American cinema, but merely to make a descriptive point about the levels on which it has habitually worked, and about the contrast with British cinema which I have already once or twice touched on. In this cinema, the comparable archetypes are, surely, not those glamorous or would-be glamorous stars whom we have notoriously not known what to do with, but people like this trio in *The Blue Lamp*— Jack Warner, Gladys Henson, Jimmy Hanley—and scenes like this one. (The archetypes who have more of a star status still approximate to this model— Kenneth More, Richard Todd, Jack Hawkins—and their key scenes are still ones of decorum, decency, or choking private emotion, like the death of Richard Todd's dog in *The Dam Busters*).

The Ealing scene which I would place alongside that of breaking the news of George Dixon's death comes in *It Always Rains on Sunday*. It involves one of Rose's step-daughters: Doris, the brunette, dutiful one of the contrasting pair. Early on the Sunday, she has had a row with her boyfriend, Ted, and they spend the day apart instead of going together to Southend. That evening, he returns to his lodgings, to find her waiting outside in the rain.
'Doris! I've been looking all over for you.'
'Same here. Your landlady wouldn't let me in. She said it wasn't that kind of house.'
As he lets her into the hall, she sneezes. 'You've caught cold.' 'Can't be helped.' Ted turns up the dim gaslight; they talk, and start apologising to each other for their quarrel. When she sneezes again, he invites her up to his room: 'I'll make a nice cup of tea.' At this point, we are made aware of his landlady who has been

listening at her door in the background shadows: she cuts in with 'No you will not, Mr Edwards.' He starts to answer her angrily, but Doris quickly restrains him, and they go out of the house together. The landlady comes forward, reaches up, and turns the gas down again. Fade out.

It is a superb distillation of a certain ideal of decency closely bound up with restraint. This is exemplified in the generous way they both start to make up the quarrel simultaneously, in the fact that there was patently, despite the landlady, no sexual thought in their minds in deciding to go up to his room (make tea not love, as Raymond Durgnat wrote in evocation of *Brief Encounter*), and in the restraint of *not* answering the landlady back. And the feeling is reinforced in every detail of performance and staging. From the moment the couple enter the hall, Hamer takes the scene in a single fixed-camera shot. As they move to the stairs, he pans slightly left with them; as they are called back by the landlady, he pans back again. The landlady herself simply emerges from the background of the shot. The movement is thus similar to that in the scene of breaking the news to Mrs Dixon: left and then right, unobtrusively responsive to the movement of the characters.

In both scenes, the technique, unremarkable and even 'unimaginative' as it may seem, has a tact and balance that can be called classical. The significance of the action is allowed to emerge without any underlining of it by conventionally 'cinematic' means: for instance, in the Hamer scene there is no separate shot to pick out the presence or the intervention of the landlady (played by a significant Ealing actress, Grace Arnold), though it is her one appearance in the film. Of course, a lack of movement need not be a virtue. Indeed, one of the depressing trademarks of British cinema has commonly been a form of frozen theatricality, typified in what I have always thought of (on the evidence of his post-Ealing work) as the 'Dearden two-shot': a scene of emotion and/or revelation during which we see one character in close-shot at one side of the screen, and another in medium-shot behind his other shoulder. They talk 'to' each other, but in effect, with convenient economy, to the camera, which stays fixed—as inflexible as the bed of Procrustes, to which the drama of the scene must fit itself. And it comes to fit very appropriately: petrified technique, petrified emotions.

One can see how Dearden came to work this way. Various elements in *The Blue Lamp* would decline into stereotypes, with technique and content inter-related. But in that film, the camera is not yet like a Procrustean bed. We feel it to be responsive to the moves of the characters, respecting their particularity. In turn, these characters, their emotions and their values, may be traditional and 'cosy' but are not yet frozen into stereotypes. They are still realised with a certain freshness and sincerity. Mrs Dixon, like the others before her, instinctively chokes back her grief; but then she weeps. Likewise, the couple in the Hamer scene choke back their irritation with the landlady, but we still feel it and feel, mainly through Doris, a strength in the couple's relationship which can take the land-lady in its stride—can afford to ignore her, as the 'family' of *The Blue Lamp* is strong enough in its own values for the arrogance of the lady in the sports car not to matter to it. In short, puritanism is not just a negative force (the landlady) but a positive one (Doris), and the 'puritanism', the *alert* puritanism, of the style matches it well.

In a book with a wider frame of reference, this notion of a 'classically' restrained British style could perhaps be worked out more fully through relating Ealing to some other films of the time. A good reference point here is David

Lean: compare, for a start, his *In Which We Serve* with *San Demetrio London*. Within the very different trajectory of their careers, I have always found the comparison between his British films and Robert Hamer's an interesting one on various grounds of theme and style: the way, for instance, they handle scenes in which a distraught women comes close to throwing herself under a train (Hamer, *The Long Memory*; Lean, *Brief Encounter* and *The Passionate Friends*). In the well-known scene in *Brief Encounter*, Lean skilfully 'heightens' the drama by a range of strong cinematic devices including close-up, tilted camera, and effects of light and sound. Hamer achieves a nightmare effect of his own by totally different means of level observation and organisation of simple elements within a static frame. Each scene is characteristic.

Without claiming that the other is in principle 'better', I feel it's unfortunate that simplistic notions of what constitutes good cinema have meant that Lean's more highly wrought style was for long seen as being *ipso facto* superior art.

The two Ealing scenes in question can be placed at a point of balance or equidistance that is characteristic of the strong side of Ealing at this time: between the more conventionally cinematic, more directly dramatic style of *Brief Encounter* and the frozen stereotype of restraint or grief (reference points here might be late Dearden, or some films of the 'fifties by Lewis Gilbert, such as *Carve her Name with Pride*, featuring set-piece scenes with calculated 'triggers' for noble emotions). The scenes in *The Blue Lamp* and *It Always Rains on Sunday* are the reverse of opportunistic set-pieces: they are worked closely into a total structure. In the former there is the tight succession of scenes of 'breaking the news', and the flowers which Mrs Dixon goes to put in water are not just emotional props brought on for the occasion. They are flowers which George has grown in the back garden; they have been his main preoccupation outside his work.

I am not writing this book with George Orwell's works at my elbow for inspiration, but it is hard to immerse oneself in Ealing without being repeatedly reminded of this writer who, from his own more analytical perspective, was concerned as much as they were with Britain and the British character. Seeking ways to pin down the particular sense of ripeness and equilibrium in the community of *The Blue Lamp*, I looked again at his essay 'England Your England' (1941), which had been useful at an earlier point, and, in the middle of much that illuminates the Ealing spirit, came on this:

'Here it is worth noting a minor English trait which is extremely well marked, though not often commented on, and that is a love of flowers . . . Does it not contradict the English indifference to the arts? Not really, because it is found in people who have no aesthetic feelings whatever. What it does link up with, however, is another English characteristic which is so much a part of us that we barely notice it, and that is the addiction to hobbies and spare-time occupations, the *privateness* of English life. We are a nation of flower-lovers, but also a nation of stamp-collectors, pigeon-fanciers, amateur carpenters, coupon-snippers, darts-players, crossword-puzzle fans. All the culture that is most truly native centres round things which even when they are communal are not official—the pub, the football match, the back garden, the fireside and the "nice cup of tea".'

Very Jack Warner, very Ealing. Dixon here is both flower-lover and darts-player, and other roles come at once to mind in which the Warner character is pigeon-fancier, coupon-snipper, and amateur carpenter. Substitute greyhound meeting for football match in the second of Orwell's two lists and it covers the 'landscape' of *The Blue Lamp*. Moreover, the description of an essential *private-ness* within a social life that is *communal* without being *official* absolutely captures the ethos of the film: both the structure of the lives we are shown, and the feelings which are brought into play about home, work, the emotional life, justice and the community itself. As for *It Always Rains on Sunday*: the role in it of Orwell's 'nice cup of tea' has already been illustrated. Rose's husband is a darts-player who goes to the pub before his ritual Sunday lunch—and so on.

It is in this image of community that Ealing comes to rest, and these two films are decisive, the second consolidating and building on the resolution of the first. *It Always Rains on Sunday* also ended with the tracking down of a lone criminal; it was a chase by Jack Warner, rather than in his memory, a lonely one at night, through deserted, rain-washed streets, in the tradition of the *film noir*. How appropriate it is that Warner himself should here be the agent of the process which, by driving Tommy Swann to show his ruthlessness and then disposing of him, ends Rose's resistance to family and community. This exorcism of his memory, of the intensity of private desire that he kept alive in Rose, transforms the world. In *The Blue Lamp*, this intensity will have no place, save in the form of hysteria, comfortably held at arm's length, in Riley and his girl. As George Dixon, Warner inherits a new, cheerful, tame world and is at the centre of it.

This is the significance of the two particular scenes. They stand on either side of the decisive shift that the end of the Hamer film represents, respectively prophetic of it, and secure in it. Doris, with Ted, embodies the kind of romantic feeling, decently restrained, that *is* compatible with the Orwell/Dixon community, and demonstrates, nowhere better than in this scene with the landlady, the values that motivate such a community and keep it going. The ending of the film, not without regret, accepts this dispensation. *The Blue Lamp* does so whole-heartedly and gives the values of the dispensation a classic statement, nowhere better than in the scene with Mitchell, Mrs Dixon, and George's flowers.

As well as consolidating this shift from private to communal, or at least the adjustment of private and communal, *The Blue Lamp* makes a great advance by centring itself on an institutional job of work, the first of the post-war Ealing films to do so. The presentation of the force corresponds to that of the service organisations in the war films. Several later films follow this pattern, with recruits being initiated into the responsibilities of work like the probation service and nursing and (again) the police. This provides a strong structure which can accommodate a composite picture of society and also firmly contain the threats of sex and violence. These can themselves become 'problems' which the jobs set themselves to cope with, as in *The Blue Lamp*, while the protagonists can sublimate their own energies in their work and their institutional routine.

Orwell referred to the importance in British culture of 'things which even when they are communal are not official.' What makes *The Blue Lamp* so seductive, so perfect a period piece, is that the police themselves can still be presented in this light. It may seem a daydream, especially from the perspective of the 'seventies, but it is one which the film manages to realise consistently and whole-heartedly. It is still close enough to the war for the wartime ideals of community and patriotism and (relative) democracy to rub off on the police in this first post-war picture of a service institution. As in *The Bells Go Down*, there is a hierarchy

which avoids being obtrusive or pompous. And the district is physically compact and intimate enough for the tone of neighbourliness to seem natural and to incorporate the police. Hence the film has the confidence to carry through its breathtaking device of building to a climax in which the *entire* community symbolically unites to deliver up a single rebel against its code. It enacts Orwell's half-admiring, half-rueful comment, in the same essay of 1941, that 'the nation is bound together by an invisible chain.'

But Orwell also, after his description of the 'privateness' of English life which this film so richly illustrates, remarks that it cannot last in its traditional form:
'It is obvious, of course, that even this purely private liberty is a lost cause. Like all other modern people, the English are in the process of being numbered, labelled, conscripted, "co-ordinated".'
One can't make too close a parallel between Orwell's deepening pessimism and the change in Ealing's films, which are clearly out of scale with one another: '1984' was published at the time *The Blue Lamp* was being shot. The point is that there *were* social changes, inevitably, which rapidly made *The Blue Lamp* appear more of a daydream than it already was: the wartime spirit was receding (or declining into an increasingly sterile nostalgia), and the 'official' was already encroaching upon the 'communal', not least within the institutions to which Ealing was so attracted. Such change constitutes a special challenge to Ealing because it is a studio so rooted in the experience of the war, so much of a community itself and so concerned to make films which celebrate its notions of community: just at the time when postwar change starts to make itself un-mistakably felt, in the late 'forties, it discovers appropriate forms for embodying

these 'timeless' notions. Both *The Blue Lamp* and Ealing comedy supply forms strong enough for Ealing to go on using. The question is whether they can be responsive to change, or whether they are simply used to pretend that change is not happening.

'I'd better put these in water.' Part of the strength of that scene comes, as I have said, from the associations the flowers carry, both personal and cultural ones. Early in the film, in one of the affectionate family scenes around their tea table, Mrs Dixon complains, or pretends to, about the embarrassing habit George has of asking people for horse manure so that he can bring it home and put it on the flower beds. 'Flowers from manure' symbolises something important in the values of the film and of Ealing. But one has to interpret it Ealing's way, excluding from this process in nature a whole set of associations that would stress physicality and transcendence, as in the pervasive imagery of *Antony and Cleopatra*—

'Kingdoms are clay; our dungy earth alike
Feeds beast as man. The nobleness of life
Is to do *thus* . . .'

'How different from the home life of our own dear Queen,' was the famous response of one Victorian theatregoer to what 'doing thus' involved; equally different is it from the home life of the Dixons. The motif of the flowers stands for nothing transcendent or exotic, it is literally a *down to earth* motif, helping to

Opposite: readers meet author in Hue and Cry. *Douglas Barr as Alec, Harry Fowler as Joe, Alastair Sim as Felix H. Wilkinson. Below: Joe, still unsuspecting, with his crooked boss Mr Nightingale (Jack Warner).*

anchor Dixon in an unambitious daily routine that has its own modest satisfactions. Very relevant here is Orwell's comment that the English love of raising flowers may have little to do with 'aesthetic feeling'. The flowers in *The Blue Lamp* act as a 'sanctification' of a lifestyle that has no aesthetic or imaginative dimensions, of its very qualities of prose, duty, restraint, acceptance.

Manure in the Dixons' back garden, haddock for breakfast at the Sandigates': an essential operation of Ealing films at this time is to reconcile us with such realities, almost to rub our noses in them. This mechanism has a special place in T. E. B. Clarke's writing, as in these early scenes in the first two Ealing comedies:

In *Hue and Cry*, Joe lives at home with his staid parents, whose concern is to see him settled in a steady job. Meanwhile he is possessed by the idea, as he tells his mother over tea, that he is on the track of a gang of criminals and may be enlisted by the CID—'And with all this crime wave going on, I wouldn't be surprised if . . .' His mother interrupts impatiently: 'You've got a bit of sausage on your chin.' It is played as a punch-line, and shuts him up.

In *Passport to Pimlico*, just after finding the treasure trove, Pemberton talks airily to the Press about what he will do with the proceeds 'Oh, maybe I'll retire— sail round the world with my own yacht with a cargo of beautiful girls . . .' His wife, on her way out with a shopping bag, throws in a deflating comment over her shoulder: 'Hark at him! Seasick on the Serpentine!'

To me, that can stand as the moment which, insofar as any single one can, represents the quintessence of Ealing: 1949, comedy, T. E. B. Clarke, Stanley Holloway, the tone of wry, shared cheerfulness, the ingrained polarisation of romance and reality.

This polarisation, and this idiom, define a *baseline* for Ealing. The dramas, as already illustrated, tend to return to and endorse it. The comedies can take off from it—can play out not only 'daydreams' of timeless, seamless communities (as in *The Blue Lamp*), but bolder fantasies which Ealing in its realistic convention clamps down upon.

Thus in *Hue and Cry*, reality is not restricted to the family tea table, a steady job, and wiping sausage off one's chin. Fantasies come true. The serial that Joe reads in his 'penny dreadful' is being used by criminals to pass information; his gang does track them down, enlisting what seems like the entire boy population of London to bring them to justice.

I have always found the charm of this film very resistible, apart from Alastair Sim's small role as the innocent serial author. Despite Balcon's testimony that its TV showings bring in new fan-mail for him, it has not had the really enduring appeal of some of the later comedies, but it had, at the time, a friendly reception that was a portent. Clarke writes of its first showing early in 1947:

'The winter was exceptionally cruel—we were being rationed more severely than at any time in the war. *Hue and Cry* was first shown during the coldest, grimmest week of a vile February. There was virtually no heating at the press reception: the critics were huddled in overcoats and the supply of drink was unavoidably limited. We couldn't believe it was possible for our little effort to relieve the general gloom.

'Yet because our picture supplied what had become another rarity—laughter— it had so joyous a welcome that it became an instant hit.'

It is a fact that the flow of British film comedy had virtually dried up. As David Shipman put it, writing of George Formby (whose film career quickly declined after he left Ealing in 1941):

'The industry, during the war, had discovered that it could make more important films than George Formby comedies . . . In the immediate post-war years there was no laughter from British studios, only turgid, phoney dramas with titles like *When the Bough Breaks* and *Good Time Girl*.'

The cranky generalisation masks a valid point which helps to explain the impact of *Hue and Cry*. It offered a relief from various solemnities bound up with the experience of the war; it gave expression to the energies of children (who were necessarily somewhat submerged beneath the earnest endeavours of the war-winning pictures); it made novel use of locations such as the London bomb-site where much of the action takes place. At the same time, it risked no offence or aesthetic challenge to its audience. Despite some inflated claims that were made for it (not by Ealing), it overlaps not at all with the location aesthetic of the Italian neo-realist film-makers of the same period, being staged and acted in a perfectly conventional 'studio' manner, much of it within the studio walls. Nor is there anything very anarchic about it in content: the children create their own sort of community in a responsible cause.

These factors, which made its novelty easy to accept, result in its looking tame today. Given the story, its fatal lack is spontaneity—in acting, response to locations, and directorial 'touch': see, for instance, the protracted scene where Joe, starting work at Covent Garden market, tries unsuccessfully to carry a set of baskets on his head. A scene that cries out for lightness and spontaneity is spun out in a heavily academic action montage overlaid with insistently whimsical music. The heaviness of touch makes the film as a whole paradoxically light-weight: it lacks the vitality to set up any real tensions (except incidentally, and in retrospect, through the casting of Jack Warner as the villain, just before his policeman roles began). It is time off, a pleasant fantasy which is easily contained. It comes full circle, in the way many Ealing comedies will do. At the start, the boys are in the choir, singing under the watchful eyes of parents and vicar: at the end, they have had their adventures; they have their black eyes as badges of honour, but they are back in the choir, with the same people watching over them.

Passport to Pimlico has a similar structure but is much more complex and interesting. It's like a more considered, adult sequel to *Hue and Cry*, taking off from the point where that finished—children on a bomb-site. Now the adults of the community take over and fulfil, play through, their own fantasy. The gateway to this is again a document: in *Hue and Cry* it was a boys' comic, in *Passport* a historical parchment found with the treasure. Both adventures are 'released' by eccentrics: Alastair Sim as the writer, Margaret Rutherford as the Professor who tells the court the implication of the document: that the locality belongs legally to the ancient Duchy of Burgundy (Miss Rutherford was cast only after Sim had turned the part down).

The children's adventure was to impose, within the adult community, a sub-system of their own working by their own rules; the adults' is to impose their own independent community within Britain. The children tilted against the comic-strip bogy of a gang of colourful crooks; the adults' adversary is the more general one of ration-books and restrictions. The children defied the common-sense put-down of their elders; the adults defy the bureaucrats who administer the system.

But this is already to fall into the conventional way of talking about the film, one which I think has become lazy and misleading.

'At the time of *Passport to Pimlico* everybody wanted to share its characters' freedom from rationing and petty restrictions. And just about everybody would secretly like to rid themselves of tiresome relatives as in *Kind Hearts and Coronets*, or get hold of unlimited whisky [*Whisky Galore*] or remove a fortune in gold bars from the Bank of England [*The Lavender Hill Mob*] . . .'

This is what T. E. B. Clarke says in his book that he was told by a colleague after the release of *The Titfield Thunderbolt* (1953), contrasting the weakness of that film's central drive with the potency of the earlier comedies. The colleague was Mackendrick; it seems a little surprising that he should be happy to lump the Ealing comedies together in this way, given the differences between his and Clarke's. They do, of course, have a common *genre* structure as comic fantasies, but the wish-fulfilment of *Passport to Pimlico* operates in a radically different way from the other two comedies of Ealing's *annus mirabilis* of 1949.

The discovery that a corner of Pimlico is legally a part of the ancient Duchy of Burgundy does emancipate its citizens from British law and thus from the regulations and rationing of the time. Its inhabitants tear up their ration books, embark on some extra buying and selling, and ignore the licensing laws. In the end, they return to the fold and to the familiar restrictions. It is, of course, a familiar mechanism in comedy (and not only comedy) to impose a fatalistic or moralistic ending without thereby renouncing the gratifications that it ostensibly shuts off. *Whisky Galore*, *Kind Hearts and Coronets* and *The Lavender Hill Mob* are good examples: their conventionally moral resolutions are imposed in a tongue-in-cheek way, right at the end, without challenging our commitment to their central characters' single-minded projects or even our belief that they really got away with it successfully. How far does *Passport to Pimlico* share this pattern? The standard summaries imply that the characters break gloriously free from controls and that the audiences of the time longingly shared their release for the duration of the film before resignedly returning, for a few years at least, to the real world of rationing. On this reading, the film would work in the same manner that cricket does in this moving passage from Neville Cardus's essay on Denis Compton:

'In 1947, summer sun blessed England, which was still licking war wounds. Never have I been so deeply touched on a cricket ground as I was in this heavenly summer, when I went to Lord's to see a pale-faced crowd, existing on rations, the rocket bomb still in the ears of most folk—to see this worn, dowdy crowd watching Compton. The strain of long years of anxiety and affliction passed from all hearts and shoulders at the sight of Compton in full flow, sending the ball here, there and everywhere, each stroke a flick of delight, a propulsion of happy sane healthy life. There was no rationing in an innings by Compton.'

Passport is set in a heatwave summer which is, or is inspired by, that of 1947. The film was made in 1948 and released in the spring of 1949. It is easy to envisage people in that summer going from cricket grounds—and the game was still, like the cinema, in its postwar boom, drawing large crowds, with runs 'unrationed'—to watch *Passport to Pimlico* in the evening. As an escape from rationing, how do the experiences compare? My reason for this preamble,

Barbara Murray and Stanley Holloway (opposite) discover the document in Passport to Pimlico, *and Margaret Rutherford tells the coroner its implications.*

besides making space for a favourite image of Compton, is to start to bring out the curious nature of the release that *Passport* actually offers.

To some, it will seem over-solemn to analyse the film stage by stage and ponder over its affectionate gags. But comedy notoriously requires as tight a logic in its construction as any other form, and depends as much on gauging how to manipulate the impulses and values of the audience it foresees. We can thus attempt to read these back from a comedy that has gained a special degree of success—as *Passport* has done in being adopted with such firm affection, both abroad and at home, as a distillation of the British spirit. I don't think, either, that this is a case where one risks destroying a gossamer web of wit by ponderous analysis. To watch the film today is to find more laughter coming from the screen, as the characters laugh at themselves and each other, than from the audience. It is, like *The Blue Lamp*, strictly a period piece, which by no means diminishes its interest. Of all the Ealing shooting-scripts, this is the one that would most be worth publishing, not as the best but as the most 'typical' (that word has to go in quotes as I mean typical of only one branch of Ealing comedy, corresponding to its gentle public image), and because its writer, Clarke, is so completely the film's author. To an unusual extent, the film is *there* in its script, not least in the very rich and full descriptions, from which I will be quoting, of how each character looks, thinks and behaves.

Passport to Pimlico. The title, and the blurred image of memory across the years, evoke a confrontation between Pimlico and the State. Actually the area is only a small section of Pimlico: Miramont Place, surrounding the bomb-site. The film opens with Arthur Pemberton putting before the Borough Council his lovingly prepared scheme for recreational use of the ground by the people of the neighbourhood; this is voted down in favour of the 'fussily pompous' Mayor's plan to sell it as a factory site to gain maximum profit for the Borough as a whole. So we're already dealing with a village within a village: the tiny community of Miramont Place, where all the people know each other, and trade with each other. (Pemberton runs his own hardware store.)

The oppressions of rationing. Molly (Jane Hylton) and Edie (Hermione Baddeley) bargain over clothing coupons at the start of Passport to Pimlico. *Right: Henry Cornelius (in hat) lining up a scene on the film's location in Lambeth.*

Pemberton is disappointed as the Council votes against his scheme.

Even Miramont Place is divided. Arthur is opposed on the Council by his neighbouring bank manager, Wix. The opposition between them is the primary one of the film. One can go further and locate the division within Wix himself, who is the film's pivotal character, the only one in whom a fundamental change of heart is seen to occur. When we first see him, before the Council meeting, he is undergoing an awkward interview in his office with an inspector from the bank's headquarters. The script says this of him:

'Wix dreams of being an important person in the world of finance, but lacks the guts even to put up a show against his immediate superior when reprimanded, as now, for exceeding his own very limited powers.'

Qua timid subordinate, Wix is the 'little man' dreaming of self-respect and independence—hence in tune with his community. *Qua* financier, on the other hand, he is a 'hawk' whose ideas are inimical to this community's values, though this may not immediately be realised; indeed, it takes the main events of the film to make the realisation complete.

In the gentle opening scenes, we find the community as a whole presented in terms of this kind of opposition. All of them are business people in a small way, valuing or seeking their independence. Some are happy if they can clear enough space around them simply to 'be themselves', others are more ambitious, as traders and/or as individuals:

'Molly is a would-be glamorous girl in the early twenties who has seen too many films, and is now no longer herself.'

When we first meet her she is crooning to herself, looking into a mirror: her interest in fashion is presented as vulgar. As for the milliner whose shop she patronises:

'Edie Randall herself is a woman in the early forties who makes pathetic attempts to keep abreast of modern styles, but it seems a pity that she tries . . .'
Contrast Mrs Pemberton:

'A comfortable, kind "body", with greying hair, and neat but old-fashioned clothes usually covered by an overall or apron . . .'

The contrast in dress stands for something deeper. Connie Pemberton knows herself and is happy in the unambitious routines of her daily life. (That sentence slides together easily, as though the two points automatically belong together: already the film's values are subtly imposing themselves, implying that to know yourself *is* to accept what you have; again, the action of the film will work this out openly, but it is implicit from the start.) Mrs Pemberton, first seen dispensing a cup of tea, is 'sentimental about children, dogs and the Royal Family, completely happy in her own domestic round. A country woman, she finds her escape from the drabness of Pimlico in cultivating pot plants of all kinds . . .'

These plants recall (or rather, in terms of chronology, anticipate) the domestic world of *The Blue Lamp*, as well as the George Orwell passage that so precisely characterised it. The Pembertons, who have a daughter, are very close indeed to the Dixons, and could well have been played by Jack Warner and Gladys Henson, though Stanley Holloway would be a little 'broad' for the reverse casting as George Dixon. Where his wife cultivates pot plants, Arthur's hobby is making wooden models—but the script's introductory note on him is worth giving in full.

'Arthur is the local "character", and nearly everyone likes and respects him. He is always ready for a chat or to give advice or help. He is also the local humorist, his wit being of the debunking, tongue-in-cheek order, which doesn't let him take many things seriously, least of all himself. He's clever with his hands, does elaborate lettering on the shop notices, and pictures of screws, hooks, buttons, etc, on the appropriate drawers. His hobby is making wooden models, which he does in the back parlour with a treadle fretsaw which creates a lot of noise and sawdust. In spite of his ribaldry, he is a sincere, honest man with all the right ideas, and a horror of graft or sham.'

Arthur takes his own intricately constructed model of the proposed community scheme to the Council meeting. The imagery is concentrated. His vision of community is his own modestly independent, hobby-filled, Orwellian lifestyle writ large (I am naturally using the adjective in the opposite of its more usual sense of 1984-like or totalitarian). At the meeting, Wix disdainfully drops ash from his cigar over the model.

The discovery of the ancient document seems to offer fulfilment for *everyone*'s dream. The inquest on the treasure takes place one morning; during the rest of the day, the implications sink in. Not only do these riches belong to the community rather than the State, but the State no longer has any jurisdiction at all. Hence no rationing, no controls of any kind. Everyone can be his own master. Wix can defy his superior and proclaim 'This is *my* bank.' The gloomy publican, Garland, can announce 'We close when *I* say.' The local bookie trades openly, the local policeman becomes his own chief, Molly can buy a new dress without waiting to save the coupons, and Edie in turn can order export silks to sell freely . . . In the pub, past closing time, documents are ritually destroyed. Wix and Pemberton can drink together in the glow of self-fulfilment. Pemberton revels in the atmosphere of communal excitement and solidarity, which reminds him of the Blitz, and in the prospect of being able to afford his pet community scheme. Wix revels in his new importance and in the prospect of putting money to work. Surely there is enough of it for everyone to play out their dreams? It's an apparent Utopia where dissent is submerged, where everyone has a chance to be himself, and to be free and affluent.

Next morning, they wake to find complications. Outsiders flood into the district and bring chaos. It's not so much that the pressures of the outside world impinge cruelly upon this Utopia, as that the cracks *within* the communal fantasy at once open up on the morning after, with the inevitability of a hangover. The Wix and Pemberton fantasies can't coexist. Freedom from controls works both ways. Outsiders can come in not only to buy but to sell. With the Metropolitan Police now forbidden to enter foreign territory, a free-for-all develops which delights some and scares others. The community is split down the middle, on predictable lines. Elected chairman of the negotiating committee, Pemberton at once phones Whitehall to talk surrender. The opposition is articulated by Wix and Garland. This is *my* bank, we close when *I* say: what may have seemed no more than the lovable assertion of individual identity by two 'little men' now defines itself further as aggressive economic individualism.

Pemberton insists that they must throw themselves on the mercy of the Government: 'The important thing is to get some law and order here. We don't want this place turned into a spivs' paradise.' To which Garland leads the protest: 'Here—but what about us business people? This is our big chance! All the stuff we want at export prices . . .' When Whitehall, through diplomatic hair-splitting, refuses to talk, Wix, who has been busy handing out loans to traders, registers a victory: 'Well, that seems to settle things.' And Garland, who presides at all

Phone call to Whitehall from Pemberton's Hardware Store. Garland (Frederick Piper), Wix (Raymond Huntley), Huggins (John Slater), with Pemberton, father and daughter.

Pimlico defies the bureaucrats: Pemberton and Wix, now shoulder to shoulder, facing Gregg and Straker (Basil Radford, Naunton Wayne).

hours over a pub packed with visitors, draws with equal satisfaction the moral, 'It's every man for himself.'

This last line seems well calculated to mark off Garland and what he stands for as heretical. If this isn't clear now, it will become so later in the film when he gets an unmistakable comeuppance; but it surely *is* clear, even at this point. 'Every man for himself' is anathema to the community, just as we would expect it to be to Ealing. The images of crowds milling chaotically around in the streets are 'fun', but sinister too: the scene has a distinctly hard edge. It's Huggins, a fishmonger in a small way ('shy, unassuming, with a quiet voice, which gains confidence when talking about fish, which are not only his work, but his hobby and delight') who is the crowd's most poignant victim, physically battered by them, then given unfair competition on his own doorstep by a spiv who offers a false description of his wares and answers Huggins's outrage by challenging him to do anything about it in the prevailing anarchy.

Insofar as the anti-controls, anti-rationing feeling means outright acquisitiveness, every man for himself, Ealing plainly means to present it as frightening. For many it does mean this, both within the film (not only Wix and Garland) and presumably within the audience, though they may not—being unused to it in practice—have thought the issue through. If not, the film enables them to; indeed, this is the main thing it does. An audience which may well have come to the cinema in a mood to dream about Free Enterprise (the dominant Tory slogan in the next election) is pulled up short—and this is less than half-way through the film.

At the same time, this isn't the only pleasure that the device of independence has released. The anti-controls feeling, so startlingly gratified for this tiny community, has a benevolent as well as an aggressive side to it, and this can continue to be safely indulged. Arthur at this stage seems craven, a spoilsport, in being ready to surrender independence and the sheer fun and pride of being Burgundy.

The film continues to play skilfully with its audience in resolving the deadlock. What happens now is that Whitehall takes fright at the existence of this un-restricted trading area inside London, and imposes its own frontier controls unilaterally. Arthur's first reaction is one of relief: action at last. But when he finds out what this means in detail, he isn't so happy: the controls, like the earlier lifting of them, are double-edged, restricting the Burgundians as well as alien spivs and threatening not only Wix and Garland's expansionist trade but his own steady ticking-over: 'What about all our customers who live outside this area?' When an official starts patronising the Burgundians as 'foreigners', even Pemberton is at last stung into defiance: 'In future we'll ruddy well *be* foreigners.'

His daughter Shirley breaks into delighted rhetoric: 'Great stuff, Dad! We'll fight them on the tramlines, we'll fight them in the local . . .' The Churchillian echo creates a typical allusive 'English' gag with a profound import that is ultimately a very melancholy one. The Burgundians from this point engage in a diplomatic war: they recover the spirit, the resilience and local autonomy and *unity* of wartime London. References back to the war, visual and verbal, come thick and fast ('Don't you know there's a siege on?') as 'plucky little Burgundy' unites against the apparatus of Whitehall. I use the word melancholy because the absolute clarity of the structure demonstrates that only by reverting to the pressures and privations of wartime can the community find the self-fulfilment it longs for, submerging differences that are otherwise intractable. In the news-reel film which carries much of the story at this point (some 'evacuated' Burgundian children go to see it in a West End cinema), we are shown images of Attlee and Churchill, Bevin and Eden, hurrying to Downing Street ostensibly to debate the issue of Burgundy, while the commentary tells us that 'For the first time since the war, party differences have been forgotten.' In its whimsical way, that detail touches on a deep-rooted nostalgia for consensus, which we still see in the recurrent appeals of the 'seventies to abandon sterile party opposition and exploit the energies of the British people in a government of national unity. We did it in the war, why not again? But no modern 'crisis' has yet returned us to anything like the constraints and the psychology of the war itself. In a modern consumer society, people's interests and priorities conflict too much for unity to be more than a sham. *Passport to Pimlico* catches this issue at exactly the critical time when these conflicts are starting to make themselves felt.

'It was difficult to believe in a time of national inspiration and unity that this inspiration and unity would ever fade'—the community we see at the start of the film is still conditioned by this feeling. The question is whether it can reconcile the desire to maintain the wartime spirit with the desire to be freer and more affluent. The 'Burgundy' device tests this out, by accelerating the processes that were already starting to happen in England at large: phasing out of rationing, bonfire of controls, Free Enterprise, the dawn of affluence. Result: free-for-all, incipient chaos, dissension. Then comes the film's second, less spectacular, device: the contrivance that causes Britain not to accept the Burgundian sur-render but lets relations deteriorate to the point of siege. Unity is rediscovered as the community re-enacts, in word and deed, the rituals of wartime, with communal feeding, strict rationing, evacuation of children, and defiance of the enemy. Wix and Pemberton, Tory and Labour, are one again: since neither can trade at all, there is no cause to argue about their different conceptions of how the economy, and society, should operate if they could. Which re-enacts, in miniature, the war experience of Britain itself.

There is, however, one exception to this unity: Garland, the publican. The man who articulated most starkly the philosophy of 'Every man for himself' is the one who turns defeatist as soon as pressure is put on. He slinks away across the frontier, jeered, the only adult to be evacuated along with the local children: Ealing is drawn to this pattern through which certain values that conflict with the community are concentrated into one individual who is then eliminated from it, symbolically rejected. If possible, bring everyone into the fold (the central wartime films); when tension persists, isolate the attitudes which seem to cause it, and reject or exorcise them. What is being exorcised in Garland, diagnosed in its pure form as anti-social and unpatriotic, is free-market acquisitiveness. Like Riley's criminal associate in *The Blue Lamp*, Wix turns against him, his 'natural' adherence to the community values (or to use Matthew Arnold's apt term, his 'best self') coming out. When Garland asks what will happen to his property in his absence, it is Wix who taunts him: 'We've got a government now. That'll be nationalised.' As the script prescribes, here as in many places, 'There is a roar of laughter,' but it's another joke with profound, teasing implications.

Richard Winnington, always the most interesting of contemporary critics of Ealing films, found *Passport* disappointing because of the feebleness of the release it offered: 'The apex of Burgundian emancipation is a song and dance in the local after hours.' Absolutely true, but in the end that is the whole point. The prime 'fantasy' of the film, which caught the imagination so firmly, is not— whatever publicity might suggest—the dream of release from rationing and restrictions. That impulse in the film is ambivalent and half-hearted, indulged even to the extent that it is only in order to be reversed: to see self-fulfilment coming in that way is a delusion. The more potent dream that takes over from it is of a return to wartime solidarity, which means an intensification of rationing and restrictions: in the course of the film, these become truly romanticised.

The narrative works by a succession of gentle gags or comic ideas, usually based on incongruity. Some of these play out the impulse of freedom, as in the long pub sequence. But the most vivid ones are surely those playing out restriction and control, as in the much-anthologised scene (which usually represents the film when a TV clip is called for) of the Burgundians stopping the underground train for border formalities. Wix and Pemberton are in significant alliance, Wix fussing about currency, Pemberton obliging an anxious European visitor by endorsing his passport with the rubber receipt-stamp from Pembertons' Stores: it's details like these which clinched the film's hold on the affection of audiences. Like the whole film, the sequence is light and playful, but could only work so effectively by appealing at a deep level: it invites laughter at controls, but indulgent laughter, resting on a fond nostalgic enjoyment, to which the structure of the plot gives real point and substance. Not least the ending.

A compromise is devised by Wix for Burgundy to come back into the British fold. An open-air dinner, for the community and the Whitehall negotiators, is laid out in celebration, with a new ration book and identity card in each place. Never was a message made more explicit than in Mrs Pemberton's dialogue here with PC Spiller, who says:

'I never thought people'd welcome the sight of these things again.'

Welcome back. Among those present: Mrs Pemberton (Betty Warren), next to her husband; P. C. Spiller (Philip Stainton); behind him, the Duke of Burgundy (Paul Dupuis).

'You never know when you're well off till you aren't.'

The irony is not at her expense: the logic of the film is behind her, as it is behind Mrs Huggett's homesick cry from the heart of Africa in Gainsborough's *The Huggetts Abroad*: 'There's something nice about a queue: something warm and friendly and all-in-the-same-boat. I wouldn't mind queuing for a bit of Icelandic cod right now.' Like *Passport*, that was shown in 1949: were people now, with the onset of affluence, waking up to what they were starting to lose?

I have referred to A. J. P. Taylor's account of the 'inspiration and unity' of the mid-war years. In May 1976, here is the same writer's response to economic crisis:

'The sensible course would be a siege economy, with import controls, rationing of essentials, direction of labour and industry, no private motoring, all sorts of lovely things. But this demands national unity and socialists who believe in socialism. Neither exists.'
(New Statesman)

It is the same tone of flippancy disguising a serious argument as characterises *Passport to Pimlico*. And the argument itself, nearly thirty years on, is extraordinarily evocative of the film—which in itself goes a long way to explaining the film's enduring, classic status. The impulses that it plays out have a recurring appeal, are deeply rooted in our culture. 'All sorts of lovely things': by using the form and the tone of comedy, the film is able to say the startling things that it does. Equally, because it's a comedy, these things can be dismissed with a laugh and even blurred in the memory, as by those who recall it as a holiday *from* restrictions and an anticipation of consumer affluence.

The heatwave ends, a storm breaks, and the thermometer visibly falls. Miramont Place, Pimlico, England, is rain and ration books: and this comes over not as a downbeat ending—one of resignation and drabness as in the early set of Ealing postwar films I have referred to—but as a romantic one. This is the achievement of the film, and its formal breakthrough: to make 'poverty of desire' into something romantic, rather than just an absence, a defeat. There is some sadness at the end in that the adventure of an independent 'Burgundy' terminates, with Pemberton ceasing to be a Prime Minister, and so on, but no sadness in the return to Government restrictions as such. Far from it: this is the consolation. Burgundy has been a minority holding out against Britain. But it is also the essence of Britain, and the resolution has the effect, not of fatalistically re-absorbing this minority into the State machine but of redefining the State in terms of this minority. Burgundy found true self-fulfilment with the replay of all the privations of wartime; by analogy, Britain is most itself when still 'defined'— in the literal sense, limited—by what is left of these privations: by these 'lovely things'. Hence the welcome to the documents at the end, stated by Mrs Pemberton on behalf of all. The sadness of the end, in fact, is that this dispensation is felt as being only temporary.

The real sadness in a wider perspective is the extent of the polarisation— between recreated past and threatening future, between the dynamism of acquisitiveness and the static nature of the community which the film romanticises. Put it another way: the sadness is that there should be so deep a compulsion to dream of consensus, to shy away from the conflicts that come up in an 'open' society rather than to follow them through clear-sightedly.

There is an Ealing film of 1955, *Lease of Life*, in which Robert Donat plays a country vicar: in the course of it, he preaches a sermon on the subject of crowds and mass emotion. Crowds can either be herds (bad) or flocks (good). This makes explicit a tension which is always central to Ealing's view of the world and which its films repeatedly dramatise. At the first crisis of *Passport to Pimlico*, when the place has turned into a 'spivs' paradise', the ancestral Duke of Burgundy, who has just arrived from France, listens to an earnest early-morning appeal from the British government over the radio for people to stay out of the area all day, to insure against disorder. He comments admiringly on what this reveals of the British way of life: you just say that, and people obey. But a window is then thrown open to reveal the chaotic sight and sound of crowds flooding in. It's a simple comic irony with, once again, a serious import. The crowd is a herd, aggressive and frightening. They cheat and exploit, and have to be expelled. Contrast the flock of the closing stages, all benevolence, rallying round to sustain gallant little Burgundy by its moral and material support. The two crowds could well consist of the same individuals: the difference is in the mood, and in the circumstances which create the mood. The flock is like the benevolent crowds at the end of *Hue and Cry* and *The Blue Lamp*, and like the crowds of wartime. But the suspicion remains that the first crowd, the herd, represents Ealing's uneasy vision of how in the real postwar world, when you open the window, venture out from behind the protective barriers, people actually behave. That is where it rests, in a polarisation that is alternately nervous and complacent.

I have been presenting, as typical of Ealing's (mainstream) philosophy, two modes of thinking which may seem at first sight to contradict one another: two forms of polarisation of romance and reality. 'Maybe I'll retire—sail round the world on my own yacht with a cargo of beautiful girls . . .' 'Hark at him! Seasick on the Serpentine!' The Pembertons here, and Ealing, belong on the 'reality' side: down-to-earth, sensible, prosaic, like the Dixons. But in terms of the wider romance/reality division they are on the 'romance' side, turning away from what is perceived (increasingly so as the war recedes in time) as an unpleasant 'real' world of conflict and acquisitiveness. Realism is a slippery concept, as indeed is romanticism: Ealing's distinctive blend is a down-to-earth 'realism' about life and its restricted possibilities, which is itself profoundly romanticised. It is the dream of a world where dreams are renounced, the romantic vision of a community which can stay safe and happy and cut off precisely through denying so much of what is conventionally associated with romance: passion, wealth, the quest for 'other' dimensions of experience. (Equally, one could say that it stays safe by denying the pressures of 'reality', these included.)

When Pemberton father and daughter go down into the bomb crater early in the film to look at the treasure, the deflating witticisms proliferate. He: 'Somebody's been saving up for a rainy day.' She, finding the crucial parchment: 'Blimey, they even had to fill up forms in those days.' With extreme ingenuity, the film succeeds in giving this style its apotheosis by recreating the protected conditions in which it can be self-sufficient, self-governing. The Pembertons rule: Arthur leads, Connie has the last word (welcoming the ration books), Shirley is courted by the Duke. Even this romance is conducted within the Pemberton idiom. One warm evening, out of doors, their conversation leads up to a kiss. At once, this is interrupted by the noise of cats on the roof, and they separate wryly. Their next effort is disturbed by another off-putting noise: they look round and see the silhouette outline of a man at his bathroom window, gargling. They smile and give up. It's like the scene in *It Always Rains on Sunday* when Rose goes out to her former lover, who is concealed in the back garden, but is frustrated by Mrs Watson leaning out of her adjacent window to talk about the Sunday joint: the sheer closeness of the community, caught up in its good-humoured daily routines, is felt as a deeply conditioning force, the source and outward sign of the community's strength, and also of its inhibitions. Of all the films, *Passport* is the one that gives the most vivid summation of this Ealing 'dispensation' and of what it plays down or leaves out: conflict, acquisitiveness, desire of all kinds.

The last thing I want to do in writing of *Passport to Pimlico* is to be patronising about the anti-acquisitive philosophy itself, which is truly the one hope of a better world, and perhaps of a continuing world at all. But if there is one lesson to draw from the anti-acquisitive and small-is-beautiful movements of recent years, it is that these ideals are not cosy, negative options which can be secured by good intentions and a change of heart, but need to be fought out with passion and intelligence, both in order to overcome the inertia of vested interests, and to give these options power to appeal widely by offering alternative satisfactions for the human energies that will otherwise go into getting and spending and wasting. This is the flaw in the Pemberton dispensation, making it ultimately so vulnerable—and this has wider implications, for Ealing and for Britain: it offers essentially a cosy retreat, a soft option, operated not by harnessing and redirecting energies, but by denying them.

WHISKY GALORE

Though I have quoted from various writers on the subject, dear to Ealing, of Britain and the British character, there is one book which I want to relate to Ealing in a more sustained manner: 'The Collapse of British Power', published in 1972 by the historian Correlli Barnett. Without mentioning Ealing, indeed without going beyond 1945, Barnett provides the essential *prolegomena* to Ealing by analysing the evolution of the 'national character' over the previous century:

'For it is character which, at grips with circumstances, governs the destiny of nations as it does of individual men. It is the key to all policies, all decisions.'

If national 'character' seems an old-fashioned, impressionistic term, it is worth noting that it could perfectly well be replaced by 'ideology'.

Barnett, like Forster, sees the ideology of the public school as central, both because it was public school products who habitually gave leadership and because certain institutionalised activities, like sport and religion, spanned the classes and in effect provided reinforcement for public school values at lower social levels. Again like Forster, he offers lists of characteristics bred into the public school man. On the one hand, 'probity, orthodoxy, romantic idealism, a strong sense of public responsibility.' On the other, 'conservatism, doctrinaire orthodoxy, rigidity, inertia and unbounded complacency.' The main cluster of key words throughout the book—soft, tender-minded, romantic, idealist, sentimental, moralistic—refer to the national character or ideology as it developed in the mid-19th century within the country's established military and industrial strength. It was this security which allowed the impact of the romantic movement, and of evangelical religion, to be so profound and lasting, and to take the 'soft' form that it did. Barnett's analysis is of a nation coming to live on its moral and material capital, able to *afford* to be tender-minded and the rest—for a time, until other powers start to challenge the superiority which Britain is used to enjoying as of right. But by then, she is too deeply conditioned to be able to change, conditioned by an ideology which has shaped and permeated her institutions, particularly educational ones.

'British educational neglect in the 19th century artificially created a stupid, lethargic, unambitious, unenterprising people for the 20th century. The consequences were insidiously to affect many fields of national performance.'

The main effects the book is concerned to trace are in the fields of strategy and diplomacy, culminating in the disastrous period between the wars:

'Other great powers did not see the world as one great human society, but—just as the British had done up to the 19th century—as an arena where, subject to the mutual convenience of diplomatic custom, nation states—the highest effective form of human society—competed for advantage. They did not believe in a natural harmony among mankind, but in national interests that might sometimes coincide with the interests of others, sometimes conflict.'

The British way of innocent trust in this 'natural harmony among mankind', and of shrinking from conflict and challenge, led directly to Munich, and to the disastrously vulnerable position she found herself in at that time—from which she has never, in spite of 'victory', recovered.

It is a thesis which it would be easy, but wrong, to caricature as simplistically hawkish and reactionary: in this context I can do small justice to its complexity and scholarship, but I believe it to be one of the seminal works on British culture. A few years ago I analysed in Screen magazine the muddled, nannyish, *wet* response to Sam Peckinpah's magnificent *Straw Dogs* on the part of British critics; it was only later, on reading Barnett's book, that I started to understand the deep-rootedness of the ideology within which these critics, with their panic at the idea of 'force' being in any circumstances justified, were operating. The book provides an equally illuminating perspective for Ealing—and for the affectionate adoption of Ealing to 'speak for England'. Barnett shows the British pulling themselves convulsively together in time of war, and then relapsing back into mildness and conservatism and good intentions—the pattern readable overall in Ealing production. I have traced how Ealing's trust in 'a natural harmony among mankind' comes to the fore after the main war films and how the films progressively suppress conflict and tension (*Scott of the Antarctic* and *Frieda*, as well as the Clarke films), in attempting to bring out the Arnoldian 'best self' in individual and community.

'His first impressions of the British were formed by the Ealing comedies . . . "I thought I knew the British character," he says, "but, since coming to live here, I have learnt that no such thing actually exists. There are simply characteristic patterns of behaviour. One of them is your instinct to go for the soft option. Everyone does it, from individuals up to governments. You avoid the harsh realities, you go in for self-delusion, you hope that good manners will solve everything . . .

'"Don't misunderstand me. I live in London for one simple reason: I love the place."'

(Erkki Toivanen of the Finnish Broadcasting Company, quoted in
Radio Times, 1976)

'Then everything along the bus route to the city upset me. The houses seemed so small, and the flower-bordered front paths, down which men in three-piece suits came hurrying off to work, seemed too bright and neat and prepared. Men were carrying umbrellas, whistling errand boys on bicycles were weaving in and out of the traffic, bright orange tile roofs curved gaily over pebble-dash fronts. Bay windows, broad clean pavements, narrow, tarmacked roadways, lurching buses, everything was just as it was in the Ealing comedy movies. It was all nice and wholesome and harmless.'

(Martin Green in 'A Mirror for Anglo-Saxons' (1961):
on a return visit from America to England)

How often have we heard—do we still hear—comments like these: the Ealing comedies invoked as creating an image of British life which, however stylised or partial, is recognised as having a continuing weird accuracy: an image (or self-image) which the observer may love, or despise, or more commonly, as in these two instances, feel ambivalent about. Compare Correlli Barnett's own summary of the historical background to Ealing:

'It was exactly because British life itself was now [between the wars] so orderly, gentle, docile, safe and law-abiding, so founded on mutual trust, that the British were less fitted to survive as a nation than their ancestors, whose characters had been formed in a coarse, tough and brutal society.'

A perfect text for *Passport to Pimlico,* whose characters seem too gentle and innocent to prosper in the 'real' world: that is their charm. Nice and wholesome and harmless or coarse, tough and brutal—do the alternatives have to be so stark? Ealing itself insists on the polarisation, embracing the first, feeling such distaste for the second as to suppress everything that seems to have a taint of coarseness or divisiveness, like sex, conflict, self-interest, class-division, even cleverness. (It is a process comparable to that which Barnett traces in British culture as a whole.) In the Pembertons and the Dixons, Ealing through T. E. B. Clarke creates memorable apotheoses of the kind of decency that excludes all these, as far as they ever can be excluded.

But—and it is a big but—this is only the mainstream of Ealing production. What *Passport*'s two contemporaries, *Kind Hearts and Coronets* and *Whisky Galore,* do is to restore what is suppressed. *Kind Hearts* is about sex and class. *Whisky Galore,* like its characters, is cruel and clever.

The curious thing is that although the reputation of these two has endured at least as well, it is *Passport* that has overwhelmingly conditioned the public image of Ealing comedy. Martin Green's words, 'nice and wholesome and harmless', are typical of many references, yet that whole passage appeals to our mental image of an *urban* comedy and, one guesses, of *Passport* in particular: neither the description nor the adjectives have any application on the face of it to *Kind Hearts* or *Whisky Galore.*

Hamer made no subsequent Ealing comedies; Mackendrick made three (*The Man in the White Suit, The Maggie, The Ladykillers*). These five films are radically distinct from the mainstream shaped by Clarke, who wrote six in all: strong where the others are weak, tough where they are gentle, intelligent where they are at best ingenious. Yet to try proving this may be an academic exercise of little value unless they have in practice operated differently on their audiences. Films are for use. One can consider three hypotheses: 1) the 'strong' comedies do successfully subvert the Ealing norms, all the more effectively for operating in a devious way, without making a show of being different; 2) in objective terms, they do this, but the Ealing image and the determination of audiences to fit them to a cosy stereotype prevent them from being properly understood; 3) the differences count for less than the similarities—these films may seem to operate in different ways but at heart they are the same old lovable Ealing. *Kind Hearts* and *Whisky Galore,* for instance, share the Ealing comedy identity to the extent of being, in David Robinson's phrase, 'quirky, local, human' and of indulging, like the Clarke scripts, the dreams of the 'little man'; as comic fantasies, they belong to the genre.

Clearly, the comparison raises questions about the experiencing of popular art which go far beyond the particular case. All I can do now is set out how I myself see the films. Broadly, where Clarke distils all the nice but weakly

Alexander Mackendrick directing Joan Greenwood and Bruce Seton in the village hall converted for use as a location studio on Whisky Galore.

romantic elements in the national character which writers like Corelli Barnett have dissected, Mackendrick's comedies are consciously *about* this character and perform a comparable analysis (compare the relation of Hamer's early films to the other Ealing output of the time).

Barnett quotes this admiring comment on Stanley Baldwin made by a political colleague of the 'twenties:

'The new PM caught the public imagination . . . His placidity, his common sense, his moderation, his modesty and his obvious sincerity caused people to say, "This is the man, a typical Englishman, for whom we have been looking for so long. We are sick of Welshmen and lawyers, the best brains and supermen. We want the old type of English statesman, who is fair-minded, judicious and responsible, rather than the man who is so clever that he thinks ahead of everyone else . . ."'

These attitudes have endured, for instance in the widely echoed criticism of another non-English politician Iain McLeod that he was 'too clever by half'. In *Passport to Pimlico*, Pemberton *is* this Baldwin type of English statesman (indeed, his rise to Prime Ministerial status has something of the romance of Baldwin's own unpredicted rise late in life). His opposite number in the negotiations is Basil Radford, epitome of the Whitehall mind. Beneath their dramatic opposition, he and Pemberton are soulmates, thinking the same way, holding to the same values, drinking tea, and able to come at the end to a cheerful accommodation which restores a 'natural' state of harmony and consensus.

Whisky Galore puts this same Basil Radford with this same sincere, fair-minded, pompous style of authority among the Celts. He is Captain Waggett, an English resident on the Hebridean island of Todday, commanding the Home

Guard there in 1943 (not literally the same character as in *Passport*, but Radford was an instantly recognisable and invariably type-cast actor, so that the part works as if he were). This sets up an English/Celtic opposition like that in the lines about Baldwin. In this film, there is no accommodation between the sides. Waggett ends up crushed and humiliated, driven out of the community. This follows the Ealing pattern of isolating a single antisocial character and ejecting him, but where the others (Tommy Swann, Riley, Garland, etc.) are condemned for their selfishness, Waggett is a very different case.

Like the Miramont Place community, the islanders suffer privations—a whisky famine—which they are miraculously presented with the chance to overcome: a cargo ship carrying whisky is wrecked offshore. Their drive to possess this never falters. Pemberton's rallying cry was Law and Order. Waggett, trying on principle to stop the cargo being looted, tells his wife: 'Once you let people take the law into their own hands, it's anarchy, anarchy!' but this impresses nobody.

The two plots can't, of course, be strictly commensurable. The desire for the whisky is less problematic than the desire to be free of all controls—if the islanders don't get the whisky, it will go to the bottom of the sea, and it seems natural justice that they should salvage some. Nor is the 'anarchy' of this united, traditional community as threatening as the free-for-all in the streets of Pimlico. You could say, then, that the difference in the resolution is conditioned by the different premises of the plot. However, the respective constructions are themselves significant: *Passport* in effect makes a *reductio ad absurdum* of all acquisitiveness or desire; *Whisky Galore* contrives to make it and keep it the central drive of the

Whisky Galore. *Opposite: Macroon (Wylie Watson) with his daughters (Joan Greenwood, Gabrielle Blunt) and their suitors (Gordon Jackson, Bruce Seton). Above: the Doctor doses Hector; Captain Waggett interrogates the constable.*

film. Above all, there is the difference in tone and values that is built into the film at every point.

There is one sequence in *Whisky Galore* which no-one who has seen the film forgets. The islanders have successfully raided the ship, and the local post-master takes the opportunity to celebrate the betrothal of both his daughters with a traditional party. Under cover of darkness, the local excise officials arrive with Waggett, who has put them up to it. At the last moment, a warning is telephoned through to the Post Office. There follows a rapid sequence of bottles being hidden in all imaginable places: hands deposit them in gutter and rainbutt, pour their contents into tank and hot-water-bottle, place them inside a cash-register and under a pie-crust and—in a final image—inside a cot, to be covered by its innocent-looking occupant: some time after last seeing the film, I can't recover all the details of the sequence, since it isn't contained in the shooting script (it was presumably left to improvisation), and on screen the images flash by in a blur, communicating a sense of urgent intuitive teamwork as the community protects its pleasures and its autonomy against the bureaucrat.

Compare the sequence in *Passport* where regulations are first defied. The legal position has been made clear in court; later, Wix endures another interview in his own office with his nagging superior. With the suddenness of a light-bulb illuminated over the head of a character in a comic-strip, inspiration strikes him: 'This is my bank!' The disconcerted superior leaves, ponders, and buys from Molly the entire supply of eggs set out on the counter of the shop where she works: 'Rationing? This is Burgundy!' Molly takes it in, amazed, then runs round to Edie's shop to buy the dress for which she was saving coupons. 'Coupons? This is Burgundy!' Edie in turn sees the light and phones for delivery of an export consignment. And it continues this way into the evening at the pub.

Clarke has referred to his use of the 'snowball' effect in *Hue and Cry*, and that word is appropriate to *Passport*: the whole film is built on such a principle. A problem is posed, an *idea* is thought up in response and spread around and worked through, then the process starts again, building up a new 'snowball'. This has obvious attractions as a means of telling a comedy story. The comedy is all played out on the surface, stage by stage, in dialogue. But it also means that the people come over as somewhat slow on the uptake, like chess-players unable to think even one move ahead but content to wait their turn. We cannot discount this as mere convention, like the convention of having characters in dramatic exposition tell each other for our benefit things that we know they know already. It's not that the characters' responses are artificially slowed down to give the film time to make its comedy points at leisure: the construction and the characters can't be separated. The people are slow—that is part of their sturdy charm, and the charm of the community. They are often opportunist or ingenious, never intelligent, and one would never be tempted to insult Pemberton, any more than Baldwin, by calling him 'so clever that he thinks ahead of everyone else'.

In complete contrast, the quickness of the *Whisky Galore* sequence conveys the quick-wittedness of that community. There is no dialogue: we simply see an old man spotting the excisemen's boat from his window and rushing to the nearest telephone, then the receipt of the call at the Post Office. The bottle-hiding sequence exhilaratingly transmits the speed of the group's reactions. There is no time for instructions to be passed round, and anyway they don't need it. By the time the visitors knock at the door, the operation is complete and the guests have melted away.

The official and Waggett are received by the postmaster (Macroon) and his daughter, all sleepy innocence. Their shrewdness is a delight. At last, we come to an Ealing film that affords moments of unreserved pleasure, rather than just varying degrees of admiration or amusement or interest. There is nothing dated about the confrontation between Waggett and the islanders in scenes like this: they belong, like *Kind Hearts*, on the level of the best Hollywood comedy of the 'thirties and reward repeated viewings. This is a three-way scene between the bewildered Waggett, the Macroons, who pretend to take the visit as an unexpected but pleasant social one, and the official (Farquharson), a local man who, though he has to admit defeat, talks the same language as them, a language with layers of subtlety that are quite opaque to Waggett:

Farquharson (meaningfully): 'I'll call earlier next time.'
Macroon: 'Och, I didn't mind you coming late at all.'

Macroon and Pemberton are both shopkeepers who come to represent their small communities. They, and the daughters, and the communities, could hardly be more different from one another. Macroon is a consummate diplomat, playing on his own strength and on others' self-interest. The encounters with Waggett play out deep cultural oppositions, and I can't but refer again to Barnett and 'The Collapse of British Power', so perfectly does Waggett (like Alec Guinness's Colonel Nicholson in *The Bridge on the River Kwai*) embody the list of the public school man's characteristics quoted above: 'Probity, orthodoxy, romantic idealism, a strong sense of public responsibility . . . Conservatism, doctrinaire orthodoxy, rigidity, inertia, and unbounded complacency.'

The encounters are collisions between this state of mind and that *realistic* calculation of self-interest and others' interest to which Barnett shows his Englishman repeatedly falling victim. Take the early scene in the Post Office between Macroon, Waggett, and the English Home Guard sergeant. By now it is known that the wrecked ship contains whisky. It is late on Sunday night; the islanders cannot break the Sabbath but are waiting for midnight:

Macroon wants the whisky brought ashore.
Waggett is determined to prevent this, on principle.
The Sergeant wants to marry Macroon's daughter.

Waggett's procedure is always straightforward. He says what he thinks, and orders his Sergeant to keep watch on the shoreline opposite the ship during the night. Macroon's manner is oblique. With Waggett, he is amusedly non-committal. With the Sergeant, when they are left alone together, he chats reflectively, in no hurry: 'You can't have a wedding without a *reiteach* [traditional celebration], and you can't have a *reiteach* without whisky.' The Sergeant is mildly shocked: this is 'blackmail'. Macroon remains inscrutable: the two men look levelly at one another, and the scene fades out.

The three-way exchange encapsulates the film:

Macroon 'reads' both men, and successfully conveys a message.

The Sergeant reads.

Waggett fails both in reading and communicating.

And it is a scene decisive for the plot. Soon, with elaborate carelessness, the Sergeant allows a group of raiders to put him out of action while boatloads of whisky are brought in; he has shifted definitively from Waggett's side to that of the islanders. Given its importance, it is very striking that Mackendrick should present the whole post-office scene in the neutral manner he does and refrain from 'signposting' what is going on—Waggett's obtuseness, Macroon's calculation, the temptation offered to the Sergeant—by any strong comic/dramatic emphasis in the cutting or playing.

Perhaps the best way of bringing out the distinctiveness of this strategy is to jump briefly to *The Lavender Hill Mob* (directed two years later by Charles Crichton from a T. E. B. Clarke script) and a superficially comparable scene of one character putting temptation in another's way: Holland reveals to his fellow-lodger, Pendlebury, his plan to steal bullion from the Bank of England and export it in the shape of Eiffel Tower models cast in Pendlebury's souvenir-producing machinery. Alec Guinness plays Holland; Stanley Holloway is Pendlebury, who is as close in character as in name to Pemberton in *Passport to Pimlico*: cheerful, decent and not especially quick on the uptake. The two men circle round Pendlebury's machine, Holland endlessly dropping hints, waiting to see if his friend, outwardly as respectable a character as himself, will respond. Finally, Pendlebury gets the message and looks up for a long moment into Holland's eyes: 'By Jove, Holland, it's a good job we're both honest men.' The line is successful, gaining a big laugh. The film has worked carefully for that laugh: the irony is unmissable, played out on the surface, underlined in the writing and speaking and framing—the faces are close to the camera, and the two excited expressions are held frozen through a slow fade.

The audience has the pleasure of being one move ahead of Pendlebury and waiting for him to catch up. The work that the spectator has to do in *Whisky Galore* is more complex and gives a different kind of satisfaction. He has to comprehend (not just in this scene) a continuous interplay of motives and perceptions, and the process—because of the amount that is left unsaid and unsignposted—is an active one, akin to that which faces the characters themselves. The director keeps confronting us with surfaces, appearances, to be interpreted, just as Macroon confronts people: he plays gently with our ability to perceive, to infer, to make connections and ultimately judgments. An English audience, at least, is drawn into the film in the manner of the English Sergeant: attracted to the locals from the start, and feeling amused pity for Waggett, but brought progressively to a fuller and more ruthless commitment. To win Macroon's daughter, the Sergeant has literally to 'speak her language' (a few lover's words in Gaelic), and this symbolises the wider initiation he undergoes into the locals' codes of perception and value.

All this makes it, surely, a more substantial and subversive work than *The Lavender Hill Mob* among the set of Ealing comedies that enlist our sympathy with a form of law-breaking. Clarke has recounted how he got the idea for *The Lavender Hill Mob* while he was meant to be working on the script for *Pool of London*, a crime thriller dealing with a cross-section of East End characters. Though he was at once switched from this project to write the comedy and has no script credit, the relation of the two is clear and neat. In *Pool of London*, one character persuades another to use his insider's expertise on a big robbery: 'Listen, George, you were going to be a bigshot, your own boss, with everything you wanted, and what are you now? An ex-clerk with a pension you can't buy fags on . . . Same with me. This is the chance for both of us to get our own back. It won't knock twice.'

Compare what is said to the similarly meek Holland at the start of *The Lavender Hill Mob*—ironically by a Bank official persuading him to accept a slightly less menial post:
'The trouble with you, Holland, is that you haven't enough ambition. When a good opportunity comes along, grab it with both hands—it may not occur again.'
'Very good, Sir: I'll follow your advice.'

Both the worms turn; they decide to grab their chance of wealth. In *Pool of London*, it's a messy, foredoomed exercise that ends ingloriously in violence and remorse, like the irresponsible 'amateur' crime of *The Blue Lamp*. In *The Lavender Hill Mob*, the meek are allowed to inherit the earth by means of a massive crime that hurts and offends no-one. There is no contradiction between the two films or the two sides of mainstream Ealing that they represent: they are perfectly complementary. The drama is Ealing's picture of how things have to be in a society which rightly inhibits individual drives and desires for self-fulfilment. The comedy is a daydream, a fantasy outlet for those urges. Its good humour has the effect of continuously endorsing the 'social' values even while the plot is ostensibly defying them. The two professional criminals, enlisted by Holland and Pendlebury on a visit to their local greyhound stadium, are gentle individuals, preoccupied with the last bus home and with the Test Match; there is no hardness or shrewdness in the 'Mob' that could lead us to think they might seriously carry off their enterprise—this simply isn't an issue.

The functioning of comedy as daydream is legitimate and common, but it is not how *Whisky Galore* works, and the distinction runs through the whole output of Mackendrick and Clarke: if Clarke's comedy is daydream, Mackendrick's is dream, in the sense of a playing-out, in compressed or symbolic forms, of conflicts as they in fact are.

'Personally I am very attracted by comedy, at least a certain form of comedy, because I think there are things which comedy alone can say. It allows you to make things happen that are too dangerous, or that a certain public cannot [otherwise] accept.'   (from a 1968 interview with Mackendrick, in *Positif*)

This will be worth returning to; one can't conceive of Clarke ever saying or thinking anything similar. His comedies celebrate the triumph of the innocent, the survival of the *un*fittest (an alternative world always being implied, in which

Alec Guinness and his fellow-lodger (Marjorie Fielding) in The Lavender Hill Mob; *also Stanley Holloway, Alfie Bass and Sid James in the same film.*

they would not be so lucky—*Pool of London* as the alternative to *The Lavender Hill Mob*); Mackendrick's show the survival of the fittest, with no implication of things 'really' being otherwise. The island community does not represent an indulgent fantasy of escape from modern pressures (like its feeble reincarnation in the quasi-Ealing *Rockets Galore*, made by Dearden, Relph and Danischewsky a decade later, just after Ealing closed); it is a community in whose capacity for survival we can believe. It embodies an ancestral Celtic shrewdness and toughness, from which we should learn, from which the Sergeant learns. Waggett does not; failing, he goes under.

Survival of the fittest: the Darwinian reference is useful, given the film's enjoyment of non-verbal communication, protective colouring, and ritual— given, too, the sense that the testing of Waggett is the testing of an obsolescent species of Englishman. Even his wife turns against him at the end, joining in the community's laughter at the rough justice of his final humiliation, when he is summoned to the mainland to face a charge of smuggling whisky. Another name to evoke is Machiavelli: not the Machiavelli of the (revealing) English stereotype of a brutal cynic, but the clear-sighted and unsentimental analyst of how social behaviour is actually motivated. What makes Mackendrick's films so refreshing, and I think unique in British cinema, is that the characters are so robustly Machiavellian in this truer sense, undermining the Ealing polarisation of nice and wholesome and harmless versus coarse, tough and brutal. *Whisky Galore* induces us to go along with deceit and cruelty and what the Sergeant identifies as 'blackmail', but these don't make the comedy cynical or amoral. They have a purpose: the well-being of the community both in the short-term (the acquisition of the life-giving whisky) and in the long-term (the survival of the fittest, the triumph of intelligence). Within this strengthened community, love and loyalty can flourish, the more convincingly for being so firmly based. The main action ends with a dance, resolving conflicts, and celebrating the marriages of Macroon's two daughters, one of them to the English Sergeant.

The ending of Whisky Galore. *The defeated Captain Waggett with the Customs Officer (Henry Mollison); and the dance.*

KIND HEARTS
AND CORONETS

'The British Cinema of that particular time . . . was completely middle-class bound. Ealing Studio comedies—for example *Kind Hearts and Coronets*, and the like. Emotionally quite frozen.

(Lindsay Anderson, talking to Joseph Gelmis)

'She was English, and a certain self-consciousness towards the world at large was borne of a morbid dread of betraying the strength of her nature to the vulgar.'

(from 'Israel Rank', by Roy Horniman)

'Israel Rank' is the novel on which Robert Hamer based his comedy of multiple murder, *Kind Hearts and Coronets*, the third of the trio of films that in mid-1949 put Ealing comedy on the map. It is as common to read that the book is a long-forgotten, humourless Victorian saga, dross transformed by Hamer into gold, as that Jack Warner dies after twenty minutes of *The Blue Lamp*, and the information is no less inaccurate. The book is a Wildean novel of the Edwardian decade which was in print again after World War II and which provides rather more than the 'germ' for the film (Balcon's word); its influence is evident in the overall structure and tone of the work, and in certain happy details. But then *Kind Hearts* has always attracted myth and mystery, and one way into it is to confront some of these. John Russell Taylor has made much of the decisive influence on it of being shot at Pinewood Studios, away from the cosy Ealing atmosphere (see his introduction to the published script); Balcon has insisted in a letter to Sight and Sound that, some locations apart, it was made entirely at Ealing.

This still leaves the question of where it stood, and stands, within the Ealing output. All the other main Ealing comedies—that is, the ones that are still revived—were either written by Clarke or directed by Mackendrick. *Kind Hearts* is on its own, the only significant overlap, apart from the casting of Alec Guinness, being that Hamer's script collaborator, the experienced Ealing staff writer John Dighton, also worked with Mackendrick on *The Man in the White Suit*. Although Balcon now describes *Kind Hearts* as a personal favourite, he was by all accounts less happy with it at the time; there were strong disagreements during production (very unusual at Ealing), and Hamer was denied the chance to follow it up with the subject he had long been preparing, a story with a strong sexual content set in the West Indies. After the success of *Kind Hearts*, his career has commonly been seen, with partial justification, as an anti-climax, one which it has been conventional to explain in terms of a personal crisis involving alcoholism. This, I feel, only pushes the question one stage back, giving a symptom not a cause, inviting conjecture about the pressures experienced by someone like Hamer working in the climate of the postwar decade in the British cinema and Ealing in particular—a climate of which the progress of mainstream Ealing gives evidence, as do Hamer's own films, *Kind Hearts* included. The tendency to look at the film in isolation has only served to build up the critical myths, of which three can be mentioned:

1) Hamer as a director with only one film in him; *Kind Hearts* as an inexplicable masterpiece, where everything miraculously clicked.

2) *Kind Hearts* as out of time, timeless; already set in the past, and immune from dating; could have been made at any period.

3) *Kind Hearts* as a *tour de force* which is, however, in Lindsay Anderson's phrase, 'emotionally quite frozen'; successful perhaps for that reason.

Though these may seem unrelated points, they each depend, I think, on seeing the film out of its 'forties context; Anderson's own review of the film at the time, in Sequence magazine, placed the emphasis rather differently, and his comment of 20 years later is no more than a seductive half-truth.

'She was English, and a certain self-consciousness towards the world at large was borne of a morbid dread of betraying the strength of her nature to the vulgar.' Roy Horniman writes this of Edith, the character played in *Kind Hearts* by Valerie Hobson; it might equally be said of other Hamer characters, like the Rose Sandigate of *It Always Rains on Sunday*. Think back over Hamer's films from *Dead of Night* on, and you find a gallery of individuals, across the range of classes, whose sexual and emotional drives are strongly repressed and as strongly burst out, only to be damped down in an adjustment to the prevailing Ealing/British dispensation which, in a consolidation of the spirit of wartime, accepts restraint on sex drive and ambition and class resentment. All of these are gloriously indulged through the story of Louis Mazzini, suburban shop assistant, murdering his way through the mass of relatives (the d'Ascoynes) who stand between him and the title of Duke of Chalfont. The form is black comedy; perhaps Hamer could only carry this off, and Louis carry through his plan, by being devoid of feeling, could only work on the spectator by denying him or her any feeling. Allow any genuine feeling in, this argument runs, and the whole edifice collapses. Surely an over-simplification. Of course, the manner of the film is cool and ironic. But you can't split things off so neatly and exclude the 'emotions' from the deep satisfactions the film gives. Why labour this point, which is only raised by a casual remark thrown out during an interview? Partly it's the fact that Anderson is the person talking, the Anderson whose own first feature, *This Sporting Life* (1963), makes a tremendous gritty show of being unafraid of raw feeling and bold statement but ends up seeming rather hollow. I say this not in order to write that enterprise off, but to suggest that the relation of 'old' and 'new' British cinema, as represented by these two directors and these two landmark films, is a lot more complex than the conventional account of the arrival of new vigour in a moribund industry recognises. We need a reading of British cinema which explores the relation of Hamer and Anderson (and various contemporaries like Powell, Fisher, Mackendrick; Richardson, Reisz, Schlesinger) from a perspective other than that of Anderson himself, which has continued to be the dominant one, Anderson having been so powerful a voice as critic (from the later 'forties) and then as practitioner. His remark on *Kind Hearts*, then, touches on all manner of questions about where the *life* of British cinema is to be found. No-one likes to be diagnosed as emotionally dried-up, and my impulse is to move to Hamer's defence, especially since his next film after

Kind Hearts, the non-Ealing *The Spider and the Fly,* has a similar reputation for being emotionally frozen: The Times's review, when the film came out, had a dismissive remark about it being, while set in France, 'a British film, an unmistakably British film in its attitudes, its values, and what passes for its emotions'—a comment which could only stem from a complacent equation of emotion displayed on the surface with emotion *tout court.* It is like ascribing to George Eliot herself, as the author of 'Middlemarch', the emotional atrophy of Mr Casaubon. It seems to me that *The Spider and the Fly* is, on the contrary, one of the most moving of British films in its sympathetic analysis of emotionally crippled protagonists, and that this points to a major critical distinction to be made within British cinema, between those films which are victims of emotional atrophy and those which diagnose it, Hamer's (at least most of them) belonging to the latter class. We don't, I think, take from *The Spider and the Fly,* or from *Kind Hearts,* the sense of a cold film. Indeed, place *Kind Hearts* beside the comedies of murder with which it is commonly bracketed—Capra's *Arsenic and Old Lace,* Chaplin's *Monsieur Verdoux,* Sacha Guitry's *Roman d'un Tricheur*—let alone such pale British imitations as *Nothing but the Best* and *Drop Dead Darling,* and it seems much less brittle, more powerfully motivated, less cerebral, warmer.

Kind Hearts is told in a flashback. Louis Mazzini, Tenth Duke of Chalfont, awaits execution for murder. The opening is quiet and slow, using the deference of governor and hangman alike towards their noble charge to present the prison as a little society obsessed with ritual and class distinction.

Louis sits in his cell, ready to spend his last night reading over the memoir he has written of his rise to the Dukedom. The moment the flashback starts, we are caught up in a drive, an abundance, which never lets up until the time Louis attains his object. His narrative rains images on us from the start, showing us in rapid sequence:

(Louis in prison)
his birth; his father's death
(prison)
Louis age 5, hearing from his mother about:
her elopement, with an Italian singer, from her home at Chalfont Castle
. . . and their humble married life in suburbia, disowned by the family.
Louis as a baby: the widow taking a lodger
Louis at 5, having his ancestry explained
Louis at 10, at school with Lionel and Sibella
(prison)
Louis at 17; his mother's death; continued snubs from the family.

The sheer freedom of association—shifting back and forth in time, both between present and past and between different layers of the past—is exhilarating, especially as juxtaposed with the sedate opening. It sets the teeming energy of a subjective vision against a stuffy official surface. The start of the memoir is like the opening of a Pandora's box: memories and images fly out in wild profusion, but they are controlled, held together, by the speaking voice as Louis's narration continues.

The whole film is here in miniature: its distinctive style, energy and humour, Louis's motivation, and the prominence of the spoken narration. The story soon settles down into a more linear form, but it never becomes a conventional 'objective' narrative: it continues to be the expression of Louis himself. Where we

might expect the soundtrack voice to introduce the memoir and then withdraw tactfully, leaving the story to run on under its own steam, this doesn't happen. The voice is never absent for long, and at no point do we cease to be conscious of Louis as the presenter of what we see. This weight given throughout to the narration has been found worrying from a purist point of view; after all, the cinema is supposed to be a visual medium. However, Hamer's boldness in foregrounding the commentary is liberating on every level, visuals included. He is released from the need to link and 'establish' scenes in the conventional expository way (which had as strong a hold in the British cinema of this period as anywhere). The commentary can situate us, leaving the camera, and dialogue, to go straight to the telling detail. The result is a quick, compressed, flexible style of narrative well ahead of its time, a pleasure in itself—but of course one doesn't respond to, nor can one account for, these formal pleasures in a vacuum. They lead out from, and back into, our involvement with Louis and his enterprise.

The commentary, then, does the work of exposition, while always giving us Louis's ironic viewpoint. Within the dramatised action, the 'flashback' (though that word has never seemed more inadequate), every word and every image *counts*.

The words. Hamer wrote that one of the opportunities he saw in making the film was 'that of using the English language, which I love, in a more varied and, to me, more interesting way than I had previously had the chance of doing in a film.' To show how the chance was grasped, one can point to all manner of felicitous touches in commentary and dialogue alike. From the Reverend Henry d'Ascoyne, innocently showing an incognito Louis round his country church:

'I always say that my west window has all the exuberance of Chaucer, without, happily, any of the concomitant crudities of his period.'

Guinness gives the line its full value. So does Dennis Price, delivering Louis's

Dennis Price as Louis Mazzini in Kind Hearts *and* Coronets. *Left: with the hangman (Miles Malleson) and the prison governor (Clive Morton). Above: swearing vengeance on his mother's grave, and despatching his first victim.*

comment on his first murder, which disposes of not only the objectionable Mr Ascoyne d'Ascoyne but also his lady companion:

'I was sorry about the girl, but found some relief in the reflection that she had presumably, during the weekend, already undergone a fate worse than death.'

It would be idle, however, to go through the film picking out verbal plums. Just as satisfying a use of language is in Louis's dozen successive replies of Yes or No to cross-examination at his trial, the expression given to each monosyllable eloquently varied as he tries to parry his prosecutor's thrusts. Or in the tensions of his conversation with Sibella, after she returns from her honeymoon with Lionel. How has she enjoyed it? 'Not at all.' 'Not at all?' 'Not at all.' Again the wit is in the intonation and in the rich level of evocation. Little is spoken, much is understood (notably about Lionel as a sexual partner, compared to Louis). Sibella complains she has married the most boring man in London. Louis: 'in England.' Sibella: 'in Europe.' It is a brilliant self-denial by Louis, and Hamer, to stop there and not cap the exchange in the obvious way. There is always a tension, a holding-back, a sense of things *not* expressed beneath the restrained, elegant forms of social life. This tension constitutes both the key to Louis's own cool, ironic style, and a context setting off the glorious *lack* of restraint in his actions as lover and especially as murderer.

The visual plane functions like the verbal, and in close relation to it. There is a continuous sharp play between word and image, which keeps the surface of the film continuously alive, even when the images are ostensibly doing no more than illustrating the spoken word. This is so right from the start: we see the fatal collapse of Louis's father—keeling over, as in the cut-in shot of the mother's death which anyone who has seen Truffaut's *Shoot the Pianist* will remember—a

Louis with Henry d'Ascoyne (Alec Guinness), destined to become his second victim, and his wife Edith (Valerie Hobson).

second or two before the commentary 'catches up' and explains. When Louis, later, recounts the problem he faced in trying to engineer the death of Admiral d'Ascoyne (who would shortly solve the problem himself, by his incompetence on the bridge), Hamer illustrates the scene to delightful effect by a fleeting shot of Louis poring over a torpedo design; the charm here is in the deadpan allusiveness, the train of thought set up in the margin of the story. The murders themselves are illustrated in a similar 'deadpan' style, the death generally happening offscreen or in long shot, enacting Louis's own deliberately detached perspective on them. Thus, the first victim, with his girl, topples over a weir while we, with Louis, watch from a distance. The next, the photographer Henry d'Ascoyne, blows himself up, by Louis's contrivance, in the shed at the bottom of his garden: this is brought to our attention, as to Louis's, by a column of smoke starting to rise in the background of the image of him taking tea in the garden with Henry's wife, who at this moment becomes his widow; their talk continues genteelly for a time until Louis deems it right to take notice. As with the verbal ironies, it's a style built on the tension between the formal surface and what we, and Louis, know to be going on behind that surface.

Let me make the standard disclaimer: the wit of scenes like these has to be experienced in context; it can't be reproduced or satisfactorily analysed on the page. However, I hope the process will still lead somewhere. The climax to which the film itself leads is Louis's killing of the last real obstacle in his way, the most intransigent member of the d'Ascoyne clan, Ethelred, Eighth Duke of Chalfont. As a guest at his castle, Louis contrives to lead him into one of his own mantraps for catching poachers. This is how Hamer presents the killing. Having him now at his mercy, Louis confronts the Duke, tells him all, and raises his gun; cut from Louis firing to Louis running (away from camera) back to the castle shouting 'Help'; cut to the funeral procession, which makes its point the more directly for repeating the exact set-up used for an earlier d'Ascoyne funeral. Summarised like this, one might picture it as a crisp, neat, indeed over-neat, sequence tied together by shock cuts for comic effect. The really distinctive and pleasing thing about it, though, is the deliberation of the pace, the slight but perceptible delay in making each of the two cuts, a delay which enacts *Louis*'s deliberation, mimicking the studied earnestness of his run for 'help'. The tempo is thus also exactly right for the introduction, in the same understated, deadpan manner, of the final twist in the sequence: the third shot, like the first two, is held slightly longer than we expect, time enough for a second coffin to be carried past the camera, as Louis's voice informs us that the last of the d'Ascoynes, his own aged employer, dropped dead from shock on being hailed as the Ninth Duke, and that he himself has now achieved his destiny as number ten. It's a sequence where one gains a real pleasure from the awareness of a director—whether helped by his editor (in this case Peter Tanner, an Ealing regular) or acting as his own—fully in control of his material and his audience, without being mechanical about it—indeed, precisely by refusing the mechanical. The sequence works by combining deliberation, restraint—no visual fireworks, an almost perverse slowness of pace—with an overall narrative speed: it still cuts through the whole incident, from death to double funeral, in a few seconds, reflecting the way Louis chooses to remember and to tell it. As in the opening burst of Louis's memoir, the whole film is here in miniature: its particular style and energy, the shaping effect of the subjective voice, and Louis's motivation.

I have been referring to the tension between the cool surface and what we are conscious of underneath, which is to say, the motivation. In this final murder scene, Louis has for once spoken out: having the Duke alone and at his mercy, he can give himself this satisfaction.
'You'll be the sixth d'Ascoyne that I've killed. You want to know why? In return for what the d'Ascoynes did for my mother. Because she married for love, instead of for rank, or money, or land, they condemned her to a life of poverty and slavery, in a world with which they had not equipped her to deal . . .'

Louis preparing to bring down Lady Agatha d'Ascoyne's balloon; and confronting his final victim, Ethelred.

Having told him this, straight, he fires, and at once becomes the ironist again, both within the story and in his retrospective chronicling of it. But we don't for this reason forget what he says or discount it as a piece of extraneous moralising. The mother is as important to *Kind Hearts* as to *Citizen Kane*: seen only briefly, but frequently recalled and psychologically central. Her presence helps to explain why Louis is so much more powerful a figure than the heroes of those black comedies with which *Kind Hearts* gets linked, or which derive from it, as the film itself is so much more substantial than any of them: it's a matter not just of finer 'wit', but of motivation, and meaning. I would account for the phenomenon of *Kind Hearts*—not a solitary 'miracle', but quite possibly the most memorable of British films—in terms of its compact unity, its fusion of various elements: of personal and social motivations, of the two main threads of Louis's story (the d'Ascoyne and Sibella ones), and of theme and form, as the compressed, subjective narrative carries forward with the freedom of dream the single-minded drive of the hero.

Personal and social. Like Hitchcock's *North by Northwest*, like 'Hamlet', *Kind Hearts* is an Oedipus story. (Where the former refers to 'Hamlet' in its title, the latter has a verbal echo in Louis's narration, when he ponders what he can do to inconvenience the d'Ascoynes: 'What could I take from them? Except, perhaps, their lives?') Simply by the shock of his entry into the world, Louis kills his father; he thereafter settles down into an exclusive loving relation with his mother. Lacking a father from this point, he can't work through the Oedipal conflict; the fact that the same actor, Dennis Price, plays this cut-off father helps us to see the death in terms of what happens within Louis, as if what has died is a part of himself, of his psyche (it also, of course, shows us Louis's image of 'himself' as married to his mother). The same principle applies, less speculatively, to the d'Ascoyne relatives, all eight being incarnated by Alec Guinness,

Six Guinnesses, with Edith, mourning a seventh, her dead husband.

like a monstrous father-figure whose power is belatedly encountered as Louis emerges, mother-dominated, into manhood and who recurs with the same face time after time, Hydra-like, as if in his nightmare. I wouldn't wish to work this scheme out too insistently, but the Oedipus complex is proposed by Freudians as a universal structure of the unconscious, so it seems valid to appeal to this structure in the film as having something to do with the power it exerts, without it necessarily being put in, or generally perceived, at a conscious level—especially when the free-association, wish-fulfilling form of the film is so evocative of dream. The form reinforces the affinity which cinema can anyway have with dream but which the British cinema so seldom really exploits, as its traditional concern has been with the conscious levels of the mind and with secondary rather than primary drives.

One can make sense too, I think, of the roles of the two women, Sibella and Edith, within the Freudian schema. But a more crucial factor in the film's operation is the way the social role of the d'Ascoynes reinforces their role in Louis's own family. They are not merely cruel 'fathers' to this one individual, but caricatures of a whole patriarchal culture, of an aristocratic English arrogance. We come here to a paradox implicit in the film's title:

'Kind hearts are more than coronets
And simple faith than Norman blood.'

Edith quotes this Tennyson couplet to Louis, reassuring him about his right to be on visiting terms with his social superiors. To Louis, of course, they aren't his superiors at all, and there is no evidence that he agrees with Tennyson's sentiment. He is trying to regain his rightful place as an aristocrat, not to blur the distinction between them and the rest; far from it—he shares his mother's disdain for 'trade'. But even though Louis is not subversive in intention, his actions are. It is the boorish arrogance of a junior d'Ascoyne to him as an assistant in a

Louis insulted by Ascoyne d'Ascoyne (Anne Valery as his lady friend).

Louis's trial in the House of Lords on a charge of murdering Lionel: the widow, Sibella (Joan Greenwood), gives evidence.

draper's shop that actually pushes him over the threshold from daydream into murder. His anger comes from knowing that he is really as good a man as d'Ascoyne, being (secretly) a close relative. But the anger can at the same time work with a less narrow focus, as if Louis were merely the draper of humble birth that he could, after all, well be and that he seems to d'Ascoyne to be. The offence would be no less. Discount his birth and he is still as good a man as this self-important dandy—we are all sons of Adam. Whatever Louis's motives, whatever his own snobbery, he acts as an agent for quite radical class resentments. And so it continues. The d'Ascoynes are felt as obstacles in the way of him, and of all of us: these feelings conflict, shift and overlap in a process of audience identification or (better word) association whose complexity is endemic to narrative fiction but is intensified by the particular ironic mode of *Kind Hearts*.

There are similar cross-currents in his relation with his childhood sweetheart, Sibella. As he rises in the world, he takes pleasure in rejecting her as a possible wife on class grounds: 'Yes, Sibella was pretty enough in her suburban way . . .

but her face would have looked rather out of place under a coronet . . .'—which is a d'Ascoyne sentiment, and rather sad when we look back to the romantic love which he felt for Sibella and compare her with the glacial Edith. But the rejection operates as an apt revenge for Sibella's earlier treatment of him. In itself, snobbery, but as revenge, subversive.

Lodging at her parents' middle-class home after his mother's death, the youthful Louis offers Sibella his adoration and his hand in marriage. He goes down on one knee to her, just as his father did to his mother in one of the first images of Louis's memoir: that is the image Louis has of it, and in proposing to Sibella he re-enacts that moment. His parents married for love and were cast out; now Louis wants to do the same and is spurned for the same worldly reasons. Sibella, though amused and attracted by him, dismisses him as a social inferior and chooses instead the more solid prospects of Lionel and his money. So this couple is assimilated to the d'Ascoynes, becoming part of the same personal/social enemy that Louis will infiltrate and destroy, turning their own weapons against them.

For all the ironic surface, there is a life and sexuality in the early scenes with Sibella which, like his attachment to his mother, count positively: indeed, the relationship is one of the most erotically suggestive in British cinema, although its expression is inhibited both by the social restraints of the characters' world and also, presumably, by an awareness of the censor. One says 'although', but these constraints seem rather to make it more powerfully felt, for instance in the highly-charged, enigmatic dialogue: Sibella's repeated 'Not at all' to Louis's question whether she has enjoyed her honeymoon, and Louis's earlier, innocently cheerful remark to the bridegroom on his wedding morning (Louis having slept with the bride overnight): 'You're a lucky man, Lionel, take my word for it.'

Two strands of the film—d'Ascoynes and Sibella, career and love—come neatly together in the closing stages. Lionel, through his own fault, faces financial ruin, and Louis, now a rising man in the d'Ascoyne private bank, refuses to extend his bill of loan. Panicking, Lionel drops the sycophantic mask and taunts Louis with his past: 'Rotten little counter-jumper, that's all you are. Very high and mighty now, but your mother married an Italian organ-grinder.'

Before Louis stands a financial and social parasite who took his first love and now, like the d'Ascoyne family, insults his mother. Everything comes together. Louis's anger is impressively direct and serious: 'I will not tolerate hearing my mother's name on your coarse tongue.' He strikes Lionel, and their brief struggle ironically leads to his trial for murder where his actual murders do not (Lionel, after Louis's departure, kills himself, and Sibella withholds the suicide note to have a lever for blackmailing Louis into taking her rather than Edith as his Duchess; the suicide happens off-screen and we don't hear about it until after Louis has killed Ethelred and gained the title). We move rapidly from Louis's anger at Lionel, via a row with Sibella, to the consummation of his revenge on the d'Ascoynes: 'in return for what the d'Ascoynes did to my mother. Because she married for love, instead of for rank, or money, or land . . .'

Hardly 'emotionally frozen', then. Mother-love, contempt, revenge—all very important. Except that Louis *has* hardened himself to carry out his resolution: he doesn't marry for love himself, but goes after rank, money and land. He has defeated the enemy by their own weapons and their own ruthlessness. And once he becomes Duke, he grows even more into his mask, becomes impregnable, supercool—except sometimes when he looks back, in his memoir.

There is a limit to what this form of analysis—plodding along beside the film, making connections, trying to pin down the hero's values, the film's meaning, and our responses—can achieve. *Kind Hearts* is the hardest of the Ealing films to write about: its meaning is so little set out on the surface, so little reducible to clear terms, compared with the typical commonsense film of the Ealing mainstream, compared even to Mackendrick's films. It is a particularly enigmatic and 'irreducible' work. Its structure is centred on the type of hero whose function is to tear a society apart by applying to it the logic of its own corruption, and the meaning resides in this whole action more than in any positive values he may directly embody (as in many gangster and western heroes: one of the purest examples would be Clint Eastwood in his own western *High Plains Drifter*). Its particular forms, including its 'Britishness', interact piquantly with the bold structure. We are left with a smooth, reflective surface, riddles, a set of tensions. Between Louis's different stances. Between emotion repressed or sublimated, and emotion expressed, as in the two late outbursts. Between coolness and warmth, as in Louis's affair with Sibella:

Sibella: 'What am I doing?'

Louis: 'You know very well. You're playing with fire.'

Sibella: 'At least it *warms* me.'

Above all, there are the tensions of the ending. It's left unresolved which lady Louis will choose, Sibella or Edith. (Sibella has produced the suicide note, thus freeing him, on the understanding that he will eliminate Edith and marry her; Louis reflects that he can just as easily double-cross Sibella.) By this stage, this dilemma is not in itself very interesting. Much more so is the question of whether Louis will really be able to get away with all those d'Ascoyne murders that are still undetected. Here the film achieve the neatest balancing act of all. As Louis, outside the prison gates, hesitates between the two waiting ladies, a man from Titbits steps forward to negotiate for the rights to his memoirs. Once again the film displays its verbal richness, playing on the range of meanings conveyed by intonation alone in Louis's final words:

> (puzzled) 'My memoirs?'
> (Seeing the point) 'My memoirs!'
> (as a horrified thought strikes him) 'My memoirs!'
> (and again): 'My memoirs!'

—as the camera tracks in to show the pile of papers on the table of his cell. The End.

So the story will be discovered and read, and Louis will be hanged after all: crime receives its due punishment, through the criminal's one fatal slip. Unless, that is, Louis has the presence of mind to turn back, have a word with the obsequious governor and retrieve his manuscript. Is there any question which is more likely or which Hamer intends us to think is more likely? To the end, the film teases us, and teases conventional morality (and the censor); it keeps us guessing about what to make of what we see, about what really goes on behind the external façades of its people, and of itself. What we are left with, the shot Hamer signs off with, is simply, matching the final words, the image of the memoirs: in effect, the image of the film itself, since these memoirs, prologue and epilogue apart, constitute the film. To the question of how we finally take it all, what we make of it, the answer we are left with is this: the memoirs, the film, the total artefact. The memoir is the message, the meaning *is* the film.

THE MAN IN THE WHITE SUIT

It will be clear how different *Kind Hearts* is, in its relish for ambiguity and artifice, from the self-effacing, transparent, commonsense realism of the Ealing norm; it is very different in other ways, almost every way imaginable. Diverse as they are, the three 1949 comedies, *Kind Hearts, Whisky Galore,* and *Passport to Pimlico,* are a remarkable and enduring trio, putting Ealing firmly on the map, giving it a fresh impetus and public identity. From them, we can look back and forward: they gather up familiar Ealing themes and materials, reworking and distilling them into three distinct visions, three projections of Britain and the British character, which offer three paths ahead.

We know which path Ealing will follow. If any one of the trio is the odd one out, it must be *Passport to Pimlico* with its mellow vision of consensus set against the others' more ruthless energies. But *Passport* was soon followed by *The Blue Lamp,* and these two films, both written by T. E. B. Clarke, constitute models of comedy and drama for the mainstream Ealing of Crichton, Dearden and various others: the *weight* of Ealing is overwhelmingly here, in terms of sheer quantity of films, and also of the studio's popular image.

1949 was the crossroads for Ealing, as for the country as a whole, the decisive point as it made its adjustment to the widening horizons of the postwar scene and asked: Who are we? Where are we going? The commitment to the *Passport to Pimlico* spirit was a momentous one.

Kind Hearts had no real successor. Hamer left Ealing, frustrated over his next project, though he returned for *His Excellency* (1951), but this was an anonymous stage adaptation which had little impact. Mackendrick, on the other hand, after *Whisky Galore,* made four more Ealing films, substantial works which entered into a continuing 'dialogue' with the way things were going. They amount to by far the most interesting set of films to be made by any director in England, let alone Ealing, in the dead decade of the 'fifties. After 1949, then, Mackendrick prospered while Hamer did not. This is only in part explained by the fact that *Kind Hearts* was clearly a more difficult film for Ealing to take in its stride than *Whisky Galore,* more extreme, more sexual, and more individualist. Consider the shape of the two men's careers. Hamer went to Ealing in 1941 as an editor and became a major Ealing contributor in 1943, as producer and joint writer/director of *San Demetrio London.* He was then active for six years until *Kind Hearts.* Mackendrick was employed from 1946, and was a major contributor from *Whisky Galore* until *The Ladykillers* (1955), another six-year span, after which he left for America.

The pattern is a striking one. While the mainstream directors happily go on and on, the relation of these two with Ealing is less sustained. Of course, as the most clearly talented of the team, they are under more temptations to move out

His Excellency, *set in a fictitious British colony: Sir James Kirkman (Cecil Parker) with rebel leader (Geoffrey Keen) and new Governor (Eric Portman)*

and work for others, but their talent can't be separated from the critical intelligence of their films, the tensions they display with all that Ealing represents. Both of them finish with a memorable black comedy, as if exploding these tensions in a definitive, violent statement. Clarke never ventures into black comedy, and one can't imagine him doing so: *Kind Hearts* and *The Ladykillers* form a sub-genre of their own within Ealing Comedy.

1949 is the overlap between Hamer's main Ealing work and Mackendrick's. Hamer's films deal more with the psychology of individuals, Mackendrick's with groups. The sexuality of Hamer's is powerful; Mackendrick's contain virtually no sexual element at all. One could say this is a difference of temperament and 'personal themes'; it also reflects the time in which they were working at Ealing.

From the *Dead of Night* story onward, Hamer's films are tense struggles between social conformism and the 'mirror' world of desires that opens up to tempt or haunt the protagonists. The relation between individual drives and the community is felt after the war as a live question, but Ealing can't find ways of reconciling them creatively. Even Hamer's films end—in the terms of *Dead of Night*—with the smashing of the mirror, with constraint on energies. At least there is a struggle, which there won't be for much longer. By the early 'fifties the struggle is over: the self-effacement of the individual in the community has been consolidated, and sexuality is more or less excluded from the data. This is the dispensation with which Mackendrick's films—one stage on from Hamer's— engage.

Kind Hearts is a Kamikaze dive, a last defiant fling on behalf of all the selfish gratifications that Ealing is closing down upon. At the end, Louis duly makes his slip, leaving his manuscript behind in the cell. Hamer leaves it delicately open to us to decide if he is punished or not. One might say that for Hamer he isn't punished; for Ealing he is. Louis, with all his drive and sex and violence and imagination, is locked up and disposed of; the Pandora's box is closed. Hamer wrote of the pleasure of 'making a picture which paid no regard whatever to established, though not practised, moral convention'—an idea which, though Ealing may let it through once, is too dangerous, too alien, to adjust to. As *The Blue Lamp* soon confirms, Ealing is *for* established moral convention, and believes that it can be practised.

The climax of *Kind Hearts* is Louis's confrontation with Ethelbert in the castle grounds. A new generation confronts the old. It's the image of an archetypal relationship which has its own intense inflections in British culture in view of the weight that this culture traditionally attaches to established authority. For Ealing the image is a particularly pregnant one and from it we can survey the generation conflicts at different stages in the studio's history. The early films of Balcon's Ealing are full of such confrontations. Ironside father and Ironside son in *Cheer Boys Cheer*; the traitor-politician and the patriot who kills him and steps into his shoes in *The Four Just Men*; the workers and mine-owners of *The Proud Valley*; old and new generations in the Robert Stevenson films. Patriarchal authority is rotten and decadent, ready to be knocked over, and the characteristic movement is that of *Cheer Boys Cheer*, from deference to defiance on the part of the son: a powerful gesture of revolt, which is actually carried through.

The insistence on national unity in the wartime films makes, up to a point, for a consolidation of this same radical analysis. The elimination of corrupt figureheads becomes all the more urgent—hence such powerful images as that of the shooting of the squire in *Went the Day Well?* And the most successful positive images of unity, as in *San Demetrio London* and *Nine Men*, are based on a new social mix, where authority is exercised responsibly and without arrogance. However, this creates its own problems, especially as the years pass. Complacency says: we threw out the old guard, won the war, breathed the new radical air of that time, and elected a new Government. Everything is changed. But how radical has the weeding-out process, the change of structure and spirit, really been? Consider again George Orwell's 1942 account of England as 'a family in which the young are generally thwarted, and most of the power is in the hands of irresponsible uncles and bedridden aunts.' The war films seemed to end by eliminating this decadent older generation from power, and by 'closing ranks' in a genuinely democratic way. The experience was so euphoric that the British remained fixated on it, reluctant to risk sacrificing it by rocking the boat. But the break with the old order turned out not to have been as radical as it seemed. Those aunts and uncles began to creep out of the woodwork again (or the system remained such that as a younger generation grew older, it turned into them). What does Alec Guinness play in the d'Ascoyne family but a string of 'irresponsible uncles'? (I don't believe that setting the film in the past has any safety distancing effect: it is a statement for its time). And what does *The Lady killers* show but the uncanny authority exercised by a group of 'bedridden aunts' (Mrs Wilberforce, and the frail little old ladies who gather at her house for tea and music)?

Another visionary image is this: the mixed-up schools of *The Happiest Days of Your Life* (1949)—prototype of the St Trinians films, and sharper and fresher than any of them—with Alistair Sim and Margaret Rutherford as rival headmaster and headmistress. This is not an Ealing film, but it was written as a play, then as a film, by the Ealing staff writer John Dighton, who was clearly an influential figure around this time: he collaborated both with Hamer on *Kind Hearts* and with Mackendrick on *The Man in the White Suit* (1951). All three films construct a delirious, nightmarish confrontation of youth and age which uses the vision of comedy to express the underlying logic of the society as a corrective to the 'consensus' complacency enshrined in the Boulting Brothers' school film *The Guinea Pig* (1948), and in the Ealing films written by Clarke.

The image of Louis and Ethelbert remains a deeply evocative one. The young man will speak out his grievance against the old, shoot him and supplant him. *The Blue Lamp* deals in as compressed a way with tradition, father and son figures. The father is Dixon: the figure of the son is split into two, Mitchell and Riley, good and evil. Time seems to stand still as Riley, trapped at the scene of his crime, confronts Dixon with a gun. Dixon advances like a stern parent, and is shot, whereupon Mitchell dedicates himself to revenge. Both Louis in *Kind Hearts* and Mitchell here are shown as explicitly filling the place of a dead son: Louis in the family banking business, Mitchell in the Dixons' home (their own son has died in the war). Both end by assuming the father's authority: Louis by violence, Mitchell by reverent succession.

It may be said that Dixon is a good 'father' and the d'Ascoynes are not, so that the films naturally have divergent attitudes to them. But of course the terms in which a film presents its issues are as significant as what it does with them; we generalise from what we are shown. We read *The Blue Lamp* as an image of how society is, especially as it deals with as powerful a social force as the police. From the start, the film defuses all revolt of new against old, simplifying it into aberrancy, delinquency. Sex and ambition go into that package too. Mitchell has no love life, and no apparent aim except to step into Dixon's shoes, which he does at the end. Even with the hostile lady driver, he won't allow himself the *verbal* satisfaction that Louis does both with Lionel and with Ethelbert before he moves on to physical violence. What seemed in its own context a dignified restraint comes in a wider one to look like cravenness, a reluctance to answer back not just the benevolent authority of police superiors, but any figure of authority at all.

From the time of *The Blue Lamp*, the balance at Ealing is overwhelmingly on the side of accepting authority and the way things are run: the young don't stand up to the old, but learn from them. Whether there is sufficient dynamic in a society operating on this basis to stop it from seizing up and growing stagnant, and what quality of life these benevolent authority figures actually promote are questions which are nowhere analysed more illuminatingly than from within Ealing itself, by Mackendrick and his collaborators in *The Man in the White Suit* (he wrote the script, together with John Dighton and Roger Macdougall, the author of the unperformed play on which it was based; for convenience, I will, after the normal fashion, be referring to the film as though he had sole, instead of the main, responsibility for it).

The Man in the White Suit is one of the few British films to be centred on industrial relations and the creation of wealth; it conveys a comprehensive vision of interactions within a society. Possibly, when one starts looking for a pattern, one can see it in everything. But the film really is both a statement about England—an England governed by consensus, as depicted by T. E. B. Clarke—and a work built on the oppositions of old and new, father and son.

The father and son are respectively Birnley, a paternalistic mill-owner and captain of industry (Cecil Parker), and Sidney Stratton, a young scientist (Alec Guinness). He's not literally a son, but Birnley comes to treat him like one, and he has a tentative romance with Birnley's daughter. His own family is never referred to; in a curious way, he is reminiscent of the Terence Stamp character in Pier

The first sight of Sidney Stratton's pirate apparatus in The Man in the White Suit. *Daphne Birnley (Joan Greenwood), Alan Birnley (Cecil Parker), Corland officials (Roddy Hughes, Colin Gordon), and Corland himself (Michael Gough).*

Paolo Pasolini's enigmatic *Teorema*, who arrives unannounced in the household of a rich industrialist's family and transforms all their lives. Sidney is an 'angel' put down among the family of England.

Like *Kind Hearts*, Mackendrick's film has a voice-over narration leading into a flashback; the voice is that of Birnley. He refers to a period of disruption in the textile industry which has fortunately been hushed up. The story itself opens with a sketch of a stuffy, hierarchic society. Birnley is being shown round a neighbouring mill by its owner, his prospective son-in-law, Michael Corland. In both men, ignorance about what actually goes on is thinly veiled but protected by an elaborate deferential chain of command. Contrast with this surface the literally bubbling energy of creative work and imagination in the unauthorised research apparatus, which is found unattended in a corner, disturbing the graduated order of the place; it is eventually traced to the dedicated Sidney.

The pattern of the opening is akin to that of *Kind Hearts*: stuffy surface, and disruptive energy undermining it. But here the story is being told by Birnley, not Sidney. Although this time the narration is not sustained, it sets up a double perspective which continues. The story does not express Sidney's own vision and drive; there is no liberation for him or the spectator. The story never quite escapes from Birnley's control. Instead of the single-minded onward drive of *Kind Hearts*, there is always this double pull. *The Man in the White Suit* remains a story of frustration, blockage and stagnation.

Half an hour goes by before the title begins to be explained; Mackendrick could no doubt count on publicity and word of mouth having made audiences aware of what was coming (as in *Passport to Pimlico*). But the first section of the picture, even without this knowledge, is interesting enough on its own, as it builds up a dizzying picture of the inbuilt obstructiveness of the system to research and vitality, irrespective of what the research is doing. We know that Sidney has a burning ambition in his field and that he has at least a technical competence (he knows more about the electron microscope than those officially in charge of it). But because his work can't be contained by the official research channels, he has become a 'pirate', slipping in unnoticed. He can manage to do so simply enough since the official channels are easy to deceive because of their bureaucratic ignorance. Thrown out of Corland's, he makes a corner for this still unidentified research in Birnley's own laboratories. At last, his experiment works. He synthesises a unique new compound which will obviously, whatever it is, be of potential value to the firm. So he breaks cover joyfully, ready to take it to Birnley (whom he hasn't met). What happens?

Through his triumphant noises, the irregularity of his position is discovered. The Head of Research goes into action. He sends for the medical department. Nurse Gamage appears, buxom and bossy, to slap Sidney's face and administer a sedative. Nanny rules! The Research man takes one incurious look at the liquid and pours it down the sink. Sidney's pure and disinterested scientific drive is still intense. We next find him laying siege to Birnley's house, just in order to tell him, to lay his discovery at the man's feet. A magnificent protective apparatus is brought into play to protect the boss's inviolability. In a quite surreal sequence, Sidney struggles with bells, doors, stairs and the butler, like a man in a dream putting all his energies into running but making no progress. Birnley is upstairs at a board meeting, under pressure because of a discrepancy in the accounts of several thousand pounds. Gradually, the sum is traced to the Research Department. Meanwhile, below, Sidney is working on the butler, persuading him to take a note to Birnley, asking to be seen. On the telephone, Birnley reaches the Head of Research and is told about Sidney. The butler comes in with the note. In the same breath, Birnley says down the phone 'send him out here' and to the butler 'tell him to go away'.

As an example of the mechanics of comedy, it's a consummate piece of contrivance, worthy of Alan Ayckbourn at his best, but the wit goes much deeper than the mechanical, compressing into this farcical *coup* the total movement and meaning of the film. The sequence offers an image for the whole structure of industry, and, by extension, society: seized up, at cross-purposes, chasing its own tail, the left hand not knowing what the right is doing . . . we have plenty of such cliché metaphors for these states of confusion. It's equally easy to generalise about 'the system' and its frustrations: the brilliance of the film is in constructing its system on such a scale and showing it in action so lucidly, creating such precise images for the logic of its working, both in the overall movement of the story and in particular moments, like the Head of Research pouring the precious fruits of research down the sink, and Birnley's mutually-cancelling commands.

At this point, the boss's daughter, Daphne, intervenes. She has already met Sidney and listened to him, and she insists that her father should listen to him now. For the first time, with Birnley, we hear the significance of the work, as Daphne stops him in his tracks. Sidney has devised a fabric that repels dirt and will never wear out.

Testing the new formula, with Birnley's blessing. Left: Sidney Stratton with his associate Wilson (John Rudling). Right: Alec Guinness, Alexander Mackendrick.

Everything now changes, as Birnley sees a chance to scoop the market. The middle part of the film charts the work of developing the fabric (not without explosive setbacks) and making a prototype suit. This suit is dazzling white and tailored to fit Sidney, who wears it for the film's final section.

Here he is, then, the man in the white suit. It's a very powerful visual image, but image of what? What do we make of the suit, of the man in it, and of what happens to them now? The suit seems to offer a dazzling future, a resource for the world. Daphne tells Sidney that people will bless him for the invention and look on him as a knight in shining armour; and this is the way he looks, with the suit evidently symbolising purity, innocence, and the disinterested truth of science.

As the story unfolds, all this falls victim to the restrictive practices of the place. Everlasting suits mean fewer new ones to be bought and less work for the factories. (A topical parallel: the manufacturers' cartel against long-life light bulbs, on which the Monopolies Commission reported in 1951, the year of the film's release.) The owners hastily get together, sort Birnley out and combine to suppress the invention. The unions give whole-hearted support. Sidney is bribed, abducted, and kept silent. The crucial scene here has Sidney, in brilliant white, confronting a roomful of devious captains of industry, all in black: first trusting them, then resisting their bribes, and finally being subjected to naked force.

White against black: the symbolism certainly operates powerfully, in line with the issues as I have summarised them. But it isn't the whole story: it is not simply a tale of virtue frustrated by worldliness. There is an ironic dimension to Sidney's white. His 'innocence' shades into stupidity, contrasting with the Machiavellian realism of his opponents, or at least of their leader: they are not simply black villains. The considerable power and moral tension of the film comes from the way it merges or superimposes the two structures: a black/white fable of virtue against corruption, and the rather different opposition of *Whisky Galore*, where the 'innocent' Waggett got what he deserved at the hands of the shrewd islanders. Even in that film, there is a moral tension which I have perhaps over-simplified in writing of it: Mackendrick has recalled becoming increasingly

Sidney at his lodgings, with the Union official Bertha (Vida Hope) and, back to camera, his landlady Mrs Watson (Edie Martin).

melancholy during the shooting, as he came to realise the strength of his sympathy with the Englishman and his honest principles. How much more acute is the balance of sympathies in *The Man in the White Suit*. The balance, the unresolved ambiguities, make it operate as a comprehensive analysis of a society. It doesn't ultimately take sides; given the data, it couldn't. Its satire is at the expense of both, of the *disposition* of these sides, old and new, and of the disposition of their qualities: i.e. at the expense of (in the fullest sense) the system, as shown in action.

We can't play down the excitement of Sidney's work, his energy and creativity, or the social possibilities of his invention. Obviously Daphne is right; the material could become a blessing for the world (as well as giving Britain a world market), and the objections come over as the narrowest obscurantism and vested interest. At the same time, we can't play down the flaws in Sidney's position. By resting his work, and his life, purely on the principle of following research where it leads, he renders himself vulnerable, both morally and practically. He has no vision of the social implications of his work and shows no interest in them when they start to be spelled out for him by Daphne on the one hand, and by the owners and union people on the other. Like Waggett, he simply doesn't operate on this level, doesn't 'read' people and their motivations. Secure in their principles and pure motives, both these men live in a fools' paradise.

This may sound like a display of fence-sitting, on the part of both the film itself and this analysis of it. I will try to bring out the dynamic nature of the film's tensions and suggest a more positive reading than one that works towards selecting a 'correct' position at a point in between two extreme ones, a certain shade of grey between the too dark black and the too brilliant white.

We can start by considering the ending. After his escape (contrived by Daphne), Sidney's concern is to reach the newspapers and publicise the fact of the new material. Characteristically, he allows himself to be thrown by petty frustrations (like not having the full fare to the nearest newspaper office)—in common with Waggett, he lacks the wit to overcome them by strategem. Cornered, finally, by a united band of bosses and workers—and the brilliance of the suit makes him an easy quarry—he is chased down an alleyway. At the end of it materialises a familiar figure, his former landlady, already established as a washerwoman and holding some washing now. (Her name is Mrs Watson, and she is played by the old, frail and magnificent Edie Martin, Ealing's quintessential little old lady—same name, same actress as the neighbour of Rose Sandigate in *It Always Rains on Sunday* who emerges at Sunday lunchtime.) Mrs Watson refuses to help him: 'Why can't you scientists leave things alone? What's to become of my bit of washing when there's no washing to do?' There follows a long close-up of Sidney, drained of the will to resist. The crowd closes in and jostles him. As they do, the structure of the cloth suddenly breaks down: bits of the suit come away in their hands. They pull it apart, jeering. Sidney is left trouserless and humiliated, and Birnley's voice-over narration returns to tie up the ending.

At one level, it is a breath-taking evasion. Mrs Watson's argument apparently settles the moral issue (Sidney seeming so impressed by it), and the profound question raised in the film can thereupon be the more easily swept out of sight and out of mind because the fabric wasn't stable anyway. Compare the moral coward-ice of medical inquiries which gloss over negligence in the treatment of emergency cases by stressing the likelihood that the patient was going to die anyway, even if treated, so what does it all matter? Ending the film so abruptly after the last twist of the plot looks like a comparable evasion.

Take each incident in isolation, at face value, and this would be fair criticism. If Mrs Watson's point were meant to tip the moral scales, then it would be a piece of sentimental nonsense out of key with the rest of the film; but it is more complex than this. We can see her appearance simply as forcing on Sidney, for the first time, the fact of other people's existence as people, with their own motivations, which can't be taken away from them. The long close-up of Sidney then implies not 'Yes, an unanswerable argument' (as it could well do, according to the 'grammar' of film), but the dawn of a new recognition on Sidney's part: of society as a network of vested interests which, however narrow, sectional and bloody-minded they may be, exist, and are part of the data. It is a recognition which the 'diplomat' or Machiavel (the Macroon of *Whisky Galore*) possesses and exploits, and which his opposite number, the 'idealist', can't do without if he is to achieve anything of his ideals. Sidney has gone through the film like a zombie in his personal relationships, a scientist with no private dimension at all. Now for the first time, *in extremis*, he has to look at someone as another human being, someone whom he has taken for granted as a friend and who is now inexplicably hostile. Mrs Watson sums up, in the starkest possible way, the spirit of the arguments used by unions and bosses alike, which Sidney has always managed not quite to take in, because they were expressed in oblique, wary terms. Now they are spelled out very clearly and basically. In the close-up, we can sense the machinery in his computer mind whirring and clicking as he feeds in the amazing new data.

Immediately, the suit disintegrates. This whole ending, played out at night, has the feeling of nightmare, and the succession of events has a psychic logic. The suit is the emblem of Sidney's angelic innocence; in the encounter with Mrs Watson, he loses it; the suit comes apart. The implication is not so much that the project was an impossible dream, let's be realistic about it, as that *this* project was doomed because embarked on so innocently—so ignorantly.

Perhaps one should say that the ending has two meanings superimposed, like that of *Kind Hearts* (Louis free, Louis recaptured). They correspond to the two readings of the final plot twists: a strong and a weak one, Mackendrick's ending and Ealing's. Ealing's is the simple commonsense one: it just doesn't want to know about the white suit. The dimension of idealism and inventiveness, of potential for change, simply disappears hereafter from Ealing's terms of reference.

The last shot has Sidney walking away from the camera, defeated. Then the theme music associated with Sidney's bubbling apparatus is brought up on the soundtrack—perhaps he can overcome the instability problem and start again. For Ealing, a whimsical signing-off. For Mackendrick, the chance that Sidney could start again with a new kind of understanding altogether. However, it would be a massive task, not only to achieve this, but then to overcome the inertia of the system which the film has analysed.

This may all sound like special pleading: the film certainly operates on the surface like a conventional British comedy, in terms of plot and actors, for example in the multiple stop-go frustration routines of the final chase and in the casting of so many familiar British actors in cameo roles. There are people I respect who are impatient with the film because it seems trapped by all the lazy British/Ealing comedy characteristics that they quite sensibly dislike. I would suggest that the film subverts the genre all the more effectively for working within it, that the chase routines work in terms of Sidney's psychology, and that the familiar actors are used artfully to embody the very quality of 'typecasting'— compartmentalising, fixed ideas and routines—that the film is about. Many of these familiar actors are old: well-loved veterans like Miles Malleson, Edie Martin, and Ernest Thesiger. In their persons, there is a sense of age and tradition closing in.

When the mill-owners first get wind of the challenge that the new fibre represents, they hastily summon up from London a grey eminence, the brain of the industry, Sir John Kierlaw. Played by Ernest Thesiger, he is a superb creation, a force of nature. Immensely old and wheezing, he works single-mindedly to head off the threat of change. If Birnley is like a capricious father to Sidney—indulging him to a certain point, then disciplining him sternly—then Kierlaw is a grandfather. Sidney and his invention are stifled by an extraordinary 'family' structure: father and Grandad, plus Nanny and Granny (the factory nurse who sedates him, and old Mrs Watson). It is they who speak at important moments for the whole industry: they represent England as 'a family with the wrong members in control', closing ranks, not against 'the enemy', but against innovation as such—now perceived *as* the enemy.

Father (Birnley) has strayed from the traditional line, seduced by the lure of a financial coup—as big a threat to the community as the individual acquisitive-

The mill owners get together to put pressure on Birnley. Michael Gough, Cecil Parker, Howard Marion Crawford, and, seated, Ernest Thesiger as Sir John Kierlaw.

ness of *Passport to Pimlico*. Now he becomes an errant 'son' and is brought back sharply into line. He rejects one son, of his own, and reinstates another: Corland, the owner whom we saw at the start, about whom he was lukewarm as a husband for Daphne. They stand shoulder to shoulder again, as Corland takes the lead in suppressing the new fibre (it was he who took the initiative in summoning the industry's grandfather in the first place).

The family now has to deal with Sidney. Bribes having failed, the argument escalates into violence; in one of the funniest moments in the film, even Kierlaw joins in, frail but determined, taking an ineffectual swipe at Sidney from his chair with his silver-topped walking-stick. Repressive violence *by* the grandfather figure . . . It is the point to which the film has logically moved.

Kierlaw's use of force is quite unhypocritical, in contrast to Birnley's flustered insistence a moment later: 'I will not resort to violence.' When Sidney is knocked down and lies motionless, Birnley diagnoses nothing serious, to which Kierlaw's dry response is 'A pity.' The figure of this old man embodies the *logic* of the way this industry is run, cutting through all the PR pretence: he is a glorious caricature, in the spirit of *Kind Hearts*, never quite going over the edge. Out of the backwoods emerges this monstrous old gentleman, the brains of the organism, to show where the power really lies and how it is enforced when the chips are down. He acts out the impulses which Birnley disguises or feels ashamed of. He is not just old but ancient, unashamedly selfish, ready for violence, and extremely tenacious.

His encounter with Birnley's daughter, Daphne, is a fine example of the way the comic mode of the film operates. Daphne is the forgotten member of the family, the daughter who has no apparent role except to be decorative and to get married. Her earlier intervention on Sidney's behalf was a shock to her father, and she intervenes again now.

Sidney having recovered and been locked away, the question is how, short of murder, he can be silenced. Bribes have failed, but Corland has an idea: he may be susceptible, if not to money, then to women. A colleague suggests that a woman Sidney seems to get on well with is Daphne. Corland, still her fiancé, agrees that she should be asked, for the sake of the industry, to use her charms on Sidney and persuade him to see things in a new light.

When the matter is put to her, Daphne forces the spokesman to spell it out: 'You're a very attractive young woman . . .' She explains: 'I'm not experienced in these matters, but I've always understood this work was very well paid.' There is a finely orchestrated range of responses. Corland and his colleague are shocked: of course they didn't want her to take it like *that* . . . When Birnley finds out, he is duly horrified, as a protective sentimental father, at the idea having been raised in the first place, and at Corland's part in it. Kierlaw, in contrast, is delighted to find someone he can do business with so unhypocritically; he names a sum. Daphne holds out for more, and he agrees to £5000. So she is let into the room with Sidney, to work on him in privacy.

Behind the mask of Ealing comedy, this seems to me to express a vision of the logic of capitalism as extreme as anything in Buñuel or Godard. For the metaphor of prostitution, compare Godard's *Two or Three Things I Know about Her*. In its seriousness and ruthlessness, in what it does with its comedy 'licence', it is, in case a reminder is needed, light years away from anything in the work of T. E. B. Clarke.

Daphne's reason for accepting the proposition so brazenly is partly the pleasure of humiliating them, Corland especially, by making them admit the logic of what they are suggesting; mainly, it is to gain access to Sidney and set

Daphne (Joan Greenwood) with Corland; and with her father.

him free. Unlike him, she has the imagination to think of the material's practical use: since it's unbreakable, he can let himself down from the window by a single strand of it (Sidney's own use of it, from this point, is counter-productive: the suit attracts attention by its luminosity).

Daphne is the one main character to break the film's moral stalemate, undermining its polarities. She shares Sidney's disinterested delight in his research, and his integrity; she can also read people and their motives, and doesn't disdain to meet the bosses' cunning with cunning of her own. Integrity without 'innocence', cunning without corruption—cunning used in order to *protect* integrity and allow it to prosper: it is a much more realistic formula for creating the sound community to which Ealing is drawn than trusting the 'innocent' qualities of Clarke heroes like the Pembertons of *Passport to Pimlico*. Daphne seems the most direct embodiment in Mackendrick's Ealing work of the qualities he values. She is played by Joan Greenwood, who was Sibella in *Kind Hearts* and Macroon's daughter in *Whisky Galore*. In the relaxed Hebridean community, remote from the modern industrial world, her blend of cunning and integrity, exemplified in her dealings with Waggett, was part of a shared culture: in industrialised, post-war England, it seems to have no roots. Daphne has no role, no outlet for her intelligence; she is a poor little rich girl, expecting to drift into marriage with her vacuous mill-owner. Sidney, too, is doomed to disappoint her, both as a potential lover and as an inventor who might have the vision to change things. Having set Sidney free, she disappears from the film. It can find no place for her; society has no place for her. We just see her face fleetingly at the end, among the crowd observing Sidney's humiliation.

There is, however, one more character I need to mention, in order to make the account of the film's elaborate family structure complete. During Sidney's final efforts to escape, his pursuers contrive to lock him into his old room at his lodgings and mount a guard outside the door: there seems no way out. However, observing him through the impregnable outside window is a six- or seven-year-old girl whom we have seen briefly at the beginning, running errands for Mrs Watson. She now puts into effect a stratagem of her own: she tells the guard that a man has just got out of the window. He hastily opens the door, sees no-one (Sidney having hidden) and rushes out to give chase. So she tells Sidney to come out now, which he does. There is nothing cute about the incident, or the girl's performance; both are very fresh and striking. Children conventionally represent innocence against worldliness, the chance of a fresh start. The child's appearance here is pointed, set against the dead weight of age and conservatism. But the film uses her unconventionally, refusing the sentimental view of 'innocence': her significance is that she is not an innocent like Sidney, but has the cunning of Daphne. She makes an intuitive judgment in favour of Sidney and carries it out. It is very bracing to have childhood innocence given a strong rather than weak definition, implying with robust psychological realism that this fusion of integrity and cunning (Daphne's mix) is *natural*—found in the child, as in the more primitive community of *Whisky Galore*—and that the conventional, and particularly English, polarity of innocence and worldliness is not natural at all.

I don't think that I am here placing excessive weight on a tiny incident. It is important both for the structure of the film itself and for Mackendrick's subsequent work. The girl, Mandy Miller, plays the name part in his next film, *Mandy*, and he will direct several subsequent films with leading parts for children: mention the name Mackendrick to a film buff and the first response is

Alec Guinness and Mandy Miller, near the end of The Man in the White Suit.

as likely to be 'director of children' as 'Ealing comedy'. It's not just that he discovered a 'knäck' of directing them; we might forecast his gravitation towards children purely from *The Man in the White Suit.*

Like *Passport to Pimlico*, the film has used its comedy gimmick to examine the workings of a society by artificially speeding them up: the white suit, like the Burgundian document, throws society into turmoil, intensifies conflicts, forces people to declare allegiances and define their philosophies. In *Passport*, the process separates out Garland and his philosophy of 'Every man for himself', allows it to be seen clearly in its full implications and in contrast with the Pemberton vision of society. The white suit forces the industry to sort out its values and expose its true nature. The representative it throws up is Kierlaw. And the last word on the issues is given to Mrs Watson: they are two complementary figures, old and frail, confronting Sidney face to face, saying the same thing, and defeating him. The fundamental movement of the film is this widening out of the father/son conflict to bring in the grandfather generation, and then, in a further extension that is satisfying both formally/and thematically, the fourth generation, the young girl. By stretching out its range of characters in this pointed way, from very young to very old, the film brings to life the idea of a tradition into which everyone is locked. The girl is at least still young and alert enough not to have been subjected to its full weight.

I wrote above of *Passport to Pimlico*, and the implications of the way it is worked out: 'The sadness is that there should be so deep a compulsion to dream of consensus, to shy away from the conflicts that come up in an "open" society rather than to follow them through clear-sightedly.' This is what Mackendrick's film shows: a shying away from honest debate in any terms transcending those of Mrs Watson, about the issues which the white suit raises; that debate is the great vacuum at the heart of the film. In effect, the film devastatingly sets out, in terms of the real world of production, the consequences for a society of the soft *Passport to Pimlico* philosophy. The dream of consensus goes sour, leading to stagnation as people dig in to defend their own position and thus the *status quo*. Towards the end, management and unions come together to plan how to silence Sidney. A management spokesman states ingratiatingly that 'Capital and labour are hand in hand in this.' But when in the same scene Corland takes a phone call that turns out to be for one of the Union representatives and has to ask round the room for 'someone called Bertha', the tone of voice is eloquent; he can't keep the amused disdain out of it. That illustrates the kind of consensus it is: unequal, negative, and sterile.

A final point about the film. Mackendrick once revealed in a television interview that his advice to Cecil Parker in approaching the role of Birnley was 'model yourself on Mick'—on Sir Michael Balcon. The device by which his rival magnates bring to an end Birnley's commitment to the new fabric is this: Corland discovers that the crucial formula was first discovered during the period before Sidney was in Birnley's employment. He doesn't technically have the rights to it. This picks up a notorious obsession of Balcon's, of which Monja Danischewsky, in his portrait of life at 'Mr Balcon's Academy for Young Gentlemen', gives some entertaining examples:

'He has always been doctrinaire in his views of the company's rights *vis-à-vis* the employee. I remember that I once saw the film *The First of the Few* with him privately in the projection theatre at Ealing. The film was the story of Mitchell, inventor of the Spitfire fighter plane, and Leslie Howard played the part of Mitchell. There was a scene in which the inventor faced his board with the plans and a model of the prototype of the plane. The board rejected the idea. "In that case," said the screen Mitchell, "I'll take it elsewhere." Before I knew what was happening, Mick had jumped to his feet, pointing an accusing finger at Leslie Howard's retreating figure. "You come back!" Mick shouted at him, "you designed that plane in the Company's time! It isn't your copyright. It belongs to the Company!" '

Is Sidney, among other things, a satirical (self-)portrait of the harassed young Ealing director struggling to express himself, to give the world his own dazzling personal vision, in defiance of the paternalistic hand of his boss and the general inertia of the industry?

Of the films I have picked out at different stages as key or pivotal ones, *The Man in the White Suit* is the most so of all, the *definitive* Ealing film (as distinct from the most typical); the extent to which it is at one level 'about' Ealing itself contributes to this definitive status. In retrospect, it looks prophetic in its analysis of the dominant lines of force in society ('the stagnant society', to quote an influential label of the 'sixties, affixed by an economist), prophetic at least in terms of the kind of society projected from Ealing, and of the graph of Ealing's own vitality. In the chronological list of Ealing films, *The Man in the White Suit* exactly marks off the division between before and after, as if a creeping paralysis were indeed at work at that very time. The films are quite suddenly overtaken by age and weariness. Whatever their limitations, the preceding Clarke films— *Passport, The Blue Lamp, The Lavender Hill Mob*—aren't tired ones. They have a certain freshness and boldness; they do or show something ambitious, as their successors do not. With the destruction of the white suit, the dimension of inventiveness that it represents vanishes from the films.

STAGNATION

1951 was a watershed year for British films as a whole, and the period 1952-58 was an extraordinarily dead one. It would need a skilled social historian to analyse what happened to Britain and British culture at this time and relate it to the content and form of the films; there is a change too profound to be accounted for purely in terms of the internal workings of the film industry. 1951 was Festival of Britain year, and Michael Frayn, in the essay I cited at the beginning of this book, sees the Festival as the end of an era, the end of the ten-year dominance of the 'herbivores, or gentle ruminants' and their philosophy; it was the year in which the Conservative party regained office. I can best approach the change from the other end, that of Ealing, in the belief that this set of films will increasingly become accepted as a prime source of evidence for reading the inner history of the times.

Even less than before will I attempt to string together an account of all the films from 1951 in a year-by-year narrative. Instead, I will pick out some important ones, notably Mackendrick's, and meanwhile offer some general points about an output that becomes increasingly homogenous:

Distaste for commerce. Following through the logic of *Passport to Pimlico* and its retreat from the acquisitive philosophy, various kinds of 'commercial' culture

are attacked or satirised: pop clubs (*I Believe in You*, 1952), professional boxing (*The Square Ring*, 1953), commercial television (*Meet Mr Lucifer*, 1953), Hollywood-style worship of film-stars (*The Love Lottery*, 1954). Entrepreneurs are generally characterised as shady, e.g. in *The Night My Number Came Up* (1955), where the odd man out on a planeload of brasshats in the Far East, a businessman flying in quest of export orders, is presented with an extraordinarily snobbish disdain. The only form of commerce to seem untainted is the small family business which just ticks over. In particular, the small catering concern, which is such a dominant milieu in British cinema generally. (See especially *The Rainbow Jacket*, 1954.)

A horror of violence. This is particularly noticeable in the three Ealing films of 1952 which tackle political themes: *Secret People*, *His Excellency*, *The Gentle Gunman*. All are seriously weakened, not by the fact of being 'against' violence, but by the way the intensity of their recoil throws them off balance: this is what misled John Ellis into his controversial reference in Screen magazine to *Secret People* (directed by Thorold Dickinson) as a 'vicious attack' on a left-wing organisation when it is effectively, like *The Gentle Gunman*, an abandonment of the political issues as such in favour of a generalised humanism—Auden's line 'We must love one another or die' is spoken on the soundtrack at the end, an end which is closely paralleled in that of *The Gentle Gunman* (dealing with the IRA).

Emotional inhibition: the seizing up of the Ealing idea of restraint discussed above in the context of *It Always Rains on Sunday* and *The Blue Lamp*. *The Cruel Sea* contains a good instance of this (the bereavement of the middle-aged man played by Liam Redmond), but also a scene that seems to contradict it: the strongly emotional reaction by Jack Hawkins to the incident which brings

Maria (Valentina Cortese), the heroine of Secret People: *left, watching her sister Nora; right, at Scotland Yard, denouncing the left-wing organisation which has killed an innocent girl. Audrey Hepburn, Irene Worth, Reginald Tate.*

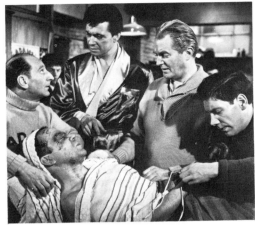

home to him the cruel responsibilities of command. But Hawkins giving way to emotion always, for me at least, feels awkward and self-conscious (as in *Man in the Sky*, 1957), which need not at all be a criticism of the actor. In his autobiography, Hawkins recounts how this same *Cruel Sea* scene was played in three ways on three successive days because Balcon and Charles Frend (the director) kept changing their minds about the amount of emotion that ought to be expressed. This suggests a certain lack of spontaneity in the handling of emotion, a suggestion which the films bear out. It links, of course, with the inhibitions on sexuality that I have already referred to. Where women appear, they are generally defined in terms of a dull polarity as respectable girl or vamp (in *The Cruel Sea*: Virginia McKenna and Moira Lister).

Deference to age and authority. There is virtually no defiance or even enterprise on the part of youth, no confrontation between father and son figures. At least, if there is, the defiance is safely 'placed' or absorbed (e.g. *I Believe in You*, on the workings of the probation service, or on a wider social canvas, *His Excellency*, both in 1952: in this respect the films grow progressively even tamer).

It is only in the early 'fifties that Ealing starts to earn its now familiar identification with the old and quaint; *The Titfield Thunderbolt* is a pioneer in this;

Violence and sexuality in 'fifties Ealing. Top: promoter, moll (Kay Kendall) and victim (Robert Beatty) in The Square Ring. *Centre: Harry Fowler in* I Believe in You, *with his girl (Joan Collins) and in the dock. Bottom: John Mills and Dirk Bogarde as brothers in the I.R.A.* (The Gentle Gunman); *romance between George Baker and Belinda Lee* (The Feminine Touch). *Below, publicity still for* Dance Hall, *Diana Dors, Jane Hylton, Natasha Parry, Petula Clark.*

but it could be forecast from *The Man in the White Suit*, and is a natural result of the conjunction of all the trends I have outlined.

The total picture is one of stagnation, of opting out of any large projects or issues, of settling for a quiet life within a society whose structure inhibits *all* forms of dynamism. The dominant fact is the power of age, authority and tradition, of an authority which is aged, in fact or spirit. Hence the importance to Mackendrick of the sensibility of the child.

Cage of Gold and *Mandy* make an interesting pair, 'before' and 'after'—released in 1950 and 1952. Dearden before, Mackendrick after. Dearden I have characterised as the director whose prolific output constitutes an Ealing norm or baseline. It is a fair summary that his postwar films up to 1951 are all interesting, but that those after this date are much less so: the closing-up, paralysing spirit seems palpably to descend upon them.

Cage of Gold is virtually the last Ealing film to give a decent part to a woman (old ladies aside)—and there are 35 films to come. Jean Simmons, as Judy, has a central role comparable with that of Googie Withers in *It Always Rains on Sunday*. She is courted and married by a glamorous cad, deserted by him (when he finds she is less rich than he thought), and then—believing him to be dead—settles down with her longtime suitor, a conscientious doctor. After a few years, the first husband returns, to be disposed of in a burst of melodramatic violence which leaves the heroine and her family unscathed.

What has changed since the Googie Withers film and since Dearden's own *Frieda* is the tightness of the structure of choices. Mainly through the actress,

Officers and their women in The Cruel Sea. *Jack Hawkins as Captain Ericsson (Meredith Edwards in attendance); Virginia McKenna and Donald Sinden; John Stratton, June Thorburn, Sinden; Moira Lister and Denholm Elliott.*

there is a real sense of the attractions of the less respectable life and the spiritual limitations of what Judy settles for, but the film loads the dice heavily the other way, constructing a set of increasingly clear polarities: French/English, sexy/solid, commercial/altruistic. The film's title is that of the French nightclub which the first husband frequents, and the phrase is used, to portentous effect, as a warning against enslavement to money values; the second husband has chosen to work in the new National Health Service rather than Harley Street; he is industrious and considerate. Compared with the early postwar films, an enormous weight has accumulated on the side of the respectable, both moral weight (a clearer polarity of vice and virtue) and institutional weight. The NHS/Harley Street opposition is fundamental. The doctor, Allan, makes his choice after carefully charted deliberation, and there is the unmistakable parallel, already mentioned, between the NHS and Ealing itself. The choice Judy is faced with, between two ways of life, is a similar one, and there is a strong (double) pressure for her to make it in the same way and fulfil the pattern, which, after a false start, she does. What she settles down to, then, is life in a large, enveloping dark house, with her baby son, her old Nanny (Gladys Henson, a solid Ealing presence—Mrs Dixon in *The Blue Lamp*) and her worthy husband. Also, at the top of the house, there is her aged father-in-law, bed-ridden, demanding but lovable, a constant reminder of the right values: opting for the NHS has meant the son taking over

Jean Simmons in Cage of Gold. *Left : with her father-in-law (Harcourt Williams).
Right : attended by second husband (James Donald) and Nanny (Gladys Henson).*

his father's practice, and following the same altruistic principles. There is even, gently underscoring the main polarities, a running gag which has the old gentleman twiddling his radio dial to get away from the ubiquitous pop music and find something classical.

But in this film the woman is at least *there*, with a spiritual and sensual existence which—simply by being represented—splits the film apart. We can decide to see the house and what it represents as inadequate for her : the film does give us data with which to undermine its own overt tying-up of everything. After 1951, there will be no place for an actress like Jean Simmons, or Joan Greenwood for that matter. The door is closing. The house, the family, the tradition, will soon be the only reality.

The reason for juxtaposing *Mandy* with *Cage of Gold* is that Mackendrick's film is dominated by this same image of a family in a house : child, parents, grandfather at the top. It is a much less benevolent structure. *Mandy* is the only non-comedy Mackendrick made at Ealing. It has usually been treated on its own as a nice little film about the education of the deaf : one whose 'documentary' core, dealing with Mandy herself and the school, is worthy and moving, but which unfortunately surrounds this with a novelettish family drama of little interest (Richard Winnington's review at the time invoked 'Mrs Dale's Diary'). Even taking the film on its own, this seems obtuse, and when one comes to it in the context of *The Man in the White Suit*, and of Ealing generally, it is hard to see it as other than a purposeful unity—in its way, as ambitious a statement about the England of its time as its comedy predecessor. It works through two sets of relationships : the adult triangle (Mandy's parents and the headmaster of her school, involved in a drama of inhibition and misunderstanding), and the ladder of the generations (Mandy, her father, her grandfather).

Though the film is certainly 'about' the education of the deaf in a serious way, its reference is wider : Mandy stands for all children, for the potential locked up inside the new (English) generation, all of whom have, after all, to learn to communicate and to relate to others. Indeed this is just what Mandy's own father has difficulty in doing. There is an intense irony in the way Mandy's slow struggle to perceive and communicate goes in parallel with, and is retarded by, the adults' elementary failure to perceive and communicate. She is a *force*, like Sidney's creativity, desperate to express itself, frustrated by more than her own limitations. Just as a comedy can classically set up (for example, through Sidney Stratton's inventive genius) an extraordinary situation which enables the forces underlying society to be played out openly, so *Mandy* takes a special case, the handicapped child, to work in this same intensified way, forcing people by the urgency of the demand made on them to reveal what they really are. It takes up issues of communication and education (in the widest sense) that are crucial to the healthy operation of the whole society. And like *The Man in the White Suit*, it works towards an image of the repressive structure of the family. The centre of gravity again shifts back, from the confused father to the grandfather—semi-invalid, a force of inertia, but still retaining authority. (He is played by Godfrey Tearle, a magistrate in his previous Ealing film and a bishop in his next one.) He has the authority that can stifle Mandy, or that can release her, if he puts the momentum of the family into reverse.

Mandy's father, Harry, is a bold sketch of the superficially attractive middle-class hero, in the line of Ralph Michael and David Farrar in earlier Ealing films, who is hollow inside: he has never matured. Faced with any problem—Mandy's deafness, then at the end the estrangement from his wife—his solution is to turn *away* from it and run back to his parents. It is clear that they have made him what he is, and they reinforce his weaknesses. Specifically, they support him in 'protecting' Mandy: giving her a private governess, not letting her meet other children or (initially) go to the school which the daughter-in-law has found. When Harry abducts Mandy from her mother and from the school, the parents complacently welcome them back. As the film establishes it, this comes over

Left: Mandy, at the training school for the deaf (Mandy Miller). Right: her father and grandfather (Terence Morgan, Godfrey Tearle).

Mandy: *the final movement. Grandfather, as usual, turned away.*

strongly as a turning away from life. It is easy to claim that a film like this is 'about' the limitations of its characters, in contrast with other films which share or condone these limitations, or exploit them in a formula way. Why shouldn't *Mandy* be seen as a conventional sentimental-suspense mechanism, making us wait for the smiling-through-tears moment of breakthrough? Conversely, couldn't one make the same sort of reading of *any* story of a handicapped child? There has to be some external obstacle to success, and thus some adult obstructiveness, to make it a drama at all. The dividing line is hard to establish, as it is with all Mackendrick's Ealing work, since he operates so much from within the conventional forms, using the same kind of actors. The adult triangle here, played by Terence Morgan, Phyllis Calvert, and Jack Hawkins (the teacher), poses a similar problem to the use of the cameo players in *The Man in the White Suit*.

Mandy's deafness is first suspected when she is still a baby, and her parents decide to make a test. Her father stands behind her, making loud noises. We get repeated close-ups of her head from his point of view: she does not turn round. The image has great weight, and we remember it: it carries the transition to the family's new life, coping with Mandy's deafness. At the end, the image is repeated: the back of the head in close-up, with someone urging it to turn round in response, and the spectator, as before, willing it to turn. This time it is the head of Mandy's father, and it is his own father who is persuading him to listen, and to 'see'. It sums up the point implicit in all that has happened: Harry is just as handicapped as his daughter. She in turn is facing, in an intensified form, the problems of all of us. The film is as much about Harry's metaphorical blindness as Mandy's real deafness.

This imagery of looking and not looking permeates the film. Mandy faced *away*. Harry habitually faces away, refuses to look at people, or issues, or to listen (hence his misunderstanding of his wife's relationship with the headmaster). His own father, too, is habitually self-absorbed and turned away from people. All three generations have come together in this old house, as in *Cage of Gold*, and it's the house itself that seems the cage. Grandfather at the top, then father, then Mandy herself, brought there by force: a remarkable image of a *sterile* continuity between generations.

It's resolved in a beautiful way. Mandy, left with nothing to do but as always showing a live curiosity, wanders into her grandfather's room. He treats her with his usual remote indulgence, then turns back to his own pursuits. But she has spotted some writing and starts to articulate sounds—to read. The received belief is that she can't read, that the school has failed. Harry's testing of her earlier to decide the point was so aggressive that she naturally froze up. Now, at last, the grandfather has to look and take notice. The vicious circle, the tight pattern of re-enactment of a pernicious upbringing, can be broken. The grandfather at last rouses himself to question his son's prejudices, both about Mandy and about the behaviour of his wife. It's at this point that we get the repetition of the long-held back-of-head shot, previously used of Mandy. Coming at the climax of a narrative of frustration and evasion of challenge, it creates considerable tension: when Harry finally turns round, the movement is a release, signifying his readiness, at last, to look and think and trust. There follows a wonderful shot with the camera simply tracking forward to the open door of the walled garden, looking out to the open space beyond. Moving from dark to light, it conveys Harry's enlightenment, the release of seeing. It is this same door which, for Mandy, leads from shelter to other people. Early in the film, she unluckily strayed through it and was overwhelmed by the world outside; now, stronger, she has passed through it, and is at this moment starting to explore and to communicate with other children. The image definitively merges the two threads of the story; it simultaneously expresses Mandy's release and her father's, and thus conveys in the clearest way possible how they are bound up together— similar, and interdependent.

So Mandy enters on the world. Harry, following her, does the same: he doesn't intervene, but stands watching her, alongside his wife (who has come in search of her)—in front of the grandparents' house. The film ends with this scene.

I find *Mandy*, especially here at the end, one of the most affecting of all British films. Its modest story is worked out with such scrupulous care and craft, and it moves to an ending which, in a very honest combination, is both momentous and tentative. The last shots, almost in diagram form, mark a realignment in the relationship of the generations: an opening out, a relaxing of the dead hand. But it can only be that: a diagram, a programme. The generations remain 'banked up' behind Mandy. She doesn't cease to be handicapped and vulnerable. Likewise, the adults remain who they are. It is a happy end in that sense overcomes prejudice; it justifies the integrity, and the ideas, of wife and teacher. However, it seems to me that the film is very conscious of the limitations of the characters as hero and heroine, of the limitations of the types they and the actors (Phyllis Calvert and Jack Hawkins) represent, and of the limits to

The adult triangle of Mandy: *Terence Morgan, Jack Hawkins, Phyllis Calvert.*

what they can achieve. Housewife dedicated to family, teacher dedicated to job, both decent, self-denying and stolidly dull—like the doctor of *Cage of Gold* and the sort of heroine which that film pressures the Jean Simmons character into becoming. *Mandy*, like *The Man in the White Suit*, indeed all Mackendrick's films at Ealing, engages unobtrusively but critically with the current orthodoxy. It is to *Cage of Gold* what *The Man in the White Suit* was to *Passport to Pimlico*, though the relation need not be a conscious one; it is an intelligent post-1951 film, with all that this implies. Its characters live in that bounded, stagnant world. *Cage of Gold* came at the culmination of a long process of closing-down, bringing everything together in one definitive, benevolent, sensible package: family and work, mutually supporting, within the house. Once the outside threats (violence, commercialism, sexuality) have been disposed of, what remains is unproblematic. *Mandy* stirs this all up. The house becomes the cage; the weight of the family is set in opposition to the growth of the child and to the enlightened work of the doctor/teacher. Nor does the film offer an alternative structure to that of the top-heavy family, the school itself being run by an obstructive board of governors. There is a strong sense of the omnipresent inertia against which wife and teacher have to struggle on Mandy's behalf, with limited equipment. The Jack Hawkins character, Searle, is (like Sidney the research scientist) good at his job, and it is a noble job, but frustrations press in upon it. This is the first of five solid, responsible leading roles that Hawkins played at Ealing. Mackendrick brings out the dimension of immaturity, of not being able to apply his strength and integrity to fulfilling effect, which always underlies his solidity, but which the later films don't seem so sensitive to, or don't know what to do with. Harry thinks his wife and Searle are having an affair. Of course, they are far too selfless and responsible for this—it's another instance of Harry's panicky jumping to conclusions. At the same time, the film conveys a wistful attraction between them which they daren't think or speak about, let alone act on. We can't help wishing, as with the couple in *Brief Encounter*, that they were capable of it, that they were therefore different people. *That* inhibition, like Sidney's blankness with women in *The Man in the White Suit*, seems bound up with the precariousness of their major effort: their struggle against the repressive forces in the child's world.

So the happy end itself is precarious, seeing in whom it is vested: these adults (Harry included), and this child, who is not only physically handicapped but marked already by the adults' culture. Contrast Mandy, quiet sad, cut-off, waiting for a chance, with the sheer tempestuous *energy* of Helen Keller, deaf, dumb and blind, in what could be seen as the American *Mandy*, *The Miracle Worker*. A momentous contrast in ways of life and of cinema underlies that comparison, even granted the ten-year gap between them. Yet Mandy remains a powerful figure, marking the level at which a fresh start has to be made within this culture. If it seems wrong to put such a representative weight on *this* child, then just produce, please, an example of English youth, child or teenager, in an Ealing or indeed British film of the next few years, who is any livelier, or freer from the dead hand. I can't think of one.

Ealing will now jog along showing immovable systems, and adults who settle for the best way of clearing a modest space for themselves within them: the films cry out for the subversive or renewing energy of children, but these are either absent, or with one—Scottish—exception, remain very 'stage-school' and lifeless. Mackendrick's apart, the films are themselves conformist and middle-aged. Perhaps the best example of this direction in mainstream Ealing drama is *The Rainbow Jacket* (1954), and the particular line of dialogue on which it ends.

This film's hero is a middle-aged jockey (Bill Owen) who forfeited his own career by taking a bribe but lives again through the success of a young protege. The first scene of the film, introducing the character, takes place at a small snackbar stall where Sidney James (an actor whose television stardom was preceded by literally hundreds of cameo roles in British films) caters for race-goers. We return to it at intervals, and each time James is heard complaining that he is anxious to sell if he can get a fair price. Owen has various ups and downs, as well as a growing relationship with the young jockey's widowed mother, but she distrusts his ambition, expressed in terms of a luxury flat and a new racing career. She prefers something steadier. At the end, in a characteristic

Bill Owen in The Rainbow Jacket. *Left: with his protégé's mother (Kay Walsh). Right: with the owner (Sid James) of the snackbar which he will eventually buy.*

Dearden climax of atonement, Owen saves the boy's future by taking on himself the blame for another bribery incident. He walks away from the racecourse, with the mother. She asks him how he will get on: how much money has he? His answer: 'Just enough to buy a little old snackbar.'

This cosy image is formally offset by the promise of the boy, whose career is at this moment advancing another stage. But his story is shot and acted in so dead a manner, and his career set within so suffocating and deference-ridden an institutional system (the racing world), that he embodies no kind of fresh life. The film is overwhelmingly with the adults and the way they resolve things: witness the final shot (the adults framed in the foreground, the boy's race deep in the background—a reverse of the formal/thematic emphasis at the close of *Mandy*) and the triumph of the final line. A little old snackbar: the adjectives count for a lot.

The Rainbow Jacket was the work of T. E. B. Clarke (original script) and Basil Dearden (direction), their first collaboration since *The Blue Lamp*. Dearden's films in the meantime have included *Cage of Gold*; we have a measure of the extent to which the complacent dispensation of those two films has now petrified. After *The Blue Lamp*, all of Clarke's other Ealing films were comedies; they reveal a progressive drain of energy and boldness which parallels that in Ealing's straight dramas, as they also centre on items that are, like the snackbar of *The Rainbow Jacket*, little and old.

Authority in The Rainbow Jacket: *the boy jockey (Fella Edmunds) up before the Jockey Club. Michael Trubshawe, Wilfred Hyde White, Robert Morley.*

LATE COMEDIES

Though Ealing, characteristically, never tried to exploit its sudden success with comedies by over-producing them (after 1951 and *The Man in the White Suit*, it made scarcely one a year, eight films out of thirty in all), the identification of the studio with comedy became increasingly complete. I would account for this by the enduring impact made by the five major ones (the 1949 trio, plus the two from 1951), by the way other studios exploited their success to make 'Ealing-style' comedies, and by the dullness of Ealing's non-comedy output, which offered little competition now that it had settled back into such unambitious formats. In fact, only three comedies of the post-1951 batch have endured, and they are less substantial than their makers' earlier comedies, but this process of attenuation is itself interesting, and they are the only remaining Ealing films I need to refer to in much detail. Two are directed by Mackendrick: *The Maggie* (1954) and *The Ladykillers* (1955). The other, written by Clarke and directed by Charles Crichton, is *The Titfield Thunderbolt* (1953). This film marks an unmistakably decadent stage, corresponding to the common identikit view of the genre, formed in retrospect, as something nice and wholesome and harmless, quaint and static and timeless.

The very title is quaint. Titfield is a small country town, and the Thunderbolt an ancient railway engine. The credit titles are displayed on a drawn background: a toy train, on a small circular layout, with a wall surrounding it. This absolutely sets the tone of the film. Offering an explanation for the fairly modest business done by the film, compared with earlier comedies, Mackendrick told Clarke this:

'Just about everybody would secretly like to rid themselves of tiresome relatives as in *Kind Hearts and Coronets*, or get hold of unlimited free whisky, or remove a fortune in gold bars from the Bank of England. But not so many people have any great desire to run a railway.'

One might ask whether a significantly greater number of people dream of operating a small cargo boat, which would be the subject of Mackendrick's own subsequent comedy, *The Maggie*. By this time, as I have suggested, Ealing had simply ceased to conceive of projects and satisfactions on a large scale, either straight or in fantasy. This certainly restricts the range of pleasures that the films offer; but clearly they still offer *some* pleasure, something to dream about.

Titfield appeals to railway enthusiasts. But beyond this, it offers a fantasy of small-town life, of a cosy rural community. Timeless and self-sufficient—like the railway of the credits, going round in circles, protected from the world outside. To set out the nature of the community and how it operates in the film is to understand both its seductive appeal (transcending that of the railway as such) and the limitations of that appeal.

The Titfield Thunderbolt. *Left: the romantic image. Right: the mobile bar-room. The Ministry Inspector John Rudling confronts (from right) Naunton Wayne, Hugh Griffith, Stanley Holloway. At the bar: Gabrielle Brune.*

Titfield has the oldest branch line in the world; it has been losing money for years, and British Railways are closing it down. A campaign is started to keep it open, and the Ministry considers whether to allow the locals to take over the line and run it themselves. The campaign has two main opponents to overcome: the bureaucrats, and the local bus company who want their rival service to enjoy a monopoly.

The set-up, then, is like that of *Passport to Pimlico*: community, bureaucrats, and free-enterprise traders. A similar quirky drama is played out, at the end of which the community wins a victory. The branch line is accepted as part of the network, and the film ends with the main line drivers saluting the gallantry of the Titfield enterprise with a chorus of toots and whistles from their larger engines. The mechanism is exactly that of *Passport*: the community's defiantly human-scale values are adopted as national ones. In its loving portrayal of this plucky community, Ealing is still 'projecting Britain'.

But what a change is evident, four years after *Passport*. After its fashion, that film tested out ideas about society in a genuinely open and exploratory manner, discovering its answers in the course of the film, or at least putting the audience through a process of discovery. *The Titfield Thunderbolt* knows all the answers before it starts—knows them, in effect, from *Passport*. Like *The Man in White Suit*, it shows a society which has committed itself to the backward-

looking, soft-option path which *Passport* settled for, and is thus a warning of some of the consequences. But it in every way lacks the critical perspective of Mackendrick's film.

From the start, the commercial interests (Pearce and Crump Ltd, the bus company) are presented as shifty and corrupt: they resist the renewal of the railway service by bribery and then sabotage. And they have a sinister vision of expansion—perhaps, they daydream, in a few years' time, the place could be ready to change its name to Pearcetown. At stake, then, is the identity of the community. The sides declare themselves. Selfish, commercial, acquisitive, as Pearcetown; or, as Titfield—what, exactly?

Because, in line with the lesson of *Passport to Pimlico*, all acquisitiveness is now suspect, the benevolent side has to be totally purged of it. It's a typical late Ealing polarisation, with absurd consequences. What we get on the railway side is a set of amateurs and parasites, people who can afford to devote themselves to the railway without any sordid commercial motives coming into it. The campaign leaders are the aged Vicar (George Relph) and the local Squire, who is youngish (John Gregson) but who has an ancestral authority in the community: his great-grandfather had the line built in the first place, and the whole enterprise is thus in effect a defence of his role (The first time we see the train, the guard holds it at Titfield beyond its time: 'Can't go yet, the Squire's not here.')

The money to support the line comes from a rich local eccentric, an alcoholic named Valentine, who is played by the Pemberton of *Passport to Pimlico*, Stanley Holloway—a casting link which seems perverse, but may have an inspired logic. Valentine's money has presumably, like the Squire's, come from some commercial enterprise in the past, but he is now safely retired, a man of leisure, who spends all his time in the pub. His motivation for supporting the railway is the fact that a bar on a train doesn't have to observe pub closing times. So, the train contains a bar in a carriage of its own, where the barmaid from the pub presides and Valentine drinks. It goes backwards and forwards carrying him. The Vicar's pleasure, too, is in going back and forth. What the train is not noticeably used for is getting anyone from A to B, for instance, to work. The line starts to make a profit only when it attracts tourists, who likewise take the ride for its own sake.

There is no need to follow in detail the twists and turns of the plot, which manipulate known and labelled elements, set out at the start, towards a predictable end. On the way, the associations which the train accumulates are: little, old, slow, picturesque. This ingenious process of accumulation is the film's main satisfaction, as each of the associations is intensified. The villains wreck the train on the eve of the test run which will decide if the Ministry can sanction the service's continuing: in the emergency, the local museum is raided and the venerable Thunderbolt brought out of retirement. The regular driver is an eccentric retired railwayman who lives in a converted railway carriage; this residence forms part of the emergency replacement train. Since the driver himself is in police custody on the day, the train is driven by the Vicar, supported by his Bishop, who turns up flushed with excitement for the occasion. The ticket lady is the Vicar's old housekeeper—Edie Martin again. There are various hold-ups during the test run, caused both by outside agencies and by the frailty of the train. Will it fail the test? The Ministry man, a bowler-hatted caricature, gives nothing away. At the end, he reveals his verdict. The train passes because of being so slow. Anything faster would have broken a hitherto unexplained bureaucratic rule. The decision formally endorses the fact that the enterprise is not a practical but a symbolic one.

Logging, however accurately, what happens in a film like this can still miss the point, especially when it's a comedy, and especially when one is out of sympathy with it, as I am with this. Comedy depends so much on tone and on subjective response; by definition, it isn't to be taken 'straight'. I can just conceive of other readings of the T. E. B. Clarke comedies, of their intentions and their final import, than those I have offered, and there can obviously be conflicting valuations of them. But if any form of comedy is straightforward and unambiguous, it is surely Clarke's, particularly the 'community' films: *Passport to Pimlico, The Titfield Thunderbolt,* and the later *Barnacle Bill* (setting them out like this registers the pattern of alliteration in the titles, which already helps to create a mood: try saying them aloud). It's hard to find in them any of the ironies or ambiguities of the Hamer and Mackendrick comedies. The group is viewed with a simple, indulgent affection, the moral distinctions are clear cut, and the directors serve the scripts faithfully. In *Titfield*, the pace and style of the film (including the colour, used here for the first time in an Ealing comedy) operate in simple reinforcement of the script's image of the train and of the community: slow, uncomplicated, and picturesque.

What makes me so out of sympathy is the sheer decadence of the film's notion of community. The train operation seems broadly to have the support of the locals. At the climax, a benevolent crowd rallies round in support, just as at the climax of the earlier Clarke films: *Hue and Cry* (the boys), *Passport to Pimlico* (the people of London), and *The Blue Lamp* (the greyhound racing

Removing the Thunderbolt from the town museum

fraternity). There is an attempt to renew this pattern by building up a picture of a community with its heart in the right place, endorsing the central enterprise. A crowd cheers the train off on its test journey. Bystanders drop everything to express support—a cricket match even breaks off spontaneously, and the players stream over to watch. The passengers get off and push in a crisis. This recalls a set-piece constructed with elaborate care on an earlier run, and worth describing: when the train's water supply is sabotaged, staff and passengers together rush across the fields to the nearest farmhouse, to fetch a supply in whatever containers are to hand, things like a tea-urn, a soda siphon, and a baby's bath on the point of being used . . . the baby image, and the whole montage, is a clear echo of *Whisky Galore* (the hiding of the drink from the excise men), but the comparison is an embarrassment, as the sequence exists in a vacuum.

The trouble with all the community scenes is that insofar as we don't know the people, they remain obstinately just extras, and insofar as we do, we know them for the innocent dilettantes they are. Neither way do they have much going for them. Why should the train matter to the locals? There is no evident reason apart from sentiment and deference: contrast the motivation of *Whisky Galore*, and even *Passport to Pimlico*. There is no grasp of a *living* community in the film, or of the relevance of the train to people's daily needs. It's the hobby of a few eccentric amateurs, mainly from the church, the squirearchy, and the idle rich. An amazing difference from the three earlier Clarke films with benevolent crowds; yet Ealing seems to want to pass the enterprise off as embodying the same kind of democratic solidarity. The community spirit, which, in the war films, expelled and replaced the muddling amateur spirit and exorcised the habit of deference to squires (*Went the Day Well?*), is now being invoked to support exactly *that* kind of leadership and to celebrate a way of life that is very explicitly old and slow and innocent. This turns out to be what the logic of

Passport to Pimlico leads to. A backward-looking community, with no dynamism; a fixation on a *soft* world of fantasy which has no anchor in reality and which thus invites the real modern world to pass it by, or rather to drop into it for an occasional sentimental dip. Well, why not? The real objection to the film, as to late Ealing in general, is that it ends up promoting this polarisation, and thus discrediting, as a serious philosophy, the whole 'small is beautiful' case which it ostensibly supports. A few years after this film, Dr Beeching 'rationalised' the British Rail network by closing a large number of branch lines. *Titfield*, which seems to be an anti-Beeching film, is in effect very pro-Beeching, since it supports the (lazy) idea that such lines have a purely sentimental value. An important case goes by default.

To point the continuity of Ealing's logic there is the familiar figure of Stanley Holloway, at the centre of the train as of Pimlico. Pimlico *becomes* Titfield (a rural nowhere), which then becomes a community shut away on the end of a pier in a coastal resort. This is the weird end to Clarke's sequence of comedies: *Barnacle Bill*, made in 1957 at the tail-end of Ealing's existence, and a dismal failure at every level except that of logic. It's the film that Clarke had to make to bring a pattern to completion, but can anyone have thought it capable of grasping an audience? Alec Guinness plays a naval captain who suffers from seasickness; he takes over a down-at-heel pier, and proceeds to treat it as if it were a ship. At the beginning, Guinness goes through a little routine, impersonating six of his naval ancestors in a series of quick flashbacks. The film's determination to recreate the spirit of past Ealing successes (in the manner of the *Whisky Galore* sequence in *Titfield*) is embarrassing: the echo here is of *Kind Hearts*, but a more sustained one is of *Passport to Pimlico*. The captain contrives to get his pier registered as a ship and therefore treated as one, just as Pimlico was treated as a sovereign state. Officialdom, on the mainland, wages a sour campaign against his command, more in the spirit of the Titfield bus company than of the Whitehall officials in the earlier film. The pier becomes a refuge, taking people on as guests in a mock cruise. The film doesn't merit a long account. The point is the extraordinary central image of this community of innocents and eccentrics sustaining a life which is doubly unreal: first it's all holiday (recalling the unreality of Titfield as a working community), and, second, it pretends to move while remaining stationary. There couldn't be a better image for the static and

unrealistic nature of the Clarke/Ealing community. It's as if the tide of inevitable change—made the more inevitable by the soft, innocent philosophy of those resisting change—surrounded Pimlico, which had decided change *wouldn't* happen, and floated it off into the sea, or nearly so. It still, just, remains attached: a part of England.

Barnacle Bill marks an unmistakable end of the line for Ealing comedy. Made when the company had already left the physical environment of Ealing Studios, it is like the last twitching of the nervous system after death.

Mackendrick had already provided a fitting epitaph in the last mainstream comedy actually to be filmed at Ealing, *The Ladykillers.* Like its predecessor, *The Maggie*, this was written for and with him by William Rose, an American who came over after the war to work for a decade in British films and became the one really important addition to the close-knit, long-serving Ealing team after the arrival of Mackendrick himself in 1946. Having done minor scripting jobs here and there in British studios, he only established himself at Ealing, and as an original writer, after the 'watershed' of the early 'fifties (marked by *The Man in the White Suit*). His scripts deal very consciously with an England which has now committed itself spiritually to the old, cosy and traditional. Outside Ealing, he made *Genevieve* (1953) and *The Smallest Show on Earth* (1957), centred on an old car and an old cinema respectively; both of them are as near to Ealing films as they could be without actually being made there, having Ealing people (Cornelius and Dearden) as directors. Rose's scripts for Ealing deal likewise with picturesque symbols of age and tradition, such as the cargo boat of *The Maggie*. In effect, he picks up the T. E. B. Clarke spirit at Ealing and exploits it in a rather more detached and aware manner than Clarke himself, as someone younger, and coming from abroad.

Ealing comedy had gone down well from the start in the American market, at least at the sophisticated 'art-house' end of it. The genre evoked an affectionate, touristy response to the quirky, traditional aspects of English life—affection with a hint of patronage in it, as the tourist has no intention of giving up his own

Opposite: The Titfield Thunderbolt. Crump, the bus-owner (Jack MacGowran), mounting anti-railway propaganda. Bishop (Godfrey Tearle), Inspector, Vicar (George Relph). Below: Barnacle Bill.

All at Sea *and* High and Dry *were the rather more evocative American titles for* Barnacle Bill *(above) and* The Maggie *(opposite). Alec Guinness is chaired ashore after his pier has crossed the channel. The Maggie in a Scottish backwater.*

American standards of efficiency and actually living the Ealing life. Rose does settle in England, but.without becoming as English as Clarke: when he becomes trapped by the lack of vitality in English tradition-mindedness, he can free himself, as Clarke never will. Rose has a clear affinity with Mackendrick, who is not only a Scot but an American-born one and preserves the intelligent critical eye of an outsider and a latecomer. Both men eventually move from Ealing to America to renew their careers. At Ealing, there is a notable set of contrasts between the Clarke films, the films Rose made without Mackendrick, and the two films they made together.

The Maggie is an obvious twin of *The Titfield Thunderbolt*—old train, old boat. The structure is the same. The boat is threatened by economic pressures, is tenaciously defended, and survives into a triumphant final sequence: the Thunderbolt stands proudly at the main-line station, the Maggie puffs jauntily down the Clyde.

There is a danger of tedium if I keep hammering away at the contrast of Clarke's work and Mackendrick's: after *Titfield* and *Barnacle Bill*, this would be like hitting a man when he's down. Instead of reiterating points that I hope to have established already, I will simply take it as evident that *The Maggie* has far more life and intelligence and moral tension than its Clarke equivalents. At the same time, it is no masterpiece. One sometimes senses an impatience in

Rose and Mackendrick at what they are doing, as if they are trapped in a back-water, and with a *fiddling* set of conflicts and frustrations. This is the least satisfying of Mackendrick's quintet of Ealing films.

The Maggie is a 'puffer', a small cargo boat operating on and around the Clyde. It is falling to bits and is an object of ridicule to the shipping company to whom it looks for commissions. By a series of misunderstandings, it is engaged to carry an urgent consignment of furniture a long way up the coast, to the new vacation house of an American tycoon. The load is too much for it, but the captain won't give it up, and the story is of his insistence on trying to carry it to its destination, in spite of the boat and of all efforts to transfer the cargo to something more efficient.

The main conflict is between the captain of the Maggie, Mactaggart, and the American, Marshall, who at first gives orders from afar but then flies up in person to sort out the problem. Played out in remote Scottish villages and stretches of water, the conflict recalls *Whisky Galore*, with Marshall and Mactaggart replacing Waggett and Macroon. Like Waggett, Marshall has the law and his integrity on his side, but is systematically humiliated: the furniture goes to the bottom, his wife offers no comfort, and he gets none of his money back.

When the film was shown in America (under the title of *High and Dry*), Mackendrick wrote to Time magazine to answer a criticism that the film's treatment of its American was excessively cruel. He made the point that both he and Rose were American-born, and that they 'saw the story very much from the viewpoint of the American . . . The savagely unfair way in which (he) is treated, the sly insult added to injury and the ultimate indignity of being made to feel that he is somehow "morally" in the wrong were, for us, part of the flavour of the joke.'

All Mackendrick's comedies lead up to this kind of extreme, savage ending with triumph and humiliation, and an uncertainty about what they 'mean': compare the fate of Sidney Stratton as well as that of Waggett. The mocking

laughter of his hitherto deferential wife gave the last twist of the knife to Waggett; the crowd laughed in triumph, as they pulled Sidney's suit to bits; Marshall tells the crew at the end that 'If you laugh at me for this, I'll kill you with my bare hands.' Though Mackendrick found himself on Waggett's side in principle, this hardly shows in *Whisky Galore* as we have it, as though he were gritting his teeth and forcing the film to follow through its own logic, punishing himself for his own 'soft' sympathies through the fate of Waggett. With Marshall, as with Sidney, the tension is much more evident on the surface, as though the polarities of *Whisky Galore* have now been perceived as too simple, too neatly rounded-off.

The letter to Time magazine is right: the film is careful to keep undercutting the support we feel for Mactaggart and his boat, whether affectionate support (the *Titfield* kind) or admiring (*Whisky Galore*). He's clever but in a rather sterile, short-term way (like the cleverness of the bosses in the latter part of *The Man in the White Suit*). Early on, an interviewer talks to Marshall about the affection people feel for the puffers as the symbol of certain 'human values': the film shows us the attraction but shows the underside too, as though to expose the shallowness of the popular stereotype. When Marshall is moved by hospitality at a party, he makes a real concession—Mactaggart can go on with the job after all, provided he keeps to his solemn promise of wasting no time—but this concession is at once shamelessly exploited as the boat hangs around to wait for some profitable extra cargo. If it's argued that the American is foolish to be so soft, that he is condemned by the Darwinian laws of *Whisky Galore*, then one has to ask what the aim is to which the species is working. Hardly the survival of the fittest. Mactaggart is a seedy old rogue, and his boat a near-wreck.

Marshall, on the other hand, is even less of a blameless victim than Sidney Stratton. Indeed he combines the characteristics of Sidney and the bosses, being

Left: the crew of The Maggie: *boy (Tommy Kearins), Captain (Alex Mackenzie), Engineer (Abe Barker), Mate (James Copeland). Right: Marshall (Paul Douglas).*

a ruthless business tycoon and also a new-world innocent, like an American launched into the cultural knowingness of Europe in a Henry James story. Morally, he gets what he deserves, and Mackendrick's letter is disingenuous in playing this down; indeed it is a point about which the film is awkwardly explicit, with its repeated stress on the crudity of Marshall's belief that he can buy up everything and everyone, including their goodwill. Paul Douglas's graceless one-note performance as Marshall brings out his unsympathetic side very strongly.

This Mactaggart/Marshall opposition becomes rather sterile; it never develops. Behind this foreground conflict, though, there is an under-life to the film, created by minor and even offscreen characters, which is much more enjoyable. Mrs Marshall never appears, but through a stream of messages and of reported re-actions to her husband's phone calls from ever more remote areas, she effectively reduces the whole basis of the film to absurdity. The cottage is being furnished as a birthday present for her, but she reveals only contempt for the whole scheme. (The surreal shots of the white plumbing floating down to the sea bed at the end have an effect like the disintegration of the white suit: So what? It wasn't any use anyway.) Then there is Dougie, the under-age member of the Maggie's crew. It's impossible to think of the film without him, or to imagine Mackendrick (in the light of his last two films) not having made a point of including a child to break the story's moral deadlock. Part of the import comes from what he is: young, alert, less set in his ways than the others. He also has an important recurring role in the action. He has the good qualities of Mactaggart, not (yet?) run to seed: you could say that the 'human values' extolled by the Glasgow reporter who is covering the story—values like shrewdness and loyalty—exist positively in him while in Mactaggart they are caricatured. His perceptions are always one jump ahead of the others. It's he who makes a fool of the one Englishman in the film, Marshall's absurd business subordinate Pusey, having him arrested for poaching (shades of Waggett's arrest for smuggling). To Marshall, he is both friendly and ruthless, acting by instinct.

After Marshall has caught up with the boat and is trying to transfer the cargo to another, Dougie cheerfully cooks him breakfast. He then asks, 'Why won't you let him take the cargo?' Marshall explains at length. But each time he pauses, Dougie looks at him and repeats 'Why won't you let him take the cargo?' This comes over not as obtuseness but as moral strength. The boat is his own life and he knows that Mactaggart was actually born in it; these things transcend Marshall's reasoning. When Marshall, later, claims to be about to buy the boat himself, Dougie immediately drops the wooden hatch on his head and knocks him out. Afterwards he apologises, but quickly says he would do it again; and he is now able to tell Marshall that the boat's owner, Mactaggart's sister, has refused to sell on any terms. Why not? 'You wouldn't understand.' Again, there are loyalties and obligations that transcend Marshall's reasoning. Dougie is another of the key 'son' figures in Ealing cinema, indeed the last of any interest, standing up to Marshall, loyal to Mactaggart. The irony is that all his life and intelligence is being dedicated to the support of the tradition, embodied in Mactaggart and the Maggie, which is presented clear-sightedly by the film as being picturesque, tenacious, but senile. But at least he exists, a force for *possible* renewal and change (like Mandy Miller in her two roles), and a direct embodi-ment, more effective than any notional compromise between the two opposing sides, of the qualities the film values.

At the end, Marshall surrenders completely. He accepts the loss of his cargo and the failure to insure it, and still pays, thus enabling the Maggie to survive: he walks off towards the house, just possibly (as with Sidney at the end of *The Man in the White Suit*) to begin life afresh, but again it will be an enormous shift, which the film has to leave to the imagination. Mactaggart has survived: he will keep the boat going, rename it the Calvin B. Marshall, and potter on for a few more years. Dougie calls out 'Good luck to you,' sincerely, to the departing Marshall, and his face, merging triumph and affection, leaves the frame. The important question is where he will go.

There is no child in *The Ladykillers*. Everything is redolent of age and tradition, specifically of English tradition, and of Ealing's celebration of that tradition.

Mrs Wilberforce is a white-haired, absent-minded little old lady who lives at the end of a cul-de-sac near St Pancras station. Mr Wilberforce was a captain in the Mercantile Marine who went down with his ship in the East 29 years ago; in the picture on her wall, he looks very like the Admiral d'Ascoyne who went down stiffly with his ship in *Kind Hearts and Coronets*. At the nearby police station presides the reassuring figure of Jack Warner, and the whole cosy neighbourhood, with its small shops and colourful friendly characters, distils the spirit of *The Blue Lamp*. Katie Johnson herself, who plays Mrs Wilberforce so beautifully, seemed to come to stardom from nowhere, but she had a long experience in small roles at Ealing and elsewhere, and one in particular is worth mentioning. In *I Believe in You* (Ealing, Dearden, 1952), she puzzles a social worker by her earnest complaint that the neighbours have been systematically poisoning her cat. When he follows up the complaint and has a look at the neighbours, she is covered in confusion and admits she has got it wrong; the matter seems to be straightened out, until she reveals her new belief that they are trying to poison *her*. In *The Ladykillers*, she is the epitome of this whole tradition of English old ladies whose gentility may or may not be a mask for dottiness.

At the start of the film, she goes down to the police station to remind the officers of the story of her friend (herself?) who thought Martians had landed: it now turns out that she had only dropped off to sleep while listening to a radio play. 'The whole thing was just a dream.' They humour her charmingly and send her away. As she goes home, dark shadows of a human presence begin to track her. When she arrives there, a fantastic adventure starts to happen to her: the dark shadows materialise. At the end of the adventure, she goes down to the police station to tell them; they humour her and send her off home again. Maybe she did dream it, we can't tell—either way, it's all just a film, and one which operates in an altogether dream-like way, as so many films do, whether or not they are 'objectively' labelled as characters' dreams. What we do know is that the story was literally dreamed up one night by William Rose, then told to Mackendrick, who leaped at the chance of basing a film on it; it retains a dreamlike logic and concentration. One does not have to insist on the 'dream' dimension as such: the film is a vision, or fable, of England. Such a view is hardly controversial: *The Ladykillers* was received at home and abroad as an intensely English phenomenon. It owes its status as a classic to the inspired tightness with which story and imagery are organised to make up the picture of England.

The associations are laid on very thick. There is the idealised 'village' quality of the little street on the West End side of St Pancras, with a view from Mrs Wilberforce's front door of the station itself, a monument of Victorian Gothic.

Katie Johnson. Left: with Cecil Parker in I Believe in You. *Right: with Jack Warner in* The Ladykillers.

Mrs Wilberforce recalls the death of the old Queen being announced at her own 21st birthday dance in Pangbourne, and more little old ladies, of the same vintage, gather at her house for tea and music. Her favourite parrot is named General Gordon. The house is old and poky, cluttered up with lace and bric-à-brac; the water system is delightfully decrepit, requiring an elaborate routine of banging on the pipes and waiting for it. The whole house is unsafe, on the tilt through subsidence—the pictures won't hang straight.

It's an entrancing portrait of a Victorian civilisation lingering on, tottering, into the postwar world. It is, specifically, postwar, though it may seem timeless: the subsidence, Mrs Wilberforce tells her prospective tenant, was caused by wartime bombing, and the pavement artist prominently displays his portrait of Winston Churchill.

The plot outline of *The Ladykillers* is well known. Five men, in answer to her advertisement, come to occupy the spare rooms upstairs—ostensibly a string quintet needing a place to practise, in fact a gang planning a wages robbery nearby and needing a base and a refuge. They get their money, but then they quarrel and eliminate each other, and the money ends up with Mrs Wilberforce.

When they debate the wisdom of their leader's plan to use Mrs Wilberforce as an unwitting agent—simply an old lady collecting a trunk from the railway parcels office for a friend—the decision is put to the vote. One of them protests at the fifth man, an ex-boxer, having a vote at all because he's so thick and gets the reply: 'We've all got a vote, haven't we? It's a democracy, ain't it?' Yes, that's what it is. Let me set out an admittedly fanciful reading of the film. The gang are the post-war Labour government. Taking over 'the House', they gratify the conservative incumbent by their civilised behaviour (that nice music), and decide to use at least the façade of respectability for their radical programme of redistributing wealth (humouring Mrs W and using her as a front). Their success is undermined by two factors, interacting: their own internecine quarrels, and the startling, paralysing charisma of the 'natural' governing class, which effortlessly takes over from them again in time to exploit their gains (like the Conservatives taking over power in 1951 just as the austerity years come to an

end). The gang are a social mix, like Labour's: a mix of academic (Alec Guinness), ex-officer (Cecil Parker), manual worker (Danny Green), naive youth (Peter Sellers) and hard-liner (Herbert Lom).

I hardly need to say that this is not a dimension which needs actually to have been in the mind of anyone involved. But the film can be entertainingly read in these terms; what it undeniably does is to enact a compulsive process of the *absorption* of the dynamic by the static, of change by tradition, of the new by the old, which is the essential pattern of postwar British history, politics included. And the mechanism it constructs is haunting. The gang, above, lay out their gains; cut to Mrs Wilberforce, below, laying out the tea for her friends. It's like one of Orwell's verbal diagrams of English society, the producing class on one level, the 'dividend-drawers' (and this surely is what these ladies are) on another, ignorant of the genesis of their wealth but sublimely secure in it, and imperceptibly in control. The men hurry to get away. But the house exercises a dreamlike hold: Danny Green catches the strap of his violin case in the door, and tugs impotently until it comes apart and showers out its notes, just as Mrs Wilberforce appears.

From now on, she is the boss. The ladies arrive in force, and the men are constrained to take tea genteelly with them. Prominent among them is the familiar face of Edie Martin, who played such important tiny roles in *It Always Rains on Sunday* and *The Man in the White Suit*, both times as another inhibiting Mrs W, Mrs Watson. She was also Miss Evesham in *The Lavender Hill Mob*, landlady of the Balmoral Private Hotel, a small world of Victoriana and strict rules (wipe your feet, no business occupations may be performed on these premises) in which Guinness and Stanley Holloway nonetheless contrived to plan their bank robbery. *The Ladykillers* clamps down on that daydream: none of us can truly escape from that world. Edie Martin brings to the film all the associations of her earlier roles, feeding them in, as it were, to the authority of Mrs Wilberforce. Even if we don't take the specific associations, the direct impact of herself and the cluttered roomful of ladies is enough to conjure up the essence of all Ealing's little old ladies with their Nannyish authority and the Victorian baggage they carry round with them. Into this St Pancras home, all the imagery of age and tradition in Ealing's past films is gathered up and compressed; it overwhelms the gang and their aspirations.

When Mrs W remonstrates with the men for their crime, their deference—at first simulated out of policy while they arrange how to kill her—turns inexorably to real, paralysed deference. She becomes a triumphant Nanny, confiscating the money, slapping the hand even of Louie (the hard-liner) with impunity, the more impressive because of her moral innocence. She becomes, explicitly, 'Mum', inviolable, killed for rather than killed. Her troublesome visitors obligingly take themselves off while she sleeps, leaving her once more in control, and now with all the money.

So she walks back again from the friendly police station to the old house still on the tilt at the end of the cul-de-sac, on the way giving a pound to the pavement artist in honour of his portrait of Churchill. She is an old lady who may have dreamed an adventure or really had it, but who is confirmed in her inheritance, in an environment made in her own image. For Mackendrick, it is an appropriate valediction, both sardonic and affectionate, to Ealing and to England, cutting exhilaratingly *through* the tortured conflicts of his previous work (as Hamer did in *Kind Hearts*)—conflicts between innocence and experience, and between the dynamic of change and the inertia of the *status quo*—to show the inertia triumphant in a quaint little England where all alike, deep down, are innocents, a colourful neighbourhood community, with Jack Warner in charge, though hardly needed. And Mackendrick leaves for New York, to make *Sweet Smell of Success*.

Opposite: criminals and ladies, in The Ladykillers: *Guinness, Parker, Sellers, Lom, Green with Edie Martin, Katie Johnson. Below: disposing of the Major.*

THE END

If *The Maggie* is twin to *The Titfield Thunderbolt*, that of *The Ladykillers* is *Touch and Go*. Both of them are comedies set in one particular street in a London neighbourhood community; both were shot in colour in 1955 from an original script by William Rose, and both were produced by Seth Holt. *Touch and Go* was the only Ealing film to be directed by Michael Truman. It has never been revived, which is not surprising, but it is worth referring to as a foil to *The Ladykillers* and an example of late, mainstream Ealing at its most suffocating.

Touch and Go sets up a conflict between youth and change on the one hand and age and tradition on the other; it purports to work out a compromise, but is deeply in thrall to the latter pair. It is a victim of the process of *absorption* by tradition that is the subject of *The Ladykillers*, and illuminates this for us if we read between its lines.

Jack Hawkins is a designer with a furniture company. He tries to persuade them to turn out 'modern' furniture to his design. The boss rejects the proposal, stating baldly that 'traditional design is the best design'. Hawkins storms out and decides to emigrate with his family to Australia. Eventually, in an effort to

Father (Jack Hawkins), daughter (June Thorburn) and boyfriend (John Fraser) in a late-night confrontation in Touch and Go.

keep him, his boss offers him all he has asked for, and comes round in person to renew the offer on the day of departure, when the taxi is all loaded up to go. The family decide to stay. A third of the firm's capacity will be turned over to production of the new designs. Compromise!

I have referred to Raymond Durgnat's book on British Cinema, 'A Mirror for England'; it's indispensable and full of brilliant insights, but under the pressure of covering a mass of films which he may have seen once long ago, or not all, Durgnat contrives to smuggle in a lot of wrong information. This is unfortunate, as the book so often provides the sole available reference for an obscure British film. Of *Touch and Go*, he writes that it 'urges middle-class families to borrow money and emigrate to Australia.' (Curiously, another error on Ealing is the statement that Googie Withers, in *Joanna Godden* (1947), emigrates to Australia; she does nothing of the sort). Perhaps the wish is father to the thought. We often long for Ealing heroes and heroines to make a decisive break, but they seldom do; they stay put resignedly. Though Ealing makes several films in Australia, it never takes the opportunity of doing the story of a modern emigrant.

Not only do the family in *Touch and Go* not get to Australia, they never seem likely to. 'Australia' remains purely an abstraction, a card played. When Hawkins goes to inquire at Australia House, the camera tilts down from rooftop level to show him entering and we hear a version of Waltzing Matilda on the sound-track; there's a time lapse, and he comes out. It remains on that level of lazy abstraction. Meanwhile a great weight of influences is coming into play to keep him at home. It reminds one of the Buñuel film *The Exterminating Angel*, in which a set of characters, assembled in a building, come to realise that there is a mysterious force which inhibits them from leaving. Hawkins and family have a similar deep compulsion: they simply can't leave home, however much they say they intend to.

They're worried about leaving their old car, and their old cat, and their old parents, and their old house in this cosy London neighbourhood (with a 'village' pub, and no traffic coming through, and an onion-seller plying his wares, and crowds of stagey children), and their old friends (old in both senses), and his old job. He can't stop himself from telephoning to see how things have been going at work since his resignation. On the eve of departure, they dine with their old friends, and when the women withdraw the men finish off with brandy:
Hawkins: 'Very, very good.'
Roland Culver: 'Very, very old.'
How can Hawkins himself, this unbeatably stolid, middle-aged presence, cut himself off from a network of associations, a culture, to which he is so deeply bound? And what are we to make of his 'modern' designs? Like Australia, they remain an abstraction, a counter in the game the film is playing. When he stays, it's a victory for his design ideas—instead of going to Australia, he can be 'modern' in London—but what does this count for against (to use the boss's word) the 'traditional' weight of his own and the community's lifestyle?

If they go, their teenage daughter will be separated from her devoted boy-friend, so the decision to stay at least favours young love. Perhaps this is a counterweight, and the pair may be intended to have an effect like that of Dougie in *The Maggie*, as a new generation that can be revitalising. But they are as tame and wet and conventional as any young couple in 'fifties British cinema, which is saying a great deal. The family cat, fourteen years old, black and cunning, is called Heathcliff, making us think, as the young couple conspicuously do not, of the romantic passion of 'Wuthering Heights'. That dimension of life has by this time been drained out of the human characters and obscurely displaced on to the non-human, on to fetishes. The attachment to old pets and objects and places grows at Ealing in proportion to the decline in the expression of direct sexual feeling. The cat in the end dominates *Touch and Go*. It looks down from the family's rooftop on the scene in the street below, as they cancel the move and their friends gather round to absorb them. The last shot frames the cat. It's a depressing end: the old cat as typical of the influences which paralyse the family into staying, deceiving themselves in the process with the thought that to stay is *not* a defeat. But it could also work, subversively, as a warning end: the cat, Heathcliff, as the symbol of a buried sensuality which will one day erupt, as it does two years later in one of the first films of the new British horror cycle, *Cat Girl*, made by an Ealing graduate, Alfred Shaughnessy. (For this film, see David Pirie's very pertinent account in 'A Heritage of Horror'.)

The name of the cat, and the spread of Rose's other films, suggests that the writer must have had some awareness of what *Touch and Go* does, and of the nature of its confidence trick. It makes no difference to the experience of the film, which is completely trapped in the stagnation that it shows: to dramatise this effectively needs bolder forms, as in *The Ladykillers*, and less plodding direction. Only with Mackendrick as collaborator is Rose able, as it were, to 'get out from under' the English and Ealing traditionalism, at its deadest in the mid-'fifties, which fascinates and envelops him.

Touch and Go brings this account of Ealing full circle, to *Davy* (1957), the film I used to illustrate the played-out spirit of late Ealing: another drably polarised account of individual ambition being worn down by the drip-drip of family and cultural pressures. As in *Touch and Go*, the hero ends by deciding to call off his bold new venture and to stay in the family act, even though' its future appears dim. This, too, was an original script by William Rose. Both films play through their dramas in a stolid, foredoomed way, offering few

Mid-'fifties Ealing: images of authority. Left: the pilots of Out of the Clouds *(Robert Beatty, James Robertson Justice). Right: the matron (Diana Wynyard) addressing the new intake in* The Feminine Touch.

excitements to an audience. Both were the first films of their directors, respectively Truman and Michael Relph, neither of whom went on to much of a career in this capacity, and one might think of blaming the drabness of the films on their inexperience. I prefer to see them as being thereby all the more transparent a rendering of Rose's intentions. As craftsmen who had worked for ten years and more at Ealing, Truman and Relph were thoroughly soaked in the studio ethos; I don't think it's unfair to say that their promotion is a triumph for the principle of Buggins's turn. The fact that they constitute the Ealing idea of new blood at this time has an obvious appropriateness to the themes of the films themselves. There is something noble about the way that Rose, in these two films as in *The Ladykillers*, goes straight to the heart of the conflicts that Ealing is presenting and living at this time; he distils their essential impetus and orchestrates it with such brutal clarity, in terms of the pull of the old and familiar, which has become overwhelming to the point of sickness. Like *Barnacle Bill*, *Davy* and *Touch and Go* are unhappily characteristic of the films of Ealing's last years.

Leaving aside *Kind Hearts and Coronets*, Ealing has little enough in common with Oscar Wilde, or with the most famous of his characters. But looking back, we can see the story of post-war Ealing as the story of Dorian Gray. Ealing itself determines to remain the same, holding out against the processes of age and change. But time goes by regardless, and the Ealing *picture* inexorably acquires the marks of age.

Ealing never loses its allegiance to the ideal community defined in *Passport to Pimlico* and *The Blue Lamp*: stable, gentle, innocent, already consciously backward-looking, and based on the elaborate set of loyalties and renunciations that will by now be familiar. This community recedes inexorably into the past. Partly, the specific processes of post-war history leave it behind; partly, its own internal frailty, its lack of dynamism, renders it vulnerable to the passage of time as such, like a preserved mummy crumbling when exposed to the air. However we place the emphasis, Ealing is too committed to that community and its values—bound up with this, it is too committed to resisting change within its own community—to stop trying to project them. It goes on the same way through the middle 'fifties, portraying either 1) the values in action (the community recreated) or 2) in the absence of the values (the community betrayed). Certain films, of course, combine these two options in some form, for instance *Davy*, where the old values are asserted in a 'whistling in the dark' spirit.

Case 1) in its pure form can only seem increasingly unreal and reactionary. Pimlico becomes Titfield becomes the pier in *Barnacle Bill*. In straight drama, a similar progress is from *The Blue Lamp* to *The Feminine Touch* (1956) which offers us, through the experience of a set of new recruits, as cosy a view of nursing life, its rewards and heartaches, as *The Blue Lamp* did of the police work into which Mitchell was inducted. Lacking any of that film's confident sweep and affectionate detail, it remains stodgily conformist and deferential. It was the only film directed at Ealing by Pat Jackson, and a comparison between it and his previous hospital picture, the very fine *White Corridors* (1951), raises anew the question of what happened to England and English culture or at least to English cinema, if that formulation seems too pretentious, though I don't believe it is) in the intervening years.

Case 2) results in some more impressive films, which are honest and have a moving kind of bleakness—*Lease of Life* (1954), for instance, with Robert

Donat as a country parson given small comfort in his problems by his mainly selfish and unsentimental parishioners. The trouble is that such a film has little positive to offer except this poignant awareness of an absence, and the main character's stoicism in the face of it.

There was no way that Ealing, with such a range of films, was going to prosper in an industry encountering increasing difficulties. Ealing had reached the end of its span, and it was left to others to create new forms of British film.

The Feminine Touch was one of the last pair of films to be made at Ealing Studios. T. E. B. Clarke, one of the many who had been with the company since the war years, wrote of the move into a corner of the MGM studios at Elstree:

'I don't think any of us welcomed the change. There was little hope of the old team spirit being preserved now that we had ceased to be a self-contained unit, and the intimate atmosphere of our previous home was sadly missing from the new bleak areas of characterless buildings.'

That says it all. Time catches up: Ealing's own face has changed. Only seven more films were made. Among them were *Barnacle Bill* and *Davy*. And *Nowhere to Go*. The first film to be directed by Seth Holt, it is an impressive one, but only of incidental interest here, since it represents a quite fresh and potentially fruitful line for Ealing, embarked on, however, far too late for it to have any influence. Holt had worked at Ealing from 1943, but this doesn't show in the film, which he designed quite consciously to be 'the least Ealing film ever made', writing the script in collaboration with that not very Ealing figure, Kenneth Tynan. Holt was the brother-in-law of Robert Hamer, did some editing for him, and now suddenly emerges at the eleventh hour to carry on his torch of Ealing non-conformism. *Nowhere to Go* jettisons the preoccupation with a benevolent community altogether and offers a crime story which is neither police-centred nor moralistic; it is made with the creative enjoyment of film as a medium which, apart from Mackendrick in his unobtrusive way, 'fifties Ealing entirely lacks. Some reviews at the time accused it of being too clever, of showing off its cinematic ingenuity, but in retrospect this seems like an irrelevant puritanism, like that which deplored the bad taste of the Hammer horror films of the same period. *Nowhere to Go* is not a major film, but it has an intelligence and energy which make most British films of the 'fifties look positively geriatric.

Dunkirk, for instance. Almost Ealing's last word, it was released, like Holt's

Far left: Robert Donat, preaching his sermon on herds and flocks in Lease of Life. *Two images from near the end of the road for Ealing: left, the home life of a test pilot in* Man in the Sky *(with Jack Hawkins, Elizabeth Sellars); Richard Attenborough and Bernard Lee in* Dunkirk.

film, in 1958. How right that Ealing at the end of its span should look back to the event which in effect had made it what it was: to Dunkirk, the turning-point of the war, the transforming event which we look back on in the same wistful spirit with which we look back on the classic Ealing films themselves. Made by the most stolid of all the Ealing directors, Leslie Norman, *Dunkirk* is very dull indeed, and this dullness is rather admirable, like the unflinching drabness of the late William Rose scripts: it is honest. The film shows a dispirited, sluggish country blundering its way to disaster—a picture consistent with the films Ealing was making in those years. But the transformation we wait for obstinately refuses to come. Before and at Dunkirk, there's no sense of energies, anywhere, waiting to be channelled, simply of a uniform sourness: the bitterness of the main 'mouthpiece' figure, the loner journalist played by Bernard Lee—'what a shambles we've made of this whole rotten business'—dominates the film. The actual Dunkirk operation is characterised by bureaucracy and irritation ('Operation Dynamo—what funny names they pick') and the expected pay-off—the elation of success, of teamwork at last—is one that the film simply refuses, or finds itself unable, to deliver. A commentary voice states baldly at the end that Dunkirk was 'a great miracle' and that 'No longer were there fighting men and civilians, there were only people. A nation had been made whole.' The film has never brought this assertion to life. Instead, it ends on a dully shot, perversely protracted, sequence of parade-ground drilling, as if to say: this is all there is to look forward to, a hard, humourless grind.

I don't think that *Dunkirk* constitutes a radical new reading of the war experience, or a debunking of the notion, so dear to Ealing and England, of a unity and inspiration discovered in the course of it; rather, it is a recognition that Ealing cannot recreate that spirit and that united community any longer. The impetus has run out; the springs of the past, what Wordsworth called 'the hiding-places of my power', are for Ealing, perhaps for England too, no longer accessible.

EPILOGUE

So Ealing petered out. Nonetheless, there is a happy ending of sorts.

'I hear you're staying on with us after all.'
'Yes, I'm afraid you're going to be stuck with me for another five years.'

For five, read twenty-five. The dialogue comes from *The Blue Lamp*. PC George Dixon decides to postpone his retirement from the force. Although within the film he dies shortly afterwards, he will live again on television as *Dixon of Dock Green*, not taking his final retirement until 1976. His TV career began in 1955; it was in that year, too, that the studio at Ealing was sold, and the purchasers were the BBC, the makers of *Dixon*. It's a neat irony and it is, I suggest, symbolic of what happened to the Ealing enterprise as a whole. Ealing was taken over by television, but infiltrated its conqueror.

Ealing, it may seem, simply fell behind the times, and was superseded by bolder forms of cinema which better reflected the modern age. That can only be a partial truth. Ealing cinema became obsolete when it did, in the latter half of

Jack Hawkins in The Long Arm: *at home with Dorothy Alison and at work with subordinates John Stratton and Geoffrey Keen.*

the 1950s primarily because television was taking away its audience: the regular, respectable audience for modest British films, on which Ealing relied. For all the 'un-Ealing' vulgarity of ITV's early headline-makers, the vast new TV audience was ready for nice steady forms of drama, and increasingly they were given it.

Often they got it from Ealing people. More important, they got it increasingly in Ealing *forms*. The forms, not so much of Ealing comedy, as of Ealing drama.

The last two features made at Ealing, before the company moved out to Borehamwood and the BBC moved in, were *The Feminine Touch*, in which a group of new nurses join a training hospital, and *The Long Arm*, a sober Scotland Yard investigation ranging over a wide cross-section of society. Their appeal was distinctly limited; they looked like pilot features for a TV series, which is what, in effect, they are. During the 1970s, it has induced a strong sense of *déjà-vu* to watch, week by week, the BBC's *Angels* (a group of new nurses join a teaching hospital) and the various police shows, and to watch such Ealing veterans as Jack Warner, Gordon Jackson, and Googie Withers in their comforting, recurring, authoritative roles. Documentary drama, institutional drama, omnibus drama: everything that seemed weak and tame in these mainstream Ealing forms is a positive virtue in series television. This leads, however, into issues which would require a separate book.

Likewise, it would need more than an Epilogue to discuss the relation of Ealing's picture of Britain to the Britain we live in, almost two decades after the Ealing operation ceased. The films, charmingly dated, recede into history; but it would be hard to maintain that the analysis contained in, for instance, *The Man in the White Suit*, has nothing to say to us now.

British television, Britain itself. *Si monumentum requiris, circumspice*: if you want a monument to Ealing, look around.

RETROSPECT 1993

Since 1976, when *Ealing Studios* was written:

1) The direct links with Balcon's Ealing, as summarised in the final chapter, have been progressively weakened, through the death or retirement of most of the remaining Ealing personnel, and by the BBC's recent sale of the studio complex, which it bought from Ealing in 1955.

2) Britain has ceased to have a film industry, except in a marginal way as an offshoot of television.

3) The concept and structure of Public Service Broadcasting, which has affinities with Ealing's 'public service' form of cinema, have been steadily eroded.

These last two changes have been caused, at least in part, by government policy, a reminder that:

4) Britain has lived through Thatcherism, and continues under a right-wing Conservative rule unbroken since 1979.

Inevitably, all of this increases our distance from Ealing and changes the way we look back on the company and the films. The easiest and commonest response is a resigned nostalgia, an undifferentiated Ealing being used to stand for a now remote period of a productive film industry and of a broad political consensus.

Ealing and Thatcherism
In terms of the opposition formulated by Michael Frayn, and invoked in the book's first chapter (pp.8-9), Thatcherism was the triumph of Carnivore values over the gentler Herbivore ones; in J.B. Priestley's terms (p.50), it was the philosophy of competition obliterating that of co-operation. The Thatcherite (and post-Thatcher) state may tend towards the Little Englandism of Ealing's Pimlico, but it is a Pimlico whose ruling ideology is that of Garland the publican (*see* pp.101-102). In *Passport to Pimlico*, Garland was an isolated figure, quickly disgraced and exiled, but in 1980s Britain he returned to claim a privileged place, his line that 'It's every man for himself' being echoed in Thatcher's own dictum that 'There is no such thing as society.'

Thatcherism is so alien to Ealing, and its assault on the Herbivore values has been so ruthless, that it might seem to have wiped Ealing effectively off the map, consigning it to the museum as just another fossilised segment of a heritage culture; to counter Thatcherism effectively we surely need stronger weapons than the old sentimental dispensation can provide. This line, I think, would be mistaken.

Firstly, as the book argues, Ealing contains its own lucid critique of the Pimlico/Herbivore values, notably in the films directed by Alexander Mackendrick, which insist that kind hearts and public spirit are not enough: unless informed by a hard intelligence, they are wide open to attack by the forces of acquisitive self-interest. Alongside Garland one can set the more substantial figure of Sir John Kierlaw, who actually wins the industrial struggle of *The Man in the White Suit*. That film's analysis of the nemesis that lies in wait for the forces of progress unless they can organise themselves intelligently is no less pertinent in the 1990s than it was on its original release in 1951, the year in which the reforming post-war Labour administration gave way to thirteen years of Conservative rule.

Secondly, there is the striking compulsion of Thatcher's successor to present himself in what might loosely be called Ealing terms. I was recently, as it happens, consulted by a TV politics programme contemplating an item on John Major in relation to Ealing comedy, and looking for appropriate material. One can see the connections they had in mind. It's a matter not only of style—Major himself being such a defiantly small-scale and low-horizon figure, like Pimlico's Pemberton—but of policy as well. For instance, the rhetoric of rail privatisation, as of 1993, seems to come straight out of *The Titfield Thunderbolt*. Break down an impersonal big system into a colourful multiplicity of local units; trust the beneficent effects of small-scale local competition between transport systems. Modern Conservatism may in practice be relentlessly centralising and authoritarian, but it still feels the need—on a much wider range of issues than transport—to present itself as in favour of the diversity and autonomy of small communities. In the case of Major at least, this seems a genuine ideological confusion with deep cultural roots, akin to the confusion that permeates *The Titfield Thunderbolt* itself.

In short, the assertion of the 1976 Epilogue (penultimate paragraph, p.181) still holds good for 1993. 'The films, charmingly dated, recede into history; but it would be hard to maintain that the analysis contained in, for instance, *The Man in the White Suit*, has nothing to say to us now.' If the book's original discussion of the key films, and of the Ealing product overall in terms of its historical development and its ideological cross-currents, carries any conviction, then the continuing relevance of Ealing to the understanding of British culture and politics does not need to be spelled out chapter by chapter. Apart from the correction of a few misprints, the main text has not been altered. I would, however, like to point to two substantial inadequacies, one in the account of Ealing's role in the politics of the wartime film industry, the other in the handling of a particular group of films.

Balcon in Wartime

The book accepts far too easily the image of Michael Balcon, constructed by him and others in retrospect, and rooted in selective memories of late Ealing: that of a benevolent, avuncular figure, the embodiment of mellow consensus values. Likewise, it was lazy to suggest (p.22) that Ealing in wartime 'quickly acquired a semi-official status,' working harmoniously with the Ministry of Information and other official bodies. The relations of Ealing to officialdom were far less cosy. Throughout the war, Balcon operated as a controversial and abrasive figure. In public statements and in less public manoeuvring—always on behalf of indigenous British film production generally and of Ealing in particular—he attacked five main targets:

1) The British in Hollywood. Balcon's attacks, in the first year of the war, on 'The Britons who have run to a safe and luxurious haven in Hollywood' (Picturegoer, 11th May 1940) received wide publicity and attracted bitter replies from, among others, his former protégé Alfred Hitchcock. Balcon was sceptical of the notion that Hollywood's pro-British films might be as valuable as Britain's own, and he was the one feature film-maker to add his signature to Paul Rotha's letter to the polemical magazine Documentary News Letter (December 1940 issue) condemning the final scene of Hitchcock's interventionist *Foreign Correspondent*.

2) Services and Government. Repeatedly, Balcon made the headlines in the trade press by attacking the reluctance of the armed services to co-operate with British producers, and of the government to intervene. The page-one story in Kinematograph Weekly for 7th November 1940 is typical. Headline: 'Services Deny Facilities to British Producers / Balcon's Protest'. Quotation: 'Surely the companies capable of producing *Contraband*, *For Freedom*, *Night Train to Munich*, *Convoy*, etc. are entitled to facilities. The fact that they are British and are working here during the Battle for Britain does not, I take it, rule them out.' The sarcasm is audible.

3) More specifically, the Ministry of Information. The Films Division of the MoI was responsible for commissioning short films and for overseeing feature production. Balcon's relations with them were always edgy, and he went public at the end of 1940 in denouncing them. The lead story in the 12th December issue of Kinematograph Weekly is headlined 'War Effort Hampered by MoI's Film Policy/Ealing Attacks Lack of Planned Programme/Will Now Concentrate on Individual Effort.' Part of the problem, not revealed at the time but set out in correspondence now available at the Public Record Office, was that Ealing had been negotiating to take over control of the government-sponsored documentary film unit (formerly with the General Post Office) and felt betrayed when the MoI blocked the arrangement at a late stage. Balcon thereupon set up an independent short-film operation, and took both Cavalcanti and Watt out of the unit and on to the Ealing staff.

4) Mr Rank. The book does register the opposition of Balcon and Ealing to Rank's wartime empire-building, but to assimilate this to the struggle of the small brewer Greenleaf against the big brewer Ironside in the 1939 comedy *Cheer Boys Cheer* is to risk trivialising it. 'The benevolent paternalism of a grey-haired old man who collects Toby Jugs' (p.5) has little connection with the abrasive Balcon of this period. His was the leading industry voice in the campaign to set up a Board of Trade Inquiry into monopoly tendencies, and he spoke out (less successfully) in favour of those recommendations of the resulting Palache Committee that would have curtailed Rank's power.

5) Hollywood. In effect, all of Balcon's interventions centred on the drive to establish an effective material base for resisting American dominance of the British film industry. As in the case of Rank and his other targets, to read the pronouncements Balcon made at the time, both publicly and privately, is to be struck by the energy and realism of his campaigning, and by his willingness to

be, where necessary, offensive and divisive. In the face of American business strategy, he urges legislation and hard financial bargaining, not a sentimental appeal to goodwill.

Reassessing Basil Dearden

If I were rewriting the book from scratch, Basil Dearden's contribution to Ealing would be handled differently. Although plenty of space is given to the films he directed, notably *The Blue Lamp*, he is dealt with rather patronisingly as a prosaic representative of 'an Ealing norm or baseline' (p.72), in contrast to other more creative individuals. As with Balcon, the difficulty is, or was, to get behind the later record and the retrospective public image and to look at the war period in particular—the formative years of Ealing—in an accurate way. For Balcon, the dominant image by the 1970s was that of the mellow consensus figure; for Dearden, that of the hack British director. The scathing and highly articulate attack on him in the Editorial of the first issue of *Movie* magazine in 1962, as the epitome of everything that was worst about mainstream British cinema, had not been challenged, and although the book treats many of his pre-1951 films with respect, it still operates in the shadow of that polemic.

After the firefighting drama *The Bells Go Down*, his first solo credit as director, Dearden made *Halfway House* and *They Came to a City*, both released in 1944. Both have a strong allegorical and didactic dimension, bringing together people from diverse backgrounds and putting them through a magically intense transforming experience. On page 52, they are described as the two worst films out of the seventeen Dearden made at Ealing (a 'dismal experience . . . arid, abstract, statuesquely posed and declaimed'), and are used to illustrate 'the hypothesis that Ealing's form of cinema, like its whole mentality, is a profoundly empirical and naturalistic one, at home with people, not ideas, with the solidly realistic, not the abstract or stylised.' These judgments are altogether too glib, rooted in a prejudice which recent historical/theoretical work on theatricality and melodrama in cinema has made it difficult to sustain. The two films are certainly schematic, and do not conceal their theatrical origins, but I now find this no obstacle: they are bold, eloquent and powerful.

Page 72 gives a summary of the plot of *Halfway House*, and some remarks on the concluding speech, which are all right as far as they go, but require further commentary. The notion of cinema implicit in the speech, and in the film itself, is more subtle than I then gave it credit for. The characters who converge on the rural Welsh inn of the title step into the fantasy experience of cinema rather in the manner of the James Stewart and Grace Kelly characters in Hitchcock's 1954 film *Rear Window*, and with similarly therapeutic results. In both films, the metacinematic dimension is underscored by the use of binoculars. The first traveller to arrive, not knowing, as we do, that the inn was bombed to ruins a year ago, looks for it within the landscape and sees nothing; he then has another look through his binoculars, and a subjective panning shot brings it solidly into view. After the group have established themselves in the inn, they gradually realise, through the hotel register and the newspapers and the radio, that they have gone back a year in time and are living through the day that will end in the bombing. As darkness approaches, the proprietor confirms to them:

'You [are] in your own time but the house and gardens and Gwyneth and I are in the time of last year, the day the bomb came . . . '

At one level, it is an effective story of the uncanny. At another, it represents very neatly the experience of cinema, in which spectators living in their own present tense are witnesses to sights and sounds which necessarily belong to the past, however vivid and involving they may be. The narrative of *Halfway House* is set in June 1943, and the characters are taken back into June 1942, to the moment of, on the international scale, the Fall of Tobruk (reported on the radio), and, on the local scale, the bombing of the inn. In 1943, cinema audiences everywhere were watching films shot in 1942, ranging from *Desert Victory*, the feature documentary on the war in Africa, to Ealing's own *Went the Day Well?* and *The Bells Go Down*, both of which dramatise local defence against enemy attack. In turn, the first audiences for *Halfway House*, in 1944, would have found themselves meeting, and becoming involved with, a set of characters who were by now already 'in the time of last year' even before the plot device shifted them back a further year. In short, the film ingeniously dramatises the impact that past-tense images and sounds can have on an audience through the rather magical medium of cinema.

This double perspective is exploited for some concentrated propaganda work. *Halfway House* shows us a group of disparate people, gathered in, as it were, off the street, being affected by their cinema-type experience, and invites us to learn the same lessons alongside them. A cross-section of wartime issues are raised—among them Irish neutrality, the black market, the break-up of families, and the fear of death—and are dealt with in a variety of ways, in the manner of different kinds of wartime cinema: newsreel/documentary, direct exhortation, and fictionalised drama. A young Irish diplomat defends his country's neutral stance against the arguments of his English fiancée, an exiled French-woman and the Welsh innkeeper, who speak for their respective nations, but it is not until he is put through the experience of German bombing that he comes round. If he is changed by the bombing itself (as by an atrocity newsreel), others are persuaded into joining the war effort by the rhetoric of the innkeeper or his daughter, whose ghostly status guarantees their disinterested authority, like a voice-of-God commentator. Finally, a uniformed couple with a teenage daughter play through the moves of wartime estrangement and the temptations of promiscuity, before being reconciled by the overall experience of the people, events and *mise-en-scène* of the inn (as by a fictional drama).

Much of the propaganda is simple, even crude, notably the handling of the Irish issue, but the film's very schematism—the laying bare, as it were, of the topical manipulative devices—works to make its project more acceptable. The elaborate construction of a (wartime) community bound together by mutual responsibility—and its confidence in the power of cinema to promote and cele-brate that community—remains very affecting. The same can be said of *They Came to a City*, Ealing's adaptation of the Utopian stage play written in mid-war by J.B. Priestley. This project is summarised and contextualised, in a perfectly adequate way, on pages 51-52, but the 'theatrical' stylisation no longer seems such a problem. Ealing and Dearden are bold in retaining most of the cast, text and *mise-en-scène* of the play, and they are, once again, artful in foregrounding the mechanics of what they are doing—by, in this case, having Priestley himself on screen discussing the post-war world with the young couple in uniform, and explicitly 'summoning up' a set of characters to act out some of the main issues.

The two films can be seen as complementary. *Halfway House* is a soft-left, or liberal, film, tolerant of everyone's problems and failings, and confident that rationality and kindness can ultimately gather them all in within the benevolent community, as in due course it does. *They Came to a City* is much harder left, ruthless with those who won't compromise their wealth and position and commit themselves to the socialist dispensation. The unrepentant city man defends himself as an individualist and is at once corrected by the John Clements character (speaking for the film): no, he is a pirate. Equally suspect, to the new community, is the city man's insistence that 'woman's place is in the home.'

They Came to a City was brought to Ealing by Sidney Cole, a staff editor who was a committed socialist and a Union activist; it gave him his first non-editing credits, as adaptor and associate producer. Priestley did no subsequent work for Ealing, and Cole, although remaining a central member of the team (associate producer of a film a year until 1952), was never able to put his politics into a film in the same way, unless one makes a case for his collaboration with Mackendrick on *The Man in the White Suit. Halfway House*, on the other hand, is prophetic of later Ealing: it gave T.E.B. Clarke his first screen credit, for 'script contribution', and is a clear forerunner of films like *The Blue Lamp*.

Dearden as director is the common factor in the two films, along with Art Director Michael Relph, who does remarkable work in his construction of two quite different styles of environment for the realistic Welsh inn and for the theatrical space in front of the City. Relph was about to become a staff producer like Cole, and would form, from 1946 onwards (*The Captive Heart*), a long-term producer/director partnership with Dearden. I don't have scope here to develop an overall re-reading of the series of Relph/Dearden films, but simply want to affirm that the pair deserve more credit than the book gives them for knowing what they are doing, at two interconnected levels, those of ideas and of cinematic form. Already in the more naturalistic drama of *The Bells Go Down* there are moments of formal self-reflexivity which, while unobtrusive and in no way holding up the narrative, are remarkably sophisticated and eloquent, notably the moment when the request by the firefighter at the end of his ladder to be moved 'in a bit closer'—so that he can pick up a phone in the burning building to ring his wife—is at once 'obeyed' by the *camera* moving in a bit closer on the wife waiting at home. Moreover, the next Relph/Dearden collaboration after the two theatre adaptations would be the exhilaratingly metacinematic omnibus film *Dead of Night*, of which Dearden directed the first episode and the linking narrative.

A number of post-war Relph/Dearden films have, in the time since *Ealing Studios* was published, attracted sympathetic critical analysis, ranging from *Frieda* (1947) to *The Ship that Died of Shame* (1955) and the post-Ealing *Victim* (1961); there is no doubt that a sustained account of their Ealing work, as opposed to the intermittent and often parenthetical one that it gets in the preceding pages, would be productive. That is, they are worth foregrounding as Ealing contributors on the same scale as Clarke, Hamer, and Mackendrick. The point is not so much the promotion of another team, and another director, to a higher category in a hierarchy of authors, as to see Ealing and its evolution in a clearer light.

'The beginning, like everything about me, went back to the war.' The main character's opening voice-over in *The Ship that Died of Shame* applies, in spirit if not literally, to Ealing itself. It is important, then, to do justice to the Ealing of that formative period, and these two revisionist notes, on Balcon and Dearden, are intended to help in complementary ways. Both on and off screen, Ealing was altogether less limited, less comfortable, less conformist, than the retrospective image suggests; and if the militant campaigning and the thematic and formal boldness that were important elements in the wartime operation were destined to taper off, leaving Ealing to become primarily identified with consensus, cosiness and naturalism, this only underlines the centrality of Ealing to the cultural, social and political history of the nation since 1939.

Postscript: There are two small corrections to make to the account of *The Blue Lamp* in Chapter 5. The unnamed critic referred to on page 88, for his hostile account of the scene in which Mrs Dixon learns of her husband's death, was Lindsay Anderson, in his essay in *Declaration* (edited by Tom Maschler, 1957). I am grateful to Tim Pulleine for pointing this out, and also to Jan Read for the courteous reminder that Dixon was not 'Ted Willis's creation', as stated on page 81. Read is credited as co-author of the story, and had in fact done a full outline of story and characters before Willis, and subsequently Ealing, came in on the project. Finally, Penelope Houston's monograph on *Went the Day Well?*, for the British Film Institute, rightly observes that Wilsford, played by Leslie Banks, is established as being not an English traitor (as suggested on pages 30-33) but a German spy.

FILM CREDITS AND NOTES

Details of all the 95 feature films produced by Balcon at, or for, Ealing are given in chronological order. They are dated, as far as possible, by the month of their *first public showing* (generally in London). In what follows, Balcon's own name has been omitted; on screen, he was invariably credited as producer or—less frequently—as Executive Producer, in which case full producer credit was given to another. Likewise, the regular credit to Ealing Studios as production company has been omitted. A number of the early films, however, are labelled as CAPAD or ATP productions. The acronym CAPAD stood for Co-operative Association of Producers and Distributors, a late-1930s consortium of independents, of which Balcon was a leading member. ATP was the Ealing-based company founded by Basil Dean (*see* p.4). Balcon's early dramas at Ealing bore the CAPAD label, and the early comedies that of ATP. Once he was fully established at Ealing, every film became simply an Ealing Studios production: this applies from *Convoy* (made early in 1940) onwards, apart from the last two of the George Formby vehicles that came shortly after it.

Nov 1938: **THE GAUNT STRANGER** (73 mins)
CAPAD. Directed by Walter Forde. Associate producer S.C. Balcon. Script by Sidney Gilliat, from the play *The Ringer* by Edgar Wallace. Photographed by Ronald Neame. Art direction by O.F. Werndorff. Edited by Charles Saunders. With: Sonnie Hale (Sam Hackett), Wilfred Lawson (Maurice Meister), Louise Henry (Cora Ann Milton), Alexander Knox (Dr Lomond), Patricia Roc (Mary Lenley), Peter Croft (John Lenley), Patrick Barr (Insp Wembury), John Longden (Insp Bliss), George Merritt (Sgt Carter).

For his first production after leaving MGM to go independent, and his first at Ealing, Balcon played safe with this adaptation of an Edgar Wallace subject that was already popular in stage and screen versions. Though alienating in its staginess and in the 'mechanical convention' of the whodunit plotting which its screen adaptor, Gilliat, found so frustrating, it is still—like the second and stronger Wallace adaptation, *The Four Just Men*—fascinating for its topical political resonances, being centred on a Nazi-like tyrant (Lawson) whose assassination is condoned, and unpunished.

Dec 1938: **THE WARE CASE** (79 mins)
CAPAD. Directed by Robert Stevenson. Associate producer: S.C. Balcon. Script by Stevenson, Roland Pertwee, from the play by G.P. Bancroft. Additional dialogue by E.V.H. Emmett. Photographed by Ronald Neame. Art direction by O.F. Werndorff. Music by Ernest Irving. Edited by Charles Saunders. With: Clive Brook (Sir Hubert Ware), Jane Baxter (Lady Margaret Ware), Barry K. Barnes (Michael), Edward Rigby (Tommy Bold), Peter Bull (Eustace), John Laurie (Henson), Ernest Thesiger (Carter), Dorothy Seacombe (Mrs Slade), Athene Seyler (Mrs Pinto), C.V. France (Judge), Francis L. Sullivan (Attorney General), Elliot Mason (impatient juror), Frank Cellier (Skinner), Wally Patch (taxi driver).

Adaptation and publicity exploited the theatricality of the material in a way that would soon become alien to the studio ethos. The part of Sir Hubert had been a celebrated stage vehicle for Gerald du Maurier. Stately-home exteriors were shot in the grounds of Pinewood.

Mar 1939: **LET'S BE FAMOUS** (83 mins)
ATP. Directed by Walter Forde. Script by Roger Macdougall, Allan Mackinnon. Photographed by Ronald Neame, Gordon Dines. Art direction by O.F. Werndorff. Songs by Noel Gay. Edited by Ray Pitt. With: Jimmy O'Dea (Jimmy Houlihan), Betty Driver (Betty Pinbright), Milton Rosmer (Albert Pinbright), Lena Brown (Polly Pinbright), Sonnie Hale (Finch), Patrick Barr (Johnny Blake), Basil Radford (Watson), Garry Marsh (B.B.C. official), Hay Plumb (announcer).

Many of those involved in the film, including Jimmy O'Dea, went on to the much more substantial *Cheer Boys Cheer*. Though a tedious experience, *Let's Be Famous* is of interest in two ways: 1) for its picture of the BBC of the time, and the triangle formed by BBC stuffiness, the vulgarity of the advertising world, and the Northern genuineness of the heroine, and 2) for the generation conflict, akin to that in so many Ealing films around this time. The Milton Rosmer character is a hard businessman and stern father who exploits the media as an advertiser but won't let his family go near them as performers.

Mar 1939: **TROUBLE BREWING** (87 mins)
ATP. Directed by Anthony Kimmins. Produced by Jack Kitchin. Script by Kimmins, Angus Macphail, Michael Hogan. Photographed by Ronald Neame. Art direction by Wilfrid Shingleton. Musical director: Ernest Irving. Edited by Ernest Aldridge. With: George Formby (George), Googie Withers (Mary), Gus McNaughton (Bill Pike), Garry Marsh (A.G. Brady), C. Denier Warren (Major Hopkins), Beatrix Fielden-Kaye (housekeeper), Joss Ambler (Lord Redhill), Ronald Shiner (Bridgewater), Martita Hunt (Mme Berdi), Basil Radford (guest), Esma Cannon (maid).

Credits are nearly identical with those of the Formby vehicles made at Ealing before Balcon succeeded Dean. This was the area of production least affected by the change.

June 1939: **THE FOUR JUST MEN** (85 mins)
CAPAD. Directed by Walter Forde. Associate producer: S.C. Balcon. Script by Roland Pertwee, Angus Macphail, Sergei Nolbandov. Photographed by Ronald Neame. Art direction by Wilfrid Shingleton. Music by Ernest Irving. Edited by Charles Saunders. With: Hugh Sinclair (Humphrey Mansfield), Griffith Jones (James Brodie), Francis L. Sullivan (Leon Poiccard), Frank Lawton (Terry), Anna Lee (Ann Lodge), Basil Sydney (Frank Snell), Alan Napier (Sir Hamar Ryman M.P.), Lydia Sherwood (Myra Hastings), Roland Pertwee (Mr Hastings), Edward Chapman (B.J. Burrell), George Merritt (Inspector Falmouth), Garry Marsh (Bill Grant), Eliot Makeham (Simmons), Frederick Piper (pickpocket), Ellaline Terriss (Lady Willoughby), Percy Walsh (Prison Governor), Percy Parsons (American broadcaster), Charles Paton (platform speaker).

This is a film I was able to see only after completing the main text. It powerfully expresses Ealing's late-'thirties opposition to ruling-class decadence. The main target of the Four is the high ranking politician Sir Hamar Ryman, an appeaser and a traitor: the film enforces, irresistibly, the inference that appeasement *is* treachery. The Four are a secret band of militant patriots who resemble Leslie Howard's Pimpernel Smith both in this quality of secrecy and in their lack of conventionally robust masculinity: they are an actor, a musical dramatist, a couturier, and a consumptive. The film was re-released during the war with an updated newsreel-based ending, presenting Churchill's leadership and the Allied war effort as fulfilment of the vision of the Four. Ealing's adviser on the extensive House of Commons scenes was Aneurin Bevan.

Aug 1939: **THERE AIN'T NO JUSTICE** (83 mins)
CAPAD. Directed by Penrose Tennyson. Associate producer: Sergei Nolbandov. Script by Tennyson, Nolbandov, James Curtis, from the novel by Curtis. Photographed by Mutz Greenbaum. Art direction by Wilfrid Shingleton. Music by Ernest Irving. Edited by Ray Pitt. With: James Hanley (Tommy

Mutch), Edward Rigby (Pa Mutch), Mary Clare (Ma Mutch), Phyllis Stanley (Elsie Mutch), Edward Chapman (Sammy Sanders), Jill Furse (Connie Fletcher), Nan Hopkins (Dot Ducrow), Richard Ainley (Billy Frist), Michael Wilding (Len Charteris), Gus Macnaughton (Alfie Norton), Richard Norris (Stan), Al Millen (Perce).

Advertised as 'The film that begs to differ', a slogan picked up by Lindsay Anderson for an article on Ealing ten years later: 'the Studio that begs to differ'.

Aug 1939: **YOUNG MAN'S FANCY** (77 mins)
CAPAD. Directed by Robert Stevenson. Associate producer: S.C. Balcon. Script by Roland Pertwee; story by Stevenson; additional dialogue by E.V.H. Emmett, Rodney Ackland. Photographed by Ronald Neame. Art direction by Wilfrid Shingleton. Music by Ernest Irving. Edited by Charles Saunders, Ralph Kemplen. With: Griffith Jones (Lord Alban), Anna Lee (Ada), Seymour Hicks (Duke of Beaumont), Martita Hunt (Duchess of Beamont), Felix Aylmer (Sir Caleb Crowther), Meriel Forbes (Miss Crowther), Billy Bennett (Captain Boumphray), Edward Rigby (Gray), Phyllis Monkman (Esme), Francis L. Sullivan (Blackbeard), Athene Seyler (milliner), George Benson (booking clerk).

Aug 1939: **CHEER BOYS CHEER** (84 mins)
ATP. Directed by Walter Forde. Associate producer: S.C. Balcon. Script by Roger Macdougall, Allan Mackinnon; story by Ian Dalrymple, Donald Bull. Photographed by Ronald Neame. Art direction by Wilfrid Shingleton. Music by Ernest Irving. Edited by Ray Pitt. With: Edmund Gwenn (Ironside), Peter Coke (John Ironside), C.V. France (Greenleaf), Nova Pilbeam (Margaret Greenleaf), Jimmy O'Dea (Matt Boyle), Alexander Knox (Saunders), Graham Moffatt (Albert), Moore Marriott (Geordie), Ivor Barnard (Naseby).

Nov 1939: **COME ON GEORGE** (88 mins)
ATP. Directed by Anthony Kimmins. Produced by Jack Kitchin. Script by Kimmins, Leslie Arliss, Val Valentine. Photographed by Ronald Neame. Art direction by Wilfrid Shingleton. Music by Ernest Irving. Edited by Ray Pitt. With: George Formby (George), Pat Kirkwood (Ann), Joss Ambler (Sir Charles Bailey), Meriel Forbes (Monica Bailey), Cyril Raymond (Jimmy Taylor), George Hayes (Bannerman), George Carney (Sgt Johnson), Ronald Shiner (Nat), Gibb McLaughlin (Dr MacGregor), James Hayter (banker).

George as a nervous stableboy, who eventually rides his horse to victory.

Jan 1940: **RETURN TO YESTERDAY** (69 mins)
CAPAD. Directed by Robert Stevenson. Associate producer: S.C. Balcon. Script by Stevenson, Roland Pertwee, Angus Macphail, from the play *Goodness*

How Sad by Robert Morley. Photographed by Ronald Neame. Art direction by Wilfrid Shingleton. Music by Ernest Irving. Edited by Charles Saunders. With Clive Brook (Robert Maine), Anna Lee (Carol), David Tree (Peter Thropp), O.B. Clarence (Truscott), Dame May Whitty (Mrs Truscott), Hartley Power (Regan), Milton Rosmer (Sambourne), Olga Lindo (Grace Sambourne), Garry Marsh (Charlie Miller), Elliot Mason (Mrs Priskin), Arthur Margetson (Osbert), Frank Pettingell (Prendergast), David Horne (Morrison), H.F. Maltby (Inspector), Wally Patch (night watchman), John Turnbull (stationmaster), Patrick Curwen (guard), Molly Rankin (Christine), Eliot Makeham (Grover), Bruce Seton (journalist), Mary Jerrold (old lady at station).

Drama of a film star returning incognito to the scenes of his youth. Completed before the outbreak of war, this was the last film both of Stevenson and of his wife Anna Lee before they left for Hollywood. He would shortly direct *Back Street* (1941); she would become a regular supporting player for John Ford. Stevenson was a pacifist, and Balcon in his 1969 autobiography speaks with understanding of his dilemma; at the time, though, he had been bitterly outspoken in attacking British film-makers who were leaving, or failing to return to, their country. *Return to Yesterday* dramatises the Anglo-American theme rather effectively, without, however, referrring to the war. The star (Brook) is torn between returning to the glamour of Hollywood and working with a small theatre company in England; when he falls in love with him, the Anna Lee character is faced with the same dilemma.

Mar 1940: **THE PROUD VALLEY** (76 mins)
CAPAD. Directed by Penrose Tennyson. Associate producer: Sergei Nolbandov. Script by Tennyson, Jack Jones, Louis Goulding, story by Herbert Marshall, Alfredda Brilliant. Photographed by Glen MacWilliams and Roy Kellino. Art direction by Wilfrid Shingleton. Music: Mendelssohn and others, arranged by Ernest Irving. Edited by Ray Pitt. With: Paul Robeson (David Goliath), Edward Rigby (Bert), Edward Chapman (Dick Parry), Rachel Thomas (Mrs Parry), Simon Lack (Emlyn Parly), Janet Johnson (Gwen Owen), Dilys Davies (Mrs Owen), Clifford Evans (Seth Jones), Jack Jones (Thomas), Allan Jeayes (Mr Trevor), Edward Lexy (commissionaire), Noel Howlett (company clerk). Working title: *David Goliath*.

July 1940: **LET GEORGE DO IT** (82 mins)
Directed by Marcel Varnel. Associate producer: Basil Dearden. Script by John Dighton, Austin Melford, Angus Macphail, Dearden. Photographed by Ronald Neame. Art direction by Wilfrid Shingleton. Musical director: Ernest Irving. Edited by Ray Pitt. With: George Formby (George), Phyllis Calvert (Mary), Garry Marsh (Mendez), Romney Brent (Slim), Bernard Lee (Nelson), Coral Browne (Ivy), Diana Beaumont (Greta), Torin Thatcher (U-boat Cdr), Donald Calthrop (Strickland), Ronald

Shiner (musician), Bill Shine (steward), Albert Lieven (radio operator).

The first of the studio's comedies to deal directly with Germany and the war. George and ukelele are waiting for the train to Blackpool; a mix-up takes him to Norway, mistaken for an Intelligence recruit. A standard comic intrigue, with nice songs, including 'Grandad's Flannelette Nightshirt'; but it gives George the chance to score off both Lord Haw-Haw and Adolf Hitler. In a dream sequence, he descends from a balloon on to a Nazi rally and punches Hitler around.

July 1940: **CONVOY** (90 mins)
Directed by Penrose Tennyson. Associate producer: Sergei Nolbandov. Script by Tennyson, Patrick Kirwan. Photographed by Roy Kellino, Gunther Krampf. Art direction by Wilfrid Shingleton. Music by Ernest Irving. Edited by Ray Pitt. With: Clive Brook (Capt Armitage), John Clements (Lt Cranford), Judy Campbell (Lucy Armitage), Penelope Dudley Ward (Mabel), Allan Jeayes (Cdr Blount), Harold Warrender (Lt-Cdr Martin), Michael Wilding (Dot), Stewart Granger (Sutton), David Hutcheson (Capt Sandeman), Edward Chapman (Capt Eckersley), Edward Rigby (Mr Matthews), Charles Williams (Shorty Howard), George Carney (Bates), Al Millen (Knowles), John Laurie (Gates), Albert Lieven (U-boat Cdr), Anton Diffring (U-Boat officer), John Boxer (German Captain), Hay Petrie (minesweeper skipper), Mervyn Johns (his mate), Edward Lexy (merchant-man skipper), John Glyn Jones (his mate), Derek Elphinstone (Hawkins), John Carol (Edmonds), George Benson (Parker), Nancy O'Neil (Mary).

Prefatory title: '*Convoy* is dedicated in all gratitude to the Officers and Men of the Royal and Merchant Navies. Their cheerful co-operation made it possible to present the many scenes in our film which were taken at sea under actual wartime conditions.' It seems that it took the Service chiefs some time to approve this form of co-operation. When Sir Joseph Ball resigned in December 1939 as film chief at the Ministry of Information (to be succeeded by Kenneth Clark), Balcon made this public comment: 'Sir Joseph has done a great job of work under extraordinary difficulties. We have been told by the Government to get on with making pictures with British backgrounds, but we are getting terrific opposition from the Services.' (Publicity slogan: 'Entertainment with Authenticity'.)

Oct 1940: **SALOON BAR** (99 mins)
Directed by Walter Forde. Associate producer: Culley Forde. Script by Angus Macphail, John Dighton, from the play by Frank Harvey Jr. Photographed by Ronald Neame. Art direction by Wilfrid Shingleton. Music by Ernest Irving. Edited by Ray Pitt. With: Gordon Harker (Joe Harris), Elisabeth Allan (Queenie), Mervyn Johns (Wickers), Anna Konstam (Ivy), Joyce Barbour (Sally), Judy Campbell (Doris), Cyril Raymond (Harry Small), Helena Pickard (Mrs Small), Laurence Kitchin

(Peter), Mavis Villiers (Joan), Alec Clunes (Eddie Graves), Norman Pierce (Bill Hoskins), Felix Aylmer (Mayor), O.B. Clarence (Sir Archibald), Manning Whiley (evangelist), Al Millen (Fred), Roddy Hughes (doctor).

The last Ealing film to belong completely, both in content and in form, to the old order, an unambitious stage adaptation, most notable for the fact that it brought the writer T.E.B. Clarke to Ealing's attention. His book about pubs, 'What's Yours?', was used for reference.

Dec 1940: **SAILORS THREE** (86 mins)
Directed by Walter Forde. Associate producer: Culley Forde. Script by Angus Macphail, John Dighton, Austin Melford. Photographed by Gunther Krampf. Art direction by Wilfrid Shingleton. Musical director: Ernest Irving. Edited by Ray Pitt. With: Tommy Trinder (Tommy), Claude Hulbert ('the Admiral'), Michael Wilding (Johnny), Carla Lehmann (Jane), Henry Hewitt (Professor Pilkington), Jeanne de Casalis (Mrs Pilkington), James Hayter (Hans), John Laurie (Macnab), Harold Warrender (Mate), Manning Whiley (German Commander), Allan Jeayes (British Commander), Alec Clunes (British pilot), Derek Elphinstone (Observer), John Glyn Jones (Best Man), Julien Vedey (Resident). Danny Green (night club bouncer), E.V.H. Emmett (newsreel commentator).

Walter Forde's last Ealing feature. Like *Let George Do It*, an unsubtle blend of music-hall comedy and war propaganda, with a robust anti-pacifist slant.

Dec 1940: **SPARE A COPPER** (77 mins)
ATP. Directed by John Paddy Carstairs. Associate producer: Basil Dearden. Script by Roger Macdougall, Dearden, Austin Melford. Photographed by Bryan Langley. Art direction by Wilfrid Shingleton. Music by Louis Levy. Edited by Ray Pitt. With: George Formby (George), Dorothy Hyson (Jane), Bernard Lee (Jake), John Warwick (Shaw), Eliot Makeham (Fuller), George Merritt (Brewster), Warburton Gamble (Sir Robert Dyer), John Turnbull (Inspector Richards), Edward Lexy (night watchman), Ellen Pollock (Lady Hardstaff). Charles Carson (Admiral), Grace Arnold (music shop customer).

Introductory title: 'Merseyside 1939.' George in the Police, exposing traitors in high places. Several of the Hay and Formby plots are like comic versions of Ealing's straight war dramas; Mass Observation research at the time suggested that their films were particularly good for public morale. In exposing a pillar of the community as a traitor, *Spare a Copper* is doing similar work at a comic level to such later films as *Went the Day Well?*

Apr 1941: **THE GHOST OF ST MICHAEL'S** (82 mins)
Directed by Marcel Varnel. Associate producer: Basil Dearden. Script by Angus Macphail, John Dighton. Photographed by Derek Williams. Art direction by Wilfrid Shingleton, in consultation with Alberto Cavalcanti. With: Will Hay (William Lamb), Claude Hulbert (Hilary Teasdale), Charles Hawtrey (Percy), Derek Blomfield (Sunshine), Felix Aylmer (Dr Winter), Raymond Huntley (Mr Humphries), Elliot Mason (Mrs Wigmore), John Laurie (Jamie), Roddy Hughes (Amberley), Hay Petrie (Procurator Fiscal), Brefni O'Rourke (Sgt Macfarlane).

Hay in his familiar role as a teacher, in a school evacuated to a far corner of Scotland. Exposure of traitors.

Aug 1941: **TURNED OUT NICE AGAIN** (81 mins)
ATP. Directed by Marcel Varnel. Associate producer: Basil Dearden. Script by Austin Melford, John Dighton, Dearden, from the play *As You Are* by Hugh Mills, Wells Root. Photographed by Gordon Dines. Art direction by Wilfrid Shingleton, in consultation with Alberto Cavalcanti. Music by Ernest Irving. Edited by Robert Hamer. With: George Formby (George Pearson), Peggy Bryan (Lydia), Elliot Mason (Mrs Pearson), Edward Chapman (Uncle Arnold), O.B. Clarence (Mr Dawson), Mackenzie Ward (Gerald Dawson), Ronald Ward (Nelson), John Salew (Largon), Wilfrid Hyde White (removal man), Michael Rennie (diner), Hay Petrie (drunk).

Back to the pre-war North. The formidable Elliot Mason, a Scottish traitress in *The Ghost of St Michael's*, is now simply a stock mother-in-law figure. Set-piece scenes depict 'thirties unemployment and a honeymoon trip to Morecambe (along with mother-in-law), the kind of material that becomes increasingly valuable to the social historian. George works in the textile industry, his discovery of a wonder cloth anticipating *The Man in the White Suit* (possibly even influencing it—John Dighton worked on both scripts). His innocence is exploited; London values clash with Northern ones.

Nov 1941: **SHIPS WITH WINGS** (103 mins)
Directed by Sergei Nolbandov. Associate producer S.C. Balcon. Script by Patrick Kirwan, Austin Melford, Diana Morgan, Nolbandov. Photographed by Mutz Greenbaum and Wilkie Cooper (interiors), Roy Kellino and Eric Cross (exteriors). Art direction by Wilfrid Shingleton. Music by Geoffrey Wright. Edited by Robert Hamer. With: John Clements (Lt Stacey), Michael Wilding (Lt Grant), Michael Rennie (Lt Maxwell), Hugh Burden (Lt Wetherby), Jane Baxter (Celia Wetherby), Leslie Banks (Admiral Wetherby), Basil Sydney (Capt Fairfax), Ann Todd (Kay Gordon), Betty Marsden (Jean), Edward Chapman (Papadopoulos), Hugh Williams (Wagner), Frank Pettingell (Fields), Frank Cellier (General Scarappa), Cecil Parker (German Air

Marshal), John Stuart (Cdr Hood), Charles Victor (MacDermott), John Laurie (Reid), Ian Fleming (Colonel).

Research by Jeffrey Richards has established that however archaic this film now looks, and looked to many at the time (*see*, for instance, pp.24-26 and 53), it was in fact received with enthusiasm by audiences and by critics in the popular press. *See* Richards's article in the *Historical Journal of Film, Radio and Television* (vol.7, no.2, 1987) and also his book, co-authored with Dorothy Sheridan, *Mass Observation at the Movies* (1987).

Jan 1942: **THE BLACK SHEEP OF WHITEHALL** (80 mins)

Directed by Will Hay, Basil Dearden. Associate producer: S.C. Balcon. Script by Angus Macphail, John Dighton. Photographed by Gunther Krampf. Art direction by Tom Morahan. Edited by Ray Pitt. With: Will Hay (Davis), Henry Hewitt (Professor Davys), John Mills (Jessop), Basil Sydney (Costello), Felix Aylmer (Crabtree), Frank Cellier (Dr Innsbach), Joss Ambler (Sir John), Thora Hird (Davis's secretary), Leslie Mitchell (radio interviewer), Richard George (hospital nurse), Roddy Hughes (journalist), Katie Johnson (train passenger), Brefni O'Rorke (Ministry receptionist), John Boxer (hotel receptionist), George Merritt (stationmaster), Ronald Shiner (porter), Kenneth Griffith (butcher's boy), Margaret.Halstan (Matron), Cyril Chamberlain (BBC producer).

Comedy of mistaken identity and disguise—six Will Hays in all, two of them female—within another plot centred on traitors in high places and bumbling English complacency.

Jan 1942: **THE BIG BLOCKADE** (73 mins)

Directed by Charles Frend. Associate producer: Alberto Cavalcanti. Script by Angus Macphail, commentary by Frank Owen. Photographed by Wilkie Cooper. Art direction by Tom Morahan. Music by Richard Addinsell. Edited by Charles Crichton, Compton Bennett. With: Leslie Banks (Taylor), Michael Redgrave (Russian), John Mills (Tom), Michael Rennie (George), Will Hay (Skipper), Bernard Miles (Mate), Frank Cellier (Schneider), Robert Morley (Von Geiselbrecht), Alfred Drayton (Direktor), Marius Goring (Propaganda Officer), Austin Trevor (U-boat Captain), Albert Lieven (Gunter), Joss Ambler (Stoltenhoff), George Woodbridge (Quisling), Michael Wilding (Captain), John Stuart (naval officer), Ronald Adam (German businessman), Frederick Piper (Malta official), Ronald Shiner (shipping clerk), Manning Whiley (naval officer), George Merritt (German shelter marshal), Elliot Mason (German stationmistress), Thora Hird (German barmaid), Quentin Reynolds (American journalist).

Apr 1942: **THE FOREMAN WENT TO FRANCE** (87 mins)

Directed by Charles Frend. Associate producer: Alberto Cavalcanti. Script by John Dighton, Angus Macphail, Leslie Arliss; story by J.B. Priestley, based on the experiences of Melbourne Johns, to whom the film is dedicated. Photographed by Wilkie Cooper. Art direction by Tom Morahan. Music by William Walton. Edited by Robert Hamer. With: Tommy Trinder (Tommy), Clifford Evans (Fred Carrick, the foreman), Constance Cummings (American girl), Gordon Jackson (Jock), Robert Morley (French Mayor), Paul Bonifas (Prefect), Ernest Milton (Stationmaster), Francis L. Sullivan (Skipper), John Williams ('English' captain), Ronald Adam (Sir Charles Fawcett), Charles Victor, Bill Blewitt (spotters), Mervyn Johns (official, Passport Office), John Boxer (official, Ministry of Home Security).

The opening is set in 1942, with Carrick by now running a successful arms factory in England; for the main story we return to 1940. The French locations were filmed in Cornwall. This was the first of Trinder's several roles in straight dramas, always in the same wisecracking Cockney persona; a painful gap separates his performance from the rest, notably the excellent Constance Cummings in her one Ealing part.

May 1942: **THE NEXT OF KIN** (102 mins)

Directed by Thorold Dickinson. Associate producer: S.C. Balcon. Script by Dickinson, Angus Macphail, John Dighton, with Captain Sir Basil Bartlett (Military Supervisor). Photographed by Ernest Palmer. Art direction by Tom Morahan. Music by William Walton. Edited by Ray Pitt. With: Mervyn Johns (no 23: Mr Davis), John Chandos (no 16: his contact), Nova Pilbeam (Beppie Leemans), Stephen Murray (Mr Barratt), David Hutcheson (Intelligence Officer), Reginald Tate (Major Richards), Geoffrey Hibbert (Private John), Philip Friend (Lt Cummins), Basil Sydney (naval Captain), Jack Hawkins (Major), Brefni O'Rourke (Brigadier), Frederick Leister (Colonel), Charles Victor (seaman), Torin Thatcher (German General), Mary Clare (Miss Webster), Phyllis Stanley (Miss Clare), Thora Hird (A.T.S. girl), Joss Ambler (Mr Vernon), Basil Radford and Naunton Wayne (careless talkers).

The War Office asked Ealing to make a feature-length training film for them on the subject of security, but provided minimal funds. Ealing more than doubled the budget from its own resources, to produce a film whose appeal transcended its military function. The very large profits from commercial distribution went first to repay this outlay, then to the War Office rather than Ealing. More details of this and of Churchill's intervention are given in Balcon's book. In addition, an explosive private memorandum, written by Dickinson after finishing the film, indicates that even this far into the war the co-operation of Service authorities with film-makers was somewhat erratic: compare note on *Convoy*, above.

Aug 1942: **THE GOOSE STEPS OUT** (79 mins)
Directed by Will Hay, Basil Dearden. Associate producer: S.C. Balcon. Script by John Dighton, Angus Macphail; story by Bernard Miles, Reg Groves. Photographed by Ernest Palmer. Art direction by Tom Morahan. Music by Bretton Byrd. Edited by Ray Pitt. With: Will Hay (William Potts), Frank Pettingell (Professor Hoffman), Julien Mitchell (General von Glotz), Raymond Lovell (Schmidt), Charles Hawtrey (Max), Peter Croft (Hans), Leslie Harcourt (Vagel), Barry Morse (Kurt), Peter Ustinov (Krauss), Jeremy Hawk (A.D.C.).

Hay in Germany as a spy, using the disguise of a Professor Muller to gain access to a secret new bomb.

Oct 1942: **WENT THE DAY WELL?** (92 mins)
Directed by Alberto Cavalcanti. Associate producer: S.C. Balcon. Script by John Dighton, Diana Morgan, Angus Macphail, from a story by Graham Greene. Photographed by Wilkie Cooper. Art direction by Tom Morahan. Music by William Walton. Edited by Sidney Cole. With: Leslie Banks (Oliver Wilsford), Basil Sydney (Major Ortler), Marie Lohr (Mrs Frazer), Valerie Taylor (Nora), C.V. France (Vicar), Frank Lawton (Tom Sturry), Elizabeth Allan (Peggy), Thora Hird (Land Girl), Mervyn Johns (Sims), John Slater (German Sgt), David Farrar (German officer), Muriel George (Mrs Collins), Patricia Hayes (Daisy), Edward Rigby (poacher), Harry Fowler (George Truscott), Norman Pierce (Jim Sturry), Grace Arnold (Mrs Owen), James Donald (German officer), Hilda Bayley (Maud), Mavis Villiers (Violet).

Jan 1943: **NINE MEN** (68 mins)
Directed by Harry Watt. Associate producer: Charles Crichton. Script by Harry Watt; story by Gerald Kersh. Photographed by Roy Kellino. Art direction by Duncan Sutherland. Music by John Greenwood. Edited by Eric Cripps; supervising editor: Sidney Cole. With: Jack Lambert (Sgt Watson), Gordon Jackson (Young 'un), Frederick Piper ('Badger' Hill), Grant Sutherland (Jock Scott), Bill Blewett (Bill Parker), Eric Micklewood ('Bookie' Lee), John Varley ('Dusty' Johnstone), Jack Horsman (Joe Harvey), Richard Wilkinson (Lt Crawford), Giulio Finzi (Italian mechanic), Fred Griffiths (base sergeant).

A remarkable feat of production, costing only £20,000, with Margam Sands in North Wales standing in for the North African desert.

Apr 1943: **THE BELLS GO DOWN** (90 mins)
Directed by Basil Dearden. Associate producer: S.C. Balcon. Script by Roger Macdougall, Stephen Black. Photographed by Ernest Palmer. Art direction by Michael Relph. Music by Roy Douglas. Edited by Mary Habberfield; supervising editor: Sidney Cole. With: Tommy Trinder (Tommy Turk), Beatrice Varley (Ma Turk), James Mason

(Ted Robbins), Norman Pierce (Pa Robbins), Muriel George (Ma Robbins), Mervyn Johns (Sam), Finlay Currie (McFarlane), Billy Hartnell (Brooks), Philip Friend (Bob), Meriel Forbes (Susie), Philippa Hiatt (Nan), Ralph Michael, Charles Victor (Dunkirk survivors), Johnnie Schofield (milkman), Grace Arnold (canteen lady), Frederick Culley (vicar), Frederick Piper (Police Sgt), Richard George (P.C. O'Brien), John Salew (landlord), Lesley Brook (June).

July 1943: **UNDERCOVER** (80 mins)
Directed by Sergei Nolbandov. Associate producer: S.C. Balcon. Script by John Dighton, Monja Danischewsky; story by George Slocombe. Photographed by Wilkie Cooper. Art direction by Duncan Sutherland. Music by Frederic Austin. Edited by Eileen Boland, supervising editor: Sidney Cole. With: John Clements (Milos Petrovitch), Tom Walls (Kossan Petrovitch), Rachel Thomas (Maria Petrovitch), Stephen Murray (Dr Steven Petrovitch), Mary Morris (Anna Petrovitch), Godfrey Tearle (General von Staengel), Robert Harris (Colonel von Brock), Michael Wilding (Constantine), Charles Victor (Sergeant), Niall McGinnis (Dr Jordan), Ivor Barnard (stationmaster), Stanley Baker (Peter), Norman Pierce (Lieutenant Frank).
Yugoslav Resistance, Spring 1941. Danischewsky's book gives some of the background to the production. Location scenes were shot in Wales, and there is some attempt to invest the Yugoslav village in which the action is set with the feeling of a tight Welsh community, notably through the casting of Rachel Thomas as the mother (compare her *Proud Valley* role) and of the young Stanley Baker. The success of this ploy, as of the film as a whole, is decidedly limited.

June 1943: **MY LEARNED FRIEND** (74 mins)
Directed by Will Hay, Basil Dearden. Associate producer: S.C. Balcon. Script by John Dighton, Angus Macphail. Photographed by Wilkie Cooper. Art direction by Michael Relph. Music by Ernest Irving. Edited by Charles Hasse. With: Will Hay (William Fitch), Claude Hulbert (Claude Babbington), Mervyn Johns (Grimshaw), Laurence Hanray (Sir Norman), Aubrey Mallalieu (magistrate), Charles Victor ('Safety' Wilson), Derna Hazell (Gloria), Leslie Harcourt (barman), Eddie Phillips ('Basher' Blake), G.H. Mulcaster (Dr Scudamore), Ernest Thesiger (Ferris), Lloyd Pearson (Colonel Chudleigh), Gibb McLaughlin (butler), Maudie Edwards (Aladdin).

The opening title says 'London pre-war', and the film has no topical reference. This was Hay's last film (he died in 1949), and his persona is somewhat muted, subordinated to Claude Hulbert's silly-ass stereotype and to Mervyn Johns's multiple murderer. This man's scheme of working his way through a list of 'six little dramas of retribution, all beautifully staged' looks ahead to *Kind Hearts and Coronets*: both stories culminate at the House of Lords. Wide though the gulf is in quality and ambition between the two films, the name of John Dighton is on both scripts (cf the earlier linking of *Turned out Nice Again* and *The Man in the White Suit*), and the relation of mature to early 'Ealing comedy', and the role of men like Dighton within it, is certainly a subject for research.

Dec 1943: **SAN DEMETRIO LONDON** (104 mins)
Directed by Charles Frend. Associate producer: Robert Hamer. Script by Hamer, Frend, from the factual narrative by F. Tennyson Jesse. Photographed by Ernest Palmer. Art direction by Duncan Sutherland. Music by John Greenwood. Edited by Eily Boland. Supervising editor: Sidney Cole. With: Walter Fitzgerald (Chief Engineer Pollard), Ralph Michael (2nd Officer Hawkins), Frederick Piper (Bosun Fletcher), Gordon Jackson (Jamieson), Mervyn Johns (Boyle), Robert Beatty ('Yank' Preston), Charles Victor, James McKechnie (deckhands), Arthur Young (Captain Waite), Nigel Clarke (Dodds), David Horne (Judge), Cavan Watson (tugboat captain), John Boxer (naval officer).

Set in 1940, dedicated to the officers and men of the British Merchant Navy. The credits name the real-life Chief Engineer Pollard as adviser. The film was widely accepted as an example of 'documentary drama' at its purest; the lack of any real attempt at verisimilitude in the American scenes (set in Galveston, Texas), and the long lifeboat sequence shot in a scarcely-disguised studio tank, help to illuminate Balcon's remark (*A Lifetime of Films*, p.130) that ' "documentary" is not a label to be lightly attached to films of a specific, factual type; it is an attitude of mind to film-making.'

Apr 1944: **HALFWAY HOUSE** (95 mins)
Directed by Basil Dearden. Associate producer: Alberto Cavalcanti. Script by Angus Macphail, Diana Morgan, with Roland Pertwee, T.E.B. Clarke, from the play *The Peaceful Inn* by Denis Ogden. Photographed by Wilkie Cooper. Art direction by Michael Relph. Music by Lord Berners. Edited by Charles Hasse. Supervising editor: Sidney Cole. With Mervyn Johns (Rhys), Glynis Johns (Gwyneth), Tom Walls (Captain Meadows), Françoise Rosay (Alice Meadows), Esmond Knight (David Davies), Guy Middleton (Fortescue), Alfred Drayton (Oakley), Valerie White (Jill French), Richard Bird (Squadron-Leader French), Sally Ann Howes (Joanna), Phillippa Hiatt (Margaret), Pat McGrath (Terence), John Boxer (doctor), C.V. France (solicitor), Joss Ambler (Pinsent), Rachel Thomas (landlady), Roland Pertwee (prison governor), Eliot Makeham (Davies's dresser).

June 1944: **FOR THOSE IN PERIL** (77 mins)
Directed by Charles Crichton. Associate producer: S.C. Balcon. Script by Harry Watt, J.O.C. Orton, T.E.B. Clarke; story by Richard Hillary.

Photographed by Douglas Slocombe (exteriors), Ernest Palmer (interiors). Art direction by Duncan Sutherland. Music by Gordon Jacob. Edited by Erik Cripps; supervising editor: Sidney Cole. With: David Farrar (Murray), Ralph Michael (Rawlings), Robert Wyndham (Leverett), John Slater (Wilkie), John Batten (wireless operator), Robert Griffith (Griffiths), Peter Arne (junior officer), James Robertson Justice (operations room officer).
Publicity slogan: 'The Action is Swift, the Characters Lovable.'

Absolutely orthodox drama of the assimilation of a new boy into a service role (Air-Sea Rescue), perhaps the closest war film to the pattern adopted by *The Blue Lamp*. David Farrar dies gallantly, Ralph Michael steps into his shoes.

This was the first feature directed by Charles Crichton, a self-effacing craftsman to whom I have made little direct reference in the main text. Crichton, an ex-editor, belongs to the commercial rather than documentary wing of Ealing's wartime intake, but his early work has more in the way of classic 'documentary' sequences than anyone's. Most striking here is the early-morning montage of boats, gulls, roofscapes, etc., before the patrol sets out.

Aug 1944: **THEY CAME TO A CITY** (78 mins)
Directed by Basil Dearden. Associate producer: Sidney Cole. Script by Dearden and Cole, from the play by J.B. Priestley. Photographed by Stan Pavey. Art direction by Michael Relph. Music: Scriabin. Edited by Michael Truman. With: John Clements (Joe Dinmore), Googie Withers (Alice), Raymond Huntley (Malcolm Stritton), Renée Gadd (Mrs Stritton), A.E. Matthews (Sir George Gedney), Mabel Terry Lewis (Lady Loxfield), Frances Rowe (Philippa), Ada Reeve (Mrs Batley), Norman Shelley (Mr Cudworth), Ralph Michael and Brenda Bruce (couple on hillside), J.B. Priestley (himself).

The main cast repeated their roles from the London stage production; Ealing's last real flirtation with theatricality. In the National Film Archive records, a reason is stated for selecting each film. *They Came to a City* was chosen 'as an unusual film which represented the first attempt to carry out socialist propaganda in the British feature film.'

Aug 1944: **CHAMPAGNE CHARLIE** (105 mins)
Directed by Alberto Cavalcanti. Associate producer: John Croydon. Script by Austin Melford, Angus Macphail, John Dighton. Photographed by Wilkie Cooper. Art direction by Michael Relph. Musical director: Ernest Irving. Edited by Charles Hasse. With: Tommy Trinder (George Leybourne, alias Champagne Charlie), Stanley Holloway (The Great Vance), Betty Warren (Bessie Bellwood), Jean Kent (Dolly Bellwood), Robert Wyndham (Duckworth), Austin Trevor (the Duke), Peter de Greeff (Lord Petersfield, his son), Leslie Clarke (Fred Sanders), Eddie Phillips (Tom Sayers), Eric Boon (Clinker), Norman Pierce (landlord), Vida Hope (barmaid), Harry Fowler ('orace), Billy Shine (stage manager),

Guy Middleton, James Robertson Justice (Patrons), Frederick Piper (Learoyd), Drusilla Wills (Bessie's dresser), Andrea Malandrinos (Gatti), Paul Bonifas (Targetino).

London in the 1860s. Comedy-drama about the rivalry of music halls and their stars; the rivals join forces, however, to resist official threats to close the halls down. The film is very 'Ealing' in its plot-movement—co-operation transcends competition—and in its picture of a cheerful, insulated community, hard-drinking but basically innocent, as the official inspectors come to recognise. Music hall becomes respectable, like the cinema. Among those credited for the lyrics is T.E.B. Clarke.

Oct 1944: **FIDDLERS THREE** (88 mins)
Directed by Harry Watt. Associate producer: Robert Hamer. Script by Harry Watt, Diana Morgan. Photographed by Wilkie Cooper. Art direction by Duncan Sutherland. Music by Spike Hughes. Edited by Eily Boland. With Tommy Trinder (Tommy), Frances Day (Poppaea), Sonnie Hale (The Professor), Francis L. Sullivan (Nero), Elisabeth Welch (Thora), Mary Clare (Volumnia), Diana Decker (Lydia), Frederick Piper (auctioneer), Russell Thorndike (High Priest), Danny Green (Lictor), James Robertson Justice (centurion).

An ill-fated musical comedy, extensively reshot by Robert Hamer, who also contributed to the lyrics. Harry Watt had expressed a wish to break out from his documentary typecasting, and Balcon with characteristic liberality agreed; the experiment was not repeated. Some soldiers are transported back to Ancient Rome. The convention is that of a cleaned-up *Up Pompeii*, stuffed with contemporary references. Trinder at Stonehenge: 'Blimey, another Government housing scheme gone wrong.' In Rome, the Empress takes a milk bath and is reprimanded about the depth of the milk—and so on, *ad nauseam*.

Aug 1945: **JOHNNY FRENCHMAN** (112 mins)
Directed by Charles Frend. Associate producer: S.C. Balcon. Script by T.E.B. Clarke. Photographed by Roy Kellino. Art direction by Duncan Sutherland. Music by Clifton Parker. Edited by Michael Truman. With: Françoise Rosay (Lanec Florrie), Tom Walls (Nat Pomeroy), Patricia Roc (Sue Pomeroy), Ralph Michael (Bob Tremayne), Paul Dupuis (Yan Kervarec), Frederick Piper (Zacky Penrose), Arthur Hambling (Steven Matthews), Grace Arnold (Mrs Matthews), Judith Furse (June Matthews), Bill Blewitt (Dick Trewhiddle), Carol O'Connor (Mr Harper), Alfie Bass (Corporal), Beatrice Varley (Mrs Tremayne), Drusilla Wills (Miss Bennett), Paul Bonifas (Jerome).

Sept 1945: **PAINTED BOATS** (63 mins)
Directed by Charles Crichton. Associate producer: Henry Cornelius. Script by Stephen Black, with Micky McCarthy. Commentary written by Louis MacNeice. Photographed by Douglas Slocombe.

Art direction by Jim Morahan. Music by John Greenwood. Edited by Leslie Allen. With: Jenny Laird (Mary Smith), Bill Blewitt (Pa Smith), May Hallatt (Ma Smith), Robert Griffith (Ted Stoner), Madoline Thomas (Mrs Stoner), Harry Fowler (Alf Stoner), Grace Arnold (his sister), Megs Jenkins (barmaid), James McKechnie (narrator).

Modest drama-documentary, with sustained voice-over commentary. Starting with aerial shots of the countryside and the words 'This is England', it represents the life of English canal people through the story of two particular families, including the impact of the war on them. Compared with Crichton's later transport-based film, *The Titfield Thunderbolt*, the sense of community and the play between modern and traditional is here quite fresh and serious.

Sept 1945: **DEAD OF NIGHT** (102 mins)
Directed by Alberto Cavalcanti, Charles Crichton, Basil Dearden, Robert Hamer. Associate producers: Sidney Cole, John Croydon. Script by John V. Baines, Angus Macphail; additional dialogue by T.E.B. Clarke. Photographed by Stan Pavey, Douglas Slocombe. Art direction by Michael Relph. Music by Georges Auric. Edited by Charles Hasse.

Linking narrative: directed by Dearden, story by E.F. Benson. With: Mervyn Johns (Walter Craig), Renée Gadd (Mrs Craig), Roland Culver (Eliot Foley), Mary Merrall (Mrs Foley), Frederick Valk (Dr van Straaten), Barbara Leake (Mrs O'Hara).

Hearse Driver: directed by Dearden, story by E.F. Benson. With: Antony Baird (Hugh), Judy Kelly (Joyce), Miles Malleson (Hearse Driver/Bus Conductor), Robert Wyndham (Dr Albury).

Christmas Party: directed by Cavalcanti, story by Angus Macphail. With: Sally Ann Howes (Sally O'Hara). Michael Allan (Jimmy).

The Haunted Mirror: directed by Hamer, story by John V. Baines. With: Googie Withers (Joan), Ralph Michael (Peter), Esme Percy (antique dealer).

Golfing Story: directed by Crichton, story by H.G. Wells. With: Basil Radford (George), Naunton Wayne (Larry), Peggy Bryan (Mary).

The Ventriloquist's Dummy: directed by Cavalcanti, story by John V. Baines. With: Michael Redgrave (Maxwell Frere), Hartley Power (Sylvester Kee), Elisabeth Welch (Beulah), Magda Kun (Mitzi), Garry Marsh (Harry Parker).

A set of stories about the supernatural, within a teasing dream framework. Charles Frend was in at the start of the project, but was not free to participate; it was even more of a communal Ealing enterprise, then, than the credits would suggest. Peter Hutchings gives an excellent analysis of the film, in its historical and generic context, in his 1993 book *Hammer and After*.

Nov 1945: PINK STRING AND SEALING WAX (89 mins)

Directed by Robert Hamer. Associate producer: S.C. Balcon. Script by Diana Morgan, Hamer, from the play by Roland Pertwee. Photographed by Richard Pavey. Art direction by Duncan Sutherland. Music by Norman Demuth. Edited by Michael Truman. With: Mervyn Johns (Edward Sutton), Googie Withers (Pearl Bond), Gordon Jackson (David Sutton), Sally Ann Howes (Peggy Sutton), Mary Merrall (Mrs Sutton), Jean Ireland (Victoria Sutton), Colin Simpson (James Sutton), David Wallbridge (Nicholas Sutton), John Carol (Dan Powell), Catherine Lacey (Miss Porter), Garry Marsh (Joe Bond), Frederick Piper (Doctor), Valentine Dyall (policeman), Maudie Edwards (Mrs Webster), Margaret Ritchie (Madame Patti), Don Stannard (John Bevan), Charles Carson (Editor).

Mar 1946: THE CAPTIVE HEART (104 mins)

Directed by Basil Dearden. Associate producer: Michael Relph. Script by Angus Macphail, Guy Morgan; story by Patrick Kirwan. Photographed by Douglas Slocombe. Art direction by Michael Relph. Music by Alan Rawsthorne. Edited by Charles Hasse. With: Michael Redgrave (Captain Hasek), Mervyn Johns (Private Evans), Basil Radford (Major Dalrymple), Jack Warner (Corporal Horsfall), James Hanley (Private Matthews), Gordon Jackson (Lieutenant Lennox), Ralph Michael (Captain Thurston), Derek Bond (Lieutenant Hartley), Guy Middleton (Captain Grayson), Karel Stepanek (Forster), Jack Lambert (Padre), Rachel Kempson (Celia Mitchell), Meriel Forbes (Beryl Curtess), Gladys Henson (Mrs Horsfall), Rachel Thomas (Mrs Evans), Jane Barrett (Caroline Hartley), Grace Arnold (official).

Shot in part in the British zone of Germany; time span 1944-45. A p.o.w.-camp story with a typical Ealing/Dearden omnibus format, sketching in the past and subsequent fortunes of a set of inmates, as well as their group existence. Easily the most memorable story is the Michael Redgrave/Rachel Kempson one. Hasek, an English-speaking Czech for whom the Germans intend special treatment, is helped to assume the identity of a dead British officer: this involves keeping up a correspondence with the man's unsuspecting widow. The possibilities of this story are exploited with a rare lack of inhibition, in one of the few Ealing films to aspire to the romantic intensity of *A Young Man's Fancy*. Another prisoner is Jack Warner, in his first Ealing role. There are hints of *The Blue Lamp* ahead (and a contrast with the Redgrave story) in his stoical/cheerful persona, and his marriage to Gladys Henson.

Oct 1946: THE OVERLANDERS (91 mins)

Directed by Harry Watt. Associate producer: Ralph Smart. Script by Harry Watt; research by Dora Birtles. Photographed by Osmond Borradaile. Music by John Ireland. Edited by E.M. Inman Hunter. Supervising editor: Leslie Norman. With:

Chips Rafferty (Dan McAlpine), John Nugent Hayward (Bill Parsons), Daphne Campbell (Mary Parsons), Jean Blue (Mrs Parsons), Helen Grieve (Helen Parsons), John Fernside (Corky), Peter Pagan (Sinbad), Frank Ransome (Charlie).

During the war, the government suggested Ealing ought to make a film dramatising Australia's contribution to the war effort. Watt flew out and spent months in research before developing this reconstruction of an epic cattle drive bringing beef from the Northern Territory to Brisbane. By collecting a unit and delivering a commercial success, Watt laid the foundation for Ealing's sustained involvement in Australian film-making: they took a lease on Pagewood Studios, near Sydney. A useful reference for this area of Ealing production is John Baxter's *Australian Cinema*.

Feb 1947: HUE AND CRY (82 mins)

Directed by Charles Crichton. Associate producer: Henry Cornelius. Script by T.E.B. Clarke. Photographed by Douglas Slocombe. Art direction by Norman G. Arnold. Music by Georges Auric. Edited by Charles Hasse. With: Alastair Sim (Felix H. Wilkinson), Jack Warner (Mr Nightingale), Valerie White (Rhona), Jack Lambert (Inspector Ford), Harry Fowler (Joe), Frederick Piper (his father), Vida Hope (his mother), Gerald Fox (Dicky), Grace Arnold (his mother), Joan Dowling (Clarry), Douglas Barr (Alec), Stanley Escane (Roy), Ian Dawson (Norman), Paul Demel (Jago), Bruce Belfrage (BBC announcer).

Mar 1947: NICHOLAS NICKLEBY (108 mins)

Directed by Alberto Cavalcanti. Associate producer: John Croydon. Script by John Dighton, from the novel by Charles Dickens. Photographed by Gordon Dines. Art direction by Michael Relph. Music by Lord Berners. Edited by Leslie Norman. With: Derek Bond (Nicholas Nickleby), Cedric Hardwicke (Ralph Nickleby), Mary Merrall (Mrs Nickleby), Sally Ann Howes (Kate Nickleby), Bernard Miles (Newman Noggs), Athene Seyler (Miss la Creevy), Alfred Drayton (Wackford Squeers), Sybil Thorndike (Mrs Squeers), Vida Hope (Fanny Squeers), Roy Hermitage (Wackford junior), Aubrey Woods (Smike), Patricia Hayes (Phoebe), Cyril Fletcher (Alfred Mantalini), Fay Compton (Madame Mantalini), Catherine Nesbitt (Miss Knag), Stanley Holloway (Vincent Crummles), Vera Pearce (Mrs Crummles), Una Barr (the Infant Phenomenon), June Elvin (Mrs Snevellici), Drusilla Wills (Mrs Crudden), James Hayter (Ned Cheeryble/Charles Cheeryble), Emrys Jones (Frank Cheeryble), Roddy Hughes (Tim Linkinwater), George Relph (Mr Bray), Jill Balcon (Madeleine Bray), Michael Shepley (Mr Gregsbury M.P.), Cecil Ramage (Sir Mulberry Hawk), Tim Bateson (Lord Verisopht), John Salew (Mr Lillyvick), Dandy Nichols (Mantalini's employee), John Chandos (employment agent).

A conscientious adaptation squeezing in a large number of the characters, but lacking much drive or sparkle, and understandably overshadowed by the more linear narrative of the Lean versions of Dickens from the same period.

June 1947: **THE LOVES OF JOANNA GODDEN** (89 mins)
Directed by Charles Frend. Associate producer: Sidney Cole. Script by H.E. Bates, Angus Macphail. From the novel *Joanna Godden* by Sheila Kaye-Smith. Photographed by Douglas Slocombe. Art direction by Duncan Sutherland. Music by Ralph Vaughan Williams. Edited by Michael Truman. With: Googie Withers (Joanna Godden), Jean Kent (Ellen Godden), John McCallum (Arthur Alce), Derek Bond (Martin Trevor), Henry Mollison (Harry Trevor), Chips Rafferty (Collard), Sonia Holm (Louise), Josephine Stuart (Grace Wickens), Alec Faversham (Peter Relf), Edward Rigby (Stuppeny), Frederick Piper (Isaac Turk), Fred Bateman (Young Turk), Grace Arnold (Martha), Barbara Leake (Mrs Luckhurst), Ethel Coleridge (lighthouse keeper's wife), William Mervyn (Huxtable).

1905, Romney Marsh: Googie Withers as a feminist farmer who eventually stops going it alone and finds happiness with John McCallum. The film is characteristic of Ealing's output of this period in reaching out with genuine seriousness towards new forms and ideas but falling back into the conventional; the extensive location shooting in Kent is undercut by a very studio style, with studio inserts. As on *San Demetrio London*, Charles Frend was ill for a time, and Robert Hamer took over.

July 1947: **FRIEDA** (98 mins)
Directed by Basil Dearden. Associate producer: Michael Relph. Script by Angus Macphail, Ronald Millar, from the latter's play. Photographed by Gordon Dines. Art direction by Jim Morahan. Music by John Greenwood. Edited by Leslie Norman. With: David Farrar (Robert Dawson), Glynis Johns (Judy Dawson), Mai Zetterling (Frieda), Flora Robson (Nell Dawson), Barbara Everest (Mrs Dawson), Ray Jackson (Tony Dawson), Patrick Holt (Alan Dawson), Gladys Henson (Edith), Albert Lieven (Richard), Barry Jones (headmaster), Norman Pierce (Crawley), D.A. Clarke-Smith (Herriot), Renée Gadd (Mrs Freeman), Garry Marsh (Beckwith), Milton Rosmer (Tom Merrick), Barry Letts (Jim Merrick), Arthur Howard (official).

Nov 1947: **IT ALWAYS RAINS ON SUNDAY** (92 mins)
Directed by Robert Hamer. Associate producer: Henry Cornelius. Script by Angus Macphail, Hamer, Cornelius, from the novel by Arthur la Bern. Photographed by Douglas Slocombe. Art direction by Duncan Sutherland. Music by Georges Auric. Edited by Michael Truman. With: Googie Withers (Rose Sandigate), Edward Chapman (George Sandigate), Susan Shaw (Vi Sandigate),

Patricia Plunkett (Doris Sandigate), David Lines (Alfie Sandigate), John McCallum (Tommy Swann), Sidney Tafler (Morrie Hyams), Betty Ann Davies (Sadie, his wife), John Slater (Lou, his brother), Jane Hylton (Bessie, his sister), Meier Tzelniker (Solly, his father), Jack Warner (Det-Sgt Fothergill), Frederick Piper (Det-Sgt Leech), Michael Howard (Slopey Collins), Nigel Stock (Ted Edwards), Hermione Baddeley (doss-house keeper), Grace Arnold (landlady), Betty Baskcomb (barmaid), Edie Martin (Mrs Watson), Al Millen (Bill Hawkins), Vida Hope (Mrs Wallis), John Salew (Caleb Neesley), Gladys Henson (Mrs Neesley), James Hanley (Whitey), John Carol (Freddie), Alfie Bass (Dicey).

Feb 1948: **AGAINST THE WIND** (96 mins)
Directed by Charles Crichton. Associate producer: Sidney Cole. Script by T.E.B. Clarke, Michael Pertwee; story by J. Elder Wills; Additional dialogue by P. Vincent Carroll. Photographed by Lionel Banes. Art direction by J. Elder Wills. Music by Leslie Bridgewater. Edited by Alan Osbiston. With: Robert Beatty (Father Phillip), Jack Warner (Max Cronk), Simone Signoret (Michèle), Gordon Jackson (Johnny Duncan), Paul Dupuis (Jacques), Gisèle Preville (Julie), John Slater (Emile), Peter Illing (Andrew), James Robertson Justice (Ackerman), Eugene Deckers (Marcel), André Morell (Abbot), Sybilla Binder (Malou), Helen Hanson (Marcel), Olaf Olsen (German officer).

Neglected but efficient film looking back to a wartime mission into occupied Belgium. As in the early Clarke/Crichton collaboration *Hue and Cry*, Jack Warner is cast against type, as an Irishman sabotaging the mission from within. He still has the warm 'Dixon' exterior, which gives extra tension to the film's most striking scene: he's shaving, whistling cheerfully, when his colleague Simone Signoret receives a tip-off and has to shoot him dead. The film retains a certain 'wartime' toughness (compare the climactic killing in *Went the Day Well?*) alongside its cosier 'Ealing' characteristics; the lukewarm public response to the film evidently had the effect of discouraging the toughness, and helping Ealing, and Clarke and Crichton, along their destined path.

Sept 1948: **SARABAND FOR DEAD LOVERS** (96 mins)
Directed by Basil Dearden. Associate producer: Michael Relph. Script by John Dighton, Alexander Mackendrick, from the novel by Helen Simpson. Photographed by Douglas Slocombe, in Technicolor. Art direction by Relph, Jim Morahan, William Kellner. Music by Alan Rawsthorne. Edited by Michael Truman. With: Stewart Granger (Konigsmark), Joan Greenwood (Sophie Dorothea), Flora Robson (Countess Platen), Françoise Rosay (Electress Sophia), Frederick Valk (Elector Ernest Augustus), Peter Bull (Prince George Louis), Anthony Quayle (Durer), Michael Gough (Prince Charles), Megs Jenkins (Frau Busche) Jill Balcon (Knesbeck), David Horne (Duke George William),

Cecil Trouncer (Major Eck), Noel Howlett (Count Platen), Barbara Leake (Maria), Miles Malleson (Lord of Misrule), Allan Jeayes (Governor at Ahlden), Guy Rolfe (Envoy).

Ealing's first colour production, an expensive, worthy, ponderous and loss-making period spectacle made during a short-lived attempt to fulfil Rank's wish for 'prestige' pictures in the late 'forties. In retrospect the most interesting factor is the involvement of Mackendrick as scriptwriter. The conflict of innocence and experience, centred on Joan Greenwood, clearly relates to his own films, though they will develop it less simplistically. Mackendrick also acted as draughtsman, sketching each set-up in advance within the film's elaborate system of pre-planning. Details of this and other aspects of the film are given in the souvenir book published at the time.

Nov 1948: **ANOTHER SHORE** (77 mins)
Directed by Charles Crichton. Associate producer: Ivor Montagu. Script by Walter Meade, from the novel by Kenneth Reddin. Photographed by Douglas Slocombe. Art direction by Malcolm Baker-Smith. Music by Georges Auric. Edited by Bernard Gribble. With: Robert Beatty (Gulliver), Moira Lister (Jennifer), Stanley Holloway (Alastair McNeil), Michael Medwin (Yellow), Maureen Delaney (Mrs Gleeson), Dermot Kelly (Boxer), Michael Golden (Broderick), Wilfred Brambell (Moore), Irene Worth and Bill Shine (socialites), Edie Martin (lady in park).

Whimsical credits announce 'A Tragi-Comedy of Dublin Life.' From the reviews it is apparent that, despite Hue and Cry, the concept of 'Ealing Comedy' had not yet been formulated. Robert Beatty is miscast as a feckless Irishman who dreams of escape to the South Seas but settles in the end for marriage and a steady job. Holloway's role as a rich alcoholic anticipates Titfield rather than Pimlico. A key scene is the dinner of oysters, steak and gateau at Jammet's restaurant: Dublin being free of rationing, it offers a more solid vicarious satisfaction than all those war-film scenes where characters imagine going through the menu at the Savoy.

Dec 1948: **SCOTT OF THE ANTARCTIC** (111 mins)
Directed by Charles Frend. Associate producer: Sidney Cole. Script by Walter Meade, Ivor Montagu. Photographed by Jack Cardiff, Osmond Borradaile, Geoffrey Unsworth, in Technicolor. Art direction by Arne Akermark, Jim Morahan. Music by Ralph Vaughan Williams. Edited by Peter Tanner. With: John Mills (Captain Scott), Derek Bond (Captain Oates), Harold Warrender (Dr Wilson), James Robertson Justice (P.O. Taff Evans), Reginald Beckwith (Lieutenant Bowers), Kenneth More (Lieutenant Teddy Evans), James McKechnie (Lieutenant Atkinson), John Gregson (P.O. Green), Barry Letts (Cherry-Gerrard), Clive Morton (Ponting), Christopher Lee (Bernard Day), Bruce Seton (Lieutenant Pennell), Anne Firth (Oriana

Wilson), Diana Churchill (Kathleen Scott).

Like Saraband: an expensive colour production responding to Rank's desire for 'prestige' films, and the subject of a commemorative book. Location shooting in Norway and Switzerland. Chosen for the Royal Film Performance.

Jan 1949: **EUREKA STOCKADE** (103 mins)
Directed by Harry Watt. Associate producer: Leslie Norman. Script by Harry Watt, Walter Greenwood. Photographed by George Heath. Art direction by Charles Woolveridge. Music by John Greenwood. Edited by Leslie Norman. Additional scenes directed by Ralph Smart. With Chips Rafferty (Peter Lalor), Jane Barrett (Alicia Dunne), Jack Lambert (Commissioner Rede), Peter Illing (Raffaello), Gordon Jackson (Tom Kennedy), Ralph Truman (Governor Hotham), Sydney Loder (Vern), Peter Finch (Humffray), Dorothy Alison (Mrs Bentley).

Watt's second and much less successful Australian film, dealing with conflict between diggers and colonial government in the gold rush of 1853. Both Lindsay Anderson (issue 7 of Sequence) and Richard Winnington (News Chronicle) saw its confused good intentions as characteristic of Ealing, and wrote strongly critical reviews on these lines.

Apr 1949: **PASSPORT TO PIMLICO** (84 mins)
Directed by Henry Cornelius. Associate producer: E.V.H. Emmett. Script by T.E.B. Clarke. Photographed by Lionel Banes. Art direction by Roy Oxley. Music by Georges Auric. Edited by Michael Truman. With: Stanley Holloway (Arthur Pemberton), Betty Warren (Connie Pemberton), Barbara Murray (Shirley Pemberton), Paul Dupuis (Duke of Burgundy), Margaret Rutherford (Professor Hatton-Jones), John Slater (Frank Huggins), Jane Hylton (Molly), Raymond Huntley (Wix), Philip Stainton (P.C. Spiller), Sidney Tafler (Fred Cowan), Hermione Baddeley (Edie Randall), Frederick Piper (Garland), Charles Hawtrey (Bert Fitch), Stuart Lindsell (Coroner), Naunton Wayne (Straker), Basil Radford (Gregg), Michael Hordern (Inspector Bashford), Arthur Howard (Bassett), Bill Shine (Captain), Harry Locke (Sergeant), Sam Kydd (Sapper), Fred Griffiths (spiv), Grace Arnold (woman in underground), E.V.H. Emmett (newsreel commentator).

June 1949: **WHISKY GALORE** (82 mins)
Directed by Alexander Mackendrick. Associate producer: Monja Danischewsky. Written by Compton Mackenzie, Angus Macphail, from the former's novel. Photographed by Gerald Gibbs. Art direction by Jim Morahan. Music by Ernest Irving. Edited by Joseph Sterling. With: Basil Radford (Captain Waggett), Catherine Lacey (Mrs Waggett), Bruce Seton (Sergeant Odd), Joan Greenwood (Peggy Macroon), Gabrielle Blunt (Catriona Macroon), Wylie Watson (Joseph Macroon),

Gordon Jackson (George Campbell), Jean Cadell (Mrs Campbell), James Robertson Justice (Dr Maclaren), Morland Graham (The Biffer), John Gregson (Sammy), James Anderson (Hector), Jameson Clark (Constable Macrae), Duncan Macrae (Angus McCormac), Mary MacNeil (Mrs McCormac), Henry Mollison (Farquharson), Compton Mackenzie (Captain Buncher), A. E. Matthews (Colonel Linsey-Woolsey), Finlay Currie (narrator). Set in 1943. U.S. title: *Tight Little Island*.

A full account of the production, including the tension between his own view of the story and Mackendrick's, is given in Danischewsky's *White Russian, Red Face*. The Mobile Studio Unit system was developed for this film, interiors being shot in a converted church hall on the location island of Barra. Charles Crichton is acknowledged to have contributed a lot at the editing stage, in line with the generous Ealing tradition of uncredited mutual help.

June 1949: **KIND HEARTS AND CORONETS** (106 mins)
Directed by Robert Hamer. Associate producer: Michael Relph. Script by Hamer, John Dighton, from the novel *Israel Rank* by Roy Horniman. Photographed by Douglas Slocombe. Art direction by William Kellner. Music: Mozart. Edited by Peter Tanner. With: Dennis Price (Louis Mazzini/his father), Joan Greenwood (Sibella), Valerie Hobson (Edith), Alec Guinness (Ascoyne d'Ascoyne/Henry d'Ascoyne/Canon d'Ascoyne/Admiral d'Ascoyne/General d'Ascoyne/Lady Agatha d'Ascoyne/Lord d'Ascoyne/Ethelbert, Duke of Chalfont/the old Duke), Audrey Fildes (Mrs Mazzini), John Penrose (Lionel), John Salew (Mr Perkins), Anne Valery (girl in punt), Barbara Leake (schoolmistress), Peggy Ann Clifford (Maud), Cecil Ramage (Counsel), Hugh Griffith (Lord High Steward), Clive Morton (Governor), Miles Malleson (hangman), Arthur Lowe (reporter).

The trade press of 1949 provides two footnotes to the chapter on this film: 1) studio scenes were shot at Pinewood (*Passport to Pimlico* occupied its space at Ealing, having over-run by several weeks), 2) the US censor insisted that crime should be punished unambiguously, and a final shot was therefore added in which Louis's manuscript is placed in the hands of the authorities. The French title is a felicitous one, *Noblesse Oblige*.
   Hamer scripted a dispiriting near-remake in *A Jolly Bad Fellow*, directed by Don Chaffey in 1963, just before Hamer's death. Leo McKern plays a multiple murderer, and Dennis Price a University don who speaks a voice-over commentary.

Aug 1949: **TRAIN OF EVENTS** (88 mins)
Directed by Sidney Cole, Charles Crichton, Basil Dearden. Associate producer: Michael Relph. Script by Dearden, T.E.B. Clarke, Ronald Millar, Angus Macphail. Photographed by Lionel Banes, Gordon Dines. Art direction by Malcolm Baker-Smith, Jim Morahan. Music by Leslie Bridgewater. Edited by Bernard Gribble. Individual sections:

The Engine Driver: directed by Cole. With: Jack Warner (Jim Hardcastle), Gladys Henson (Mrs Hardcastle), Susan Shaw (Doris Hardcastle), Patric Doonan (Ron Stacey), Miles Malleson (timekeeper), Philip Dale (Hardcastle's fireman), Leslie Phillips (Stacey's fireman).

The Prisoner-of-war: directed by Dearden. With: Joan Dowling (Ella), Laurence Payne (Richard), Olga Lindo (Mrs Bailey).

The Composer: directed by Crichton. With: Valerie Hobson (Stella), John Clements (Raymond Hillary), Irina Baronova (Irina), John Gregson (Malcolm), Gwen Cherrell (Charmian), Jacqueline Byrne (TV announcer).

The Actor: directed by Dearden. With: Peter Finch (Philip), Mary Morris (Louise), Laurence Naismith (Joe Hunt), Doris Yorke (Mrs Hunt), Michael Hordern, Charles Morgan (plain-clothes men), Guy Verney (producer), Mark Dignam (Bolingbroke), Philip Ashley, Bryan Coleman, Henry Hewitt, Lyndon Brook (actors).

A train crashes; the film reconstructs the human dramas of four of the victims. The result is a much less successful omnibus film than *Dead of Night*. Henceforth, though other companies continue to use the format, Ealing will do so only indirectly, presenting the individual's story as part of a more meaningful social continuum than this, and sticking to one director at a time.

Nov 1949: **A RUN FOR YOUR MONEY** (85 mins)
Directed by Charles Frend. Associate producer: Leslie Norman. Script by Frend, Norman, Richard Hughes; story by Clifford Evans; additional dialogue by Diana Morgan. Photographed by Douglas Slocombe. Art direction by William Kellner. Music by Ernest Irving. Edited by Michael Truman. With: Donald Houston (Dai), Meredith Edwards (Twm), Moira Lister (Jo), Alec Guinness (Whimple), Hugh Griffith (Huw), Julie Milton (Bronwen), Clive Morton (editor), Joyce Grenfell (Mrs Pargeter), Dorothy Bramhall (Jane), Edward Rigby (beefeater), Gabrielle Brune (crooner), Patric Doonan (conductor).

The fourth Ealing Comedy of 1949 is a considerable anticlimax. Two callow Welsh miners win the prize of a trip to London in a newspaper competition. On arrival, they are looked after by the paper's incompetent gardening correspondent: this is not much of a role for Guinness, and the film moves through a heavy series of comic routines and encounters of innocence and experience. The Richard Hughes who shares the script credit is, surprisingly, the author of *A High Wind in Jamaica*.

Jan 1950: **THE BLUE LAMP** (82 mins)
Directed by Basil Dearden. Produced by Michael Relph. Script by T.E.B. Clarke; story by Ted Willis,

Jan Read; additional dialogue by Alexander Mackendrick. Photographed by Gordon Dines. Art direction by Tom Morahan. Music by Ernest Irving. Edited by Peter Tanner. With: Jack Warner (P.C. George Dixon), James Hanley (P.C. Andy Mitchell), Robert Flemyng (Sgt Roberts), Bernard Lee (Inspector Cherry), Dirk Bogarde (Tom Riley), Patric Doonan (Spud), Peggy Evans (Diana Lewis), Frederick Piper (Mr Lewis), Betty Ann Davies (Mrs Lewis), Dora Bryan (Maisie), Norman Shelley (Jordan), Gladys Henson (Mrs Dixon), Bruce Seton (P.C. Campbell), Meredith Edwards (P.C. Hughes), Clive Morton (Sgt Brooks), William Mervyn (Chief Inspector Hammond), Campbell Singer (Station Sgt), Michael Golden (Mike Randall), Glyn Houston (barrow boy), Muriel Aked (Mrs Waterbourne), Renée Gadd (woman driver), Tessie O'Shea (herself).

Balcon had wanted to make a film about the police's work in 1939, but the Metropolitan Police, when asked to discuss the project, delivered a crushing snub. A decade later, their co-operation was very full. Mackendrick directed the second unit, shooting the car scenes on location.

June 1950: **DANCE HALL** (80 mins)
Directed by Charles Crichton. Associate producer: E.V.H. Emmett. Written by Emmett, Diana Morgan, Alexander Mackendrick. Photographed by Douglas Slocombe. Art direction by Norman Arnold. Music: Geraldo and other orchestras. Edited by Seth Holt. With: Natasha Parry (Eve), Jane Hylton (Mary), Diana Dors (Carole), Petula Clark (Georgie), Donald Houston (Phil), Bonar Colleano (Alec), Douglas Barr (Peter), Fred Johnson (Mr Wilson), Gladys Henson (Mrs Wilson), Dandy Nichols (Mrs Crabtree), Sydney Tafler (Manager), James Carney (Mike), Kay Kendall (Doreen), Eunice Gayson (Mona), Grace Arnold (Mrs Bennett), Harold Goodwin (Jack), Michael Trubshawe (Colonel), Harry Fowler (amorous youth).

A decent film in a familiar Ealing format, following the lives of various individuals who mingle at a London Dance Hall. The unusual aspect is the fore-grounding of the women, of whom Natasha Parry, a genuine Ealing discovery, is the most memorable. Night sequences were shot at a location nearby: at the original Ealing Film Studios, built for silent production by Will Barker in 1904 and long since converted into a factory.

July 1950: **BITTER SPRINGS** (89 mins)
Directed by Ralph Smart. Associate producer: Leslie Norman. Script by W.P. Lipscomb, Monja Danischewsky; story by Smart. Photographed by George Heath. Art direction by Charles Woolveridge. Music by Ralph Vaughan Williams. Edited by Bernard Gribble. With: Tommy Trinder (Tommy), Chips Rafferty (Wally King), Gordon Jackson (Mac), Jean Blue (Ma King), Charles Tingwell (John King), Nonnie Piper (Emma King),

Nicky Yardley (Charlie), Michael Pate (Trooper), Henry Murdoch (Black Jack).

Ealing's last Australian film for seven years; the trio to date form a downward progress.

Sept 1950: **CAGE OF GOLD** (83 mins)
Directed by Basil Dearden. Associate producer: Michael Relph. Script by Jack Whittingham; story by Whittingham, Paul Stein. Photographed by Douglas Slocombe. Art direction by Jim Morahan. Music by Georges Auric. Edited by Peter Tanner. With: Jean Simmons (Judith), David Farrar (Bill Brennan), James Donald (Dr Alan Kearn), Harcourt Williams (Dr Kearn Sr), Gladys Henson (Nanny), Herbert Lom (Rahman), Gregoire Aslan (Duport), Madeleine Lebeau (Madeleine), Maria Mauban (Antoinette), Bernard Lee (Inspector Gray), Martin Boddey (Adams), Campbell Singer (Constable), Arthur Howard (registry office bridegroom). Working title: *Sacrifice*.

Oct 1950: **THE MAGNET** (79 mins)
Directed by Charles Frend. Associate producer: Sidney Cole. Script by T.E.B. Clarke. Photographed by Lionel Banes. Art direction by Jim Morahan. Music by William Alwyn. Edited by Bernard Gribble. With: Stephen Murray (Dr Brent), Kay Walsh (Mrs Brent), William Fox (Johnny Brent), Meredith Edwards (Harper), Julien Mitchell (Mayor), Wylie Watson (Pickering), Joss Ambler (businessman), Gladys Henson, Thora Hird (nannies), Joan Hickson (Mrs Ward), Grace Arnold (Mrs Mercer), Harold Goodwin (pin-table man), Michael Brooke Jr (Kit), Keith Robinson (Spike), Thomas Johnson (Perce), Sam Kydd (postman), Seumas Mor na Feasag [James Robertson Justice] (tramp).

An example, like *A Run for Your Money* and the later *Barnacle Bill*, of Charles Frend's unease with comedy; but the story, an original by T.E.B. Clarke, seems unworkable from the start. The central figure is the 10-year-old son of a psychiatrist, played by William Fox, who would grow up into the James Fox of *The Servant*. The magnet is a toy at the centre of an elaborate whimsical plot which resists economical summary and does not merit a full one.

Feb 1951: **POOL OF LONDON** (85 mins)
Directed by Basil Dearden. Associate producer: Michael Relph. Script by Jack Whittingham, John Eldridge. Photographed by Gordon Dines. Art direction by Jim Morahan. Music by John Addison. Edited by Peter Tanner. With: Bonar Colleano (Dan), Earl Cameron (Johnny), Leslie Phillips (Harry), Susan Shaw (Pat), Renée Asherson (Sally), Moira Lister (Maisie), Joan Dowling (Pamela), James Robertson Justice (Trotter), Max Adrian (Vernon), Alfie Bass (Alf), Laurence Naismith (commissionaire), Beckett Bould (watchman), Victor Maddern (tram conductor).

Like *Dance Hall*, a ripe, densely packed compendium of Ealing life, from the fertile period around 1950; another examination of the interlocking destinies of a group, this time the crew of a merchant ship who come ashore for a weekend, and the people they meet in South London. If only one film could be preserved for posterity, to illustrate the essence of Ealing from the time before decadence set in, this would be a good choice, with its clear-cut embodiment of Ealing attitudes to women, violence, social responsibility, and cinematic form. The film grew out of a documentary project, and uses London locations extensively; it's one of the last films to feature a London tram-ride.

June 1951: **THE LAVENDER HILL MOB**
(78 mins)
Directed by Charles Crichton. Associate producer: Michael Truman. Script by T.E.B. Clarke. Photographed by Douglas Slocombe. Art direction by William Kellner. Music by Georges Auric. Edited by Seth Holt. With: Alec Guinness (Holland), Stanley Holloway (Pendlebury), Sidney James (Lackery), Alfie Bass (Shorty), Marjorie Fielding (Mrs Chalk), Edie Martin (Miss Evesham), Ronald Adam (bank official), Clive Morton (Police Sgt), John Gregson (Farrow), Sidney Tafler (stallholder), Patrick Barr (Inspector), Meredith Edwards (P.C. Edwards), Robert Shaw (police scientist), Michael Trubshawe (British Ambassador), Audrey Hepburn (Chiquita).

The script won an Academy award for T.E.B. Clarke.

Aug 1951: **THE MAN IN THE WHITE SUIT**
(85 mins)
Directed by Alexander Mackendrick. Associate producer: Sidney Cole. Script by Roger Macdougall, Mackendrick, John Dighton, from Macdougall's play. Photographed by Douglas Slocombe. Art direction by Jim Morahan. Music by Benjamin Frankel. Edited by Bernard Gribble. With: Alec Guinness (Sidney Stratton), Joan Greenwood (Daphne), Cecil Parker (Birnley), Michael Gough (Michael Corland), Ernest Thesiger (Sir John Kierlaw), Howard Marion Crawford (Cranford), Henry Mollison (Hoskins, head of research), Russell Waters (Davidson), Joan Harben (Miss Johnson), Vida Hope (Bertha), Patric Doonan (Frank), Duncan Lamont (Harry), Roddy Hughes and Colin Gordon (Corland accountants), Harold Goodwin (Wilkins), Judith Furse (Nurse Gamage), Miles Malleson (tailor), Edie Martin (Mrs Watson), Mandy Miller (young girl), Olaf Olsen (Knudsen, the butler), Frank Atkinson (baker), Billy Russell (night watchman), John Rudling (Wilson).

Dec 1951: **WHERE NO VULTURES FLY**
(107 mins)
Directed by Harry Watt. Associate producer: Leslie Norman. Script by W. P. Lipscomb, Ralph Smart, Leslie Norman; story by Harry Watt. Photographed by Geoffrey Unsworth, in Technicolor. Wildlife photography by Paul Beeson. Music by Alan Rawsthorne. Edited by Gordon Stone. With: Anthony Steel (Bob Payton), Dinah Sheridan (Mary Payton), William Simons (Tim Payton), Harold Warrender (Mannering), Meredith Edwards (Gwyl), Orlando Martins (M'Kwongi) Andrew Cruickshank (Governor).

An African *Overlanders*. Ealing was approached to make a film there; Watt again set out on a long research tour, and devised a story based on fact—on the life of the Kenyan conservationist Mervyn Cowie. The film achieved a comparable robust U-certificate adventure quality, and a still greater box-office success, which tempted Watt to make an anti-climactic sequel (the counterpart of *Eureka Stockade* being *West of Zanzibar*). Bob Payton establishes himself as a game warden, overcoming bureaucratic and commercial obstacles to establish a typical benevolent Ealing dispensation.

Jan 1952: **HIS EXCELLENCY** (82 mins)
Directed by Robert Hamer. Produced by Michael Truman. Script by Hamer, W.P. Lipscomb, from the play by Dorothy and Campbell Christie. Photographed by Douglas Slocombe. Art direction by Jim Morahan. Music: Handel. Edited by Seth Holt. With: Eric Portman (George Harrison), Cecil Parker (Sir James Kirkman), Helen Cherry (Lady Kirkman), Susan Stephen (Peggy Harrison), Edward Chapman (The Admiral), Clive Morton (G.O.C.), Robin Bailey (Charles), Alec Mango (Jackie), Geoffrey Keen (Morellos), John Salew (Fernando), Elspeth March (Mrs Fernando), Eric Pohlmann (Dobrieda), Paul Demel (chef), Henry Longhurst (Lord Kynaston), Howard Marion Crawford (tea shop proprietor), Barbara Leake, Barbara Cavan (tea shop ladies), Basil Dignam (security officer), Laurence Naismith, Victor Maddern (soldiers).

Portman plays a bluff Trade Union leader, sent out by Labour to govern the colony of Arista (Malta?); he comes up against stuffy protocol on the one hand, and rebellious demagogy on the other. Though the outline sounds promising, opening up political issues rarely confronted in British cinema, it's a disappointingly tame and stagebound work on which Hamer's signature remains puzzling.

Feb 1952: **SECRET PEOPLE** (96 mins)
Directed by Thorold Dickinson, Produced by Sidney Cole. Script by Dickinson and Wolfgang Wilhelm; story by Dickinson and Joyce Cary. Photographed by Gordon Dines. Art direction by William Kellner. Music by Roberto Gerhard. Edited by Peter Tanner. With: Valentina Cortese (Maria Brentano), Serge Reggiani (Louis), Audrey Hepburn (Nora), Angela Fouldes (Nora as a child), Charles Goldner (Anselmo), Megs Jenkins (Penny), Irene Worth (Miss Jackson), Reginald Tate (Inspector Eliot), Athene Seyler (Mrs Kellick), Geoffrey Hibbert (Steenie), Sydney Tafler (Syd Burnett), John Penrose (Bill), John Chandos (John),

Michael Ripper (Charlie), Bob Monkhouse (hairdresser).

An unusual project in that it came from outside Ealing altogether, Dickinson having had no link with the studio since *Next of Kin*. Lindsay Anderson's book, *Making a Film*, gives a comprehensive account of the production, and through it of the Ealing system. The film is centred on the revulsion of the heroine when she finds that her readiness to join a plot against the right-wing dictator who killed her father years ago, and who is visiting Britain, has led her into a cell of fanatics indifferent to human suffering. It was attacked on release by left-wing groups, was cut and little seen, and has since been a subject of intermittent controversy. Today it looks a tasteful, unlucky film, made a few years too late—partaking of the lack of freshness which often affects projects nursed over a period of years, and also of a particular early-'fifties limitation discussed in the main text.

Mar 1952: **I BELIEVE IN YOU** (95 mins)
Directed by Basil Dearden. Produced by Michael Relph. Script by Relph, Dearden, Jack Whittingham, from the memoir *Court Circular* by Sewell Stokes. Additional scenes by Nicholas Phipps. Photographed by Gordon Dines. Art direction by Maurice Carter. Music by Ernest Irving. Edited by Peter Tanner. With: Cecil Parker (Henry Phipps), Celia Johnson (Matty), Harry Fowler (Hooker), Joan Collins (Norma), George Relph (Mr Dove), Godfrey Tearle (Mr Pyke), Ernest Jay (Mr Quayle), Laurence Harvey (Jordie), Ursula Howells (Hon Ursula), Sidney James (Sgt Body), Katie Johnson (Miss Mackline), Ada Reeve (Mrs Crockett) Brenda de Banzie (Mrs Hooker), Alex McCrindle (Mr Haines), Fred Griffiths (Crump), Richard Hart (Eric Stevens), Gladys Henson (Mrs Stevens), Judith Furse (athletics secretary). Working title: *One Sinner*.

Cecil Parker joins the probation service in middle age. The film has a standard double format: induction of new boy, mosaic of individual stories, making up a picture of society. Raymond Durgnat in *A Mirror for England* has a pertinent and sympathetic account of the film.

July 1952: **MANDY** (93 mins)
Directed by Alexander Mackendrick. Produced by Leslie Norman. Script by Jack Whittingham, Nigel Balchin, from the novel *The Day Is Ours* by Hilda Lewis. Photographed by Douglas Slocombe. Art direction by Jim Morahan. Music by William Alwyn. Edited by Seth Holt. With: Jack Hawkins (Searle), Terence Morgan (Harry Garland), Phyllis Calvert (Christine Garland), Mandy Miller (Mandy Garland), Godfrey Tearle (Mr Garland senior), Marjorie Fielding (Mrs Garland), Nancy Price (Miss Ellis), Dorothy Alison (Miss Stockton), Patricia Plunkett (Miss Cricker), Eleanor Summerfield (Lily), Edward Chapman (Ackland) Colin Gordon (Woollard), Gabrielle Brune (secretary). U.S. title: *Crash of Silence*.

Oct 1952: **THE GENTLE GUNMAN** (86 mins)
Directed by Basil Dearden. Produced by Michael Relph. Script by Roger Macdougall, from his own play. Photographed by Gordon Dines. Art direction by Jim Morahan. Music by John Greenwood. Edited by Peter Tanner. With: John Mills (Terence Sullivan), Dirk Bogarde (Matt Sullivan), Elisabeth Sellars (Maureen Fagan), Barbara Mullen (Molly Fagan), Robert Beatty (Shinto), Eddie Byrne (Flynn), Joseph Tomelty (Dr Brannigan), Gilbert Harding (Henry Truethorne), Liam Redmond (Tom Connolly), Michael Golden (Murphy), Jack McGowran (McGuire), James Kenney (Johnny Fagan), Patric Doonan (sentry).

The film which marks the transition in Dearden's work from open to closed, live to dead: a stiff stage adaptation, with Bogarde and Mills cast unconvincingly as Irish brothers and a platitudinously worked-out anti-violence, all-men-are-brothers message. A point of interest is the rare straight role played by the 'fifties TV personality Gilbert Harding, as a crusty anti-Irish Englishman.

Mar 1953: **THE TITFIELD THUNDERBOLT** (84 mins)
Directed by Charles Crichton. Produced by Michael Truman. Script by T.E.B. Clarke. Photographed by Douglas Slocombe, in Technicolor. Art direction by C.P. Norman. Music by Georges Auric. Edited by Seth Holt. With: Stanley Holloway (Valentine), George Relph (Weech), Naunton Wayne (Blakeworth), John Gregson (Gordon), Godfrey Tearle (Bishop), Edie Martin (Emily), Hugh Griffith (Dan), Sidney James (Hawkins), Gabrielle Brune (Joan), Jack McGowran (Crump), Ewan Roberts (Pearce), Reginald Beckwith (Coggett), Michael Trubshawe (Ruddock), John Rudling (inspector from Ministry), Frank Atkinson (Police Sgt).

Mar 1953: **THE CRUEL SEA** (126 mins)
Directed by Charles Frend. Produced by Leslie Norman. Script by Eric Ambler, from the novel by Nicholas Monsarrat. Photographed by Gordon Dines. Art direction by Jim Morahan. Music by Alan Rawsthorne. Edited by Peter Tanner. With: Jack Hawkins (Ericson), Donald Sinden (Lockhart), Denholm Elliott (Morell), John Stratton (Ferraby), Stanley Baker (Bennett), Virginia McKenna (Julie Hallam), Moira Lister (Elaine Morell), June Thorburn (Doris Ferraby), Liam Redmond (Jim Watts), Bruce Seton (Bob Tallow), Megs Jenkins (Glad Tallow), Meredith Edwards (Wells), John Warner (Baker), Glyn Houston (Phillips), Alec McCowen (Tonbridge), Andrew Cruickshank (doctor), Walter Fitzgerald (warden).

Jack Hawkins becomes Ealing's dominant hero in the last few years of its existence. One can trace the succession over 20 years: John Clements, Ralph Michael, Jack Warner, Stanley Holloway, Alec Guinness, Hawkins. It makes a nice symmetrical pattern, coming back to a strong officer-class figure (both Michael and Guinness being, in their different styles, self-effacing and relatively classless). Where Hawkins differs from Clements is in standing for the principle of meritocracy.

Though *The Cruel Sea*, a critical and commercial success, appears very different from its Ealing contemporary *The Titfield Thunderbolt*, it seems to me complementary: the sheer fuss it makes over even the unremarkable acts of professionalism of its Captain implies the easy-going amateurism we see elsewhere to be an inevitable (postwar) norm.

July 1953: **THE SQUARE RING** (83 mins)
Directed by Basil Dearden. Produced by Michael Relph. Script by Robert Westerby, from the play by Ralph W. Peterson. Additional dialogue by Peter Myers and Alec Grahame. Photographed by Otto Heller. Art direction by Jim Morahan. Edited by Peter Bezencenet. With: Jack Warner (Danny Felton), Robert Beatty (Kid Curtis), Bill Owen (Happy Burns), Maxwell Reed (Rick Martell), George Rose (Whitey Johnson), Bill Travers (Rowdie Rawlings), Alfie Bass (Frank Forbes), Ronald Lewis (Eddie Lloyd), Sidney James (Adams), Joan Collins (Frankie), Bernadette O'Farrell (Peg Curtis), Kay Kendall (Eve Lewis), Eddie Byrne (Lou Lewis), Joan Sims (Bunty), Sidney Tafler, Alexander Gauge (wiseacres), Ben Williams (Mr Lloyd), Madoline Thomas (Mrs Lloyd), Harry Herbert (de Grazos), C.M. Nichols (timekeeper).

The night's action at a professional boxing promotion; the dramatic unities are closely adhered to. One can see why Ealing snapped up the rights to this play, and why it was Dearden who filmed it: it offers a neat cross-section of boxers, from starry-eyed novice to punch-drunk veteran, and an unflattering picture of commercial exploitation. Five out of the six boxers we are involved with win, though the last one, Robert Beatty, dies after doing so. Jack Warner runs the dressing-room.

Nov 1953: **MEET MR LUCIFER** (83 mins)
Directed by Anthony Pelissier. Produced by Monja Danischewsky. Script by Danischewsky, from the play *Beggar My Neighbour* by Arnold Ridley; additional dialogue by Peter Myers, Alec Grahame. Photographed by Desmond Dickinson. Art direction by Wilfrid Shingleton. Music by Eric Rogers. Edited by Bernard Gribble. With: Stanley Holloway (Sam Hollingsworth), Peggy Cummins (Kitty Norton), Jack Watling (Jim Norton), Barbara Murray (Patricia Pedelty), Joseph Tomelty (Mr Pedelty), Gordon Jackson (Hector McPhee), Jean Cadell (Mrs Macdonald), Kay Kendall (Lonely Hearts singer), Charles Victor (Mr Elder), Humphrey Lestocq (Arthur), Raymond Huntley (Mr Patterson), Ernest Thesiger (Mr Macdonald), Frank Pettingell (Mr Roberts), Olive Sloane (Mrs Stannard), Joan Sims (Fairy Queen), Ian Carmichael (Man Friday), Geoffrey Keen (voice of Mr Lucifer), Gladys Henson (lady in bus), Edie Martin (deaf lady), Dandy Nichols (Mrs Clarke), Roddy Hughes (Billings), and TV personalities:

Gilbert Harding, Philip Harben, Macdonald Hobley, David Miller.

Stanley Holloway, playing the Demon King in an unsuccessful pantomime, indulges his grievance against television by 'dreaming' a fantasy in which it makes people unhappy. Pelissier, whose previous films include two substantial literary adaptations in *The History of Mr Polly* and *The Rocking-Horse Winner*, was evidently brought in from outside Ealing because none of the staff directors was keen to make the film, to which the studio had committed itself: in the light of the finished product, this reluctance is understandable. It does, however, preserve a valuable record of certain TV acts, and of attitudes to the medium in this crucial period just before ITV arrived. This aspect of the film is analysed in detail in my essay on 'Broadcasting and Cinema: Screens within Screens', in *All Our Yesterdays* (1986, *see* Bibliography).

Jan 1954: **THE LOVE LOTTERY** (89 mins)
Directed by Charles Crichton. Produced by Monja Danischewsky. Script by Harry Kurnitz; story by Charles Neilson-Terry and Zelma Bramley Moore; additional scenes and dialogue by Danischewsky. Photographed by Douglas Slocombe, in Technicolor. Art direction by Tom Morahan. Music by Benjamin Frankel. Edited by Seth Holt. With: David Niven (Rex Allerton), Peggy Cummins (Sally), Anne Vernon (Jane), Herbert Lom (Amico), Gordon Jackson (Ralph), Charles Victor (Jennings), Felix Aylmer (Winant), Theodore Bikel (Parsimonious), Hattie Jacques (chambermaid), John Chandos (Chinaman), Humphrey Bogart (himself).

A good quiz question: in what Ealing film does Humphrey Bogart appear? Answer, this second successive still-born comedy about the media. David Niven plays a film star whose company is the prize in a competition run by a comic/sinister international organisation; when he and the hero-worshipping winner have duly returned to their first loves, a final gag shows the head of the firm soliciting the co-operation of another film-star—Bogart.

Feb 1954: **THE MAGGIE** (92 mins)
Directed by Alexander Mackendrick. Produced by Michael Truman. Script by William Rose. Photographed by Gordon Dines. Art direction by Jim Morahan. Music by John Addison. Edited by Peter Tanner. With: Paul Douglas (Calvin B. Marshall), Alex Mackenzie (Mactaggart), Tommy Kearins (Dougie), James Copeland (Mate), Abe Barker (Engineer), Hubert Gregg (Pusey), Dorothy Alison (Miss Peters), Andrew Keir (reporter), Geoffrey Keen (Campbell), Mark Dignam (the Laird), Jameson Clark (publican), Moultrie Kelsall (Captain), Meg Buchanan (Sarah), Fiona Clyne (Sheena). US title: *High and Dry*.

Mar 1954: **WEST OF ZANZIBAR** (94 mins)
Directed by Harry Watt. Produced by Leslie
Norman. Script by Jack Whittingham, Max Catto;
story by Harry Watt. Photographed by Paul Beeson,
in Technicolor. Art direction by Jim Morahan.
Music by Alan Rawsthorne. Edited by Peter
Bezencenet. With: Anthony Steel (Bob Payton),
Sheila Sim (Mary Payton), William Simons (Tim
Payton), Orlando Martins (M'Kwongi), Edric
Connor (Ushingo), Martin Benson (Dhofar), Peter
Illing (Khingoni), Juma (Juma), Howard Marion
Crawford (Wood), Alan Webb (senior official).

This sequel to *Where No Vultures Fly* is much less
'open', technically and thematically. The back-
projection devices are obtrusive, and Watt's amaze-
ment when the Kenyan government banned the film
was surely ingenuous: it takes the Africans' side
against exploitation, as he insists, but in a deeply
paternalist way. This is another film on which
Durgnat in *A Mirror for England* has some useful
remarks.

May 1954: **THE RAINBOW JACKET** (99 mins)
Directed by Basil Dearden. Produced by Michael
Relph. Script by T.E.B. Clarke. Photographed by
Otto Heller, in Technicolor. Art direction by Tom
Morahan. Music by William Alwyn. Edited by Jack
Harris. With: Bill Owen (Sam), Kay Walsh (Barbara
Crain), Fella Edmonds (Georgie Crain), Edward
Underdown (Geoffrey Tyler), Honor Blackman
(Mrs Tyler), Robert Morley (Lord Logan), Wilfrid
Hyde White (Lord Stoneleigh), Charles Victor (Mr
Boss), Frederick Piper (Lukey), Howard Marion
Crawford (Travers), Sidney James (Harry), Michael
Trubshawe (Gresham), Gordon Richards (jockey).

Two real-life stars of the racing world are used:
Raymond Glendenning as a commentator, and
Gordon Richards as a jockey. The latter is wasted,
however, by so clearly doing his riding in the studio.

Oct 1954: **LEASE OF LIFE** (94 mins)
Directed by Charles Frend. Associate producer: Jack
Rix. Script by Eric Ambler; story by Frank Baker,
Patrick Jenkins. Photographed by Douglas
Slocombe, in Eastmancolor. Art direction by Jim
Morahan. Music by Alan Rawsthorne. Edited by
Peter Tanner. With: Robert Donat (Rev William
Thorne), Kay Walsh (Mrs Thorne), Adrienne Corri
(Susan Thorne), Denholm Elliott (Martin Blake),
Walker Fitzgerald (Dean), Cyril Raymond
(headmaster), Reginald Beckwith (journalist),
Richard Wattis (solicitor), Frank Atkinson (verger),
Frederick Piper (jeweller), Alan Webb (Dr
Pembury), Beckett Bould (Mr Sproatley), Vida
Hope (Mrs Sproatley), John Salew (their doctor),
Richard Leech (Carter), Jean Anderson (Miss
Calthorp), Edie Martin (her friend), Russell Waters
(Russell), Robert Sandford (boy with book).

This story of an 'undistinguished country parson',
who learns he has a fatal illness, is to me Frend's
most impressive post-war film, his forte being certainly

not comedy, not spectacular heroism, but the charting
of modest, dutiful work. The film's attitude to authority is unusual for late Ealing. Thorne consciously
offends both the local headmaster and his bishop, and
thus sacrifices a promotion that is virtually settled,
by preaching a sermon that ridicules the idea of a
'headmaster God'.

Nov 1954: **THE DIVIDED HEART** (89 mins)
Directed by Charles Crichton. Produced by Michael
Truman. Script by Jack Whittingham, with Richard
Hughes. Photographed by Otto Heller. Art direction
by Edward Carrick. Music by Georges Auric. Edited
by Peter Bezencenet. With: Cornell Borchers (Inga),
Yvonne Mitchell (Sonja), Armin Dahlen (Franz),
Michel Ray (Toni), Alexander Knox (Chief Justice),
Liam Redmond (1st Justice), Eddie Byrne (2nd
Justice), Geoffrey Keen (Marks), Theodore Bikel
(Josip), Ferdy Mayne (Dr Muller), Martin Stephens
(Hans), John Welsh (Chief Marshal), John
Schlesinger (ticket collector), Alec McCowen
(reporter).

Germany 1952—then flashbacks, mainly to wartime
Yugoslavia. A child smuggled out for safety, and
adopted by a German couple, is reclaimed by his
Yugoslav mother, a survivor of Auschwitz: the film
deals with the tug-of-love between two equally
deserving mothers, and with its eventual resolution
by the judges of the U.S. Control Commission in
Germany, in favour of the Yugoslav. On the film, the
verdict has to be: worthy but tame—sober, academic,
actressy, afraid of getting into any deep emotional
water. Balcon's own involvement with the project
was close. 'Again we based our film on an actual
story taken from the newspapers. Part of its appeal
for me was that it was about the mother-child
relationship, a theme close to my heart and which, I
recognise, was a recurring one in Ealing films' (from
A Lifetime of Films).

Feb 1955: **OUT OF THE CLOUDS** (88 mins)
Directed by Basil Dearden. Produced by Michael
Relph. Script by Relph, Michael Eldridge.
Photographed by Paul Beeson, in Eastmancolor. Art
direction by Jim Morahan. Music by Richard
Addinsell. Edited by Jack Harris. With: Anthony
Steel (Gus Randall), Robert Beatty (Nick
Milbourne), David Knight (Bill), Margo Lorenz
(Leah), James Robertson Justice (Brent), Eunice
Gayson (Penny), Isabel Dean (Mrs Malcolm),
Marie Lohr (rich passenger), Esma Cannon (her
companion), Bernard Lee (customs officer),
Gordon Harker (taxi driver), Abraham Sofaer
(Indian), Megs Jenkins (landlady), Melissa Stribling
(Jean), Sidney James (gambler), Nicholas Phipps
(Foreign Office man), Jill Melford (Eleanor), Arthur
Howard (booking clerk), Cyril Luckham (doctor),
Jack Lambert (designer), Katie Johnson (passenger).

The Relph/Dearden 'omnibus' formula progressively
seizes up, the little human dramas becoming more
schematic and the containing authority structure
more rigid, as in this drama of airline pilots and

passengers, their work, love-life and peccadilloes. Like *Meet Mr Lucifer*, though, this film has acquired value as a period piece, presenting a Heathrow where each flight is still an event and each traveller gets personal attention. It gives Katie Johnson her last pre-*Ladykillers* role as a nervous passenger insisting 'But I always sit with my back to the engine.'

Mar 1955: **THE NIGHT MY NUMBER CAME UP** (94 mins)
Directed by Leslie Norman. Associate producer: Tom Morahan. Script by R.C. Sherriff; story by Air Marshal Sir Victor Goddard. Photographed by Lionel Banes. Art direction by Jim Morahan. Music by Malcolm Arnold. Edited by Peter Tanner. With: Michael Redgrave (Air Marshal Hardie), Sheila Sim (Mary Campbell), Alexander Knox (Robertson), Ursula Jeans (Mrs Robertson), Denholm Elliott (Mackenzie), Ralph Truman (Lord Wainwright), Michael Hordern (Commander Lindsay), Nigel Stock (pilot), George Rose (businessman), Bill Kerr, Alfie Bass (soldiers), Victor Maddern (steward), Stratford Johns (sergeant).

Air travel again, in the Far East: a story in the *Dead of Night* tradition about a dream—a plane crashing—which gradually starts to become true in all its details. This framework, with panic and the irrational disrupting the profound complacencies of a set of British brass-hats and camp-followers, has fine possibilities, but the film itself (Leslie Norman's first as director) is so much at one with the group's own ethos that this dimension is stifled.

Apr 1955: **THE SHIP THAT DIED OF SHAME** (95 mins)
Directed by Basil Dearden. Produced by Michael Relph. Script by John Whiting, Relph, Dearden, from the novel by Nicholas Monsarrat. Photographed by Gordon Dines. Art direction by Bernard Robinson. Music by William Alwyn. Edited by Peter Bezencenet. With: Richard Attenborough (George Hoskins), George Baker (Bill Randall), Bill Owen (Birdie), Virginia McKenna (Helen), Roland Culver (Fordyce), Ralph Truman (Sir Richard), Bernard Lee, Harold Goodwin (customs officers), John Chandos (Raines), John Longden (detective), David Langton (man in bar), Stratford Johns (garage worker).

The George Baker character starts his voice-over introduction: 'The beginning, like everything about me, went back to the war,' and the film continues to work over characteristic Ealing materials. For the main trio, everything is anti-climax: after their intense naval experiences: they drift back together, buy up their old wartime boat, and use it for smuggling trips and worse, before eventually having to come to their senses.

Sept 1955: **TOUCH AND GO** (85 mins)
Directed by Michael Truman. Associate producer: Seth Holt. Script by William Rose; story by William

and Tania Rose. Photographed by Douglas Slocombe, in Technicolor. Art direction by Edward Carrick. Music by John Addison. Edited by Peter Tanner. With: Jack Hawkins (Jim Fletcher), Margaret Johnston (Helen Fletcher), June Thorburn (Peggy Fletcher), John Fraser (Richard Kenyon), Roland Culver (Reg Fairbright), Alison Leggatt (Alice Fairbright), Henry Longhurst (Mr Pritchett), Margaret Halstan (Mrs Pritchett), James Hayter (Kimball), Basil Dignam (Stevens), Bessie Love (Mrs Baxter), Gabrielle Brune (waitress), Heather Sears (student), Margaret Courtenay (Kimball's secretary).

Dec 1955: **THE LADYKILLERS** (97 mins)
Directed by Alexander Mackendrick. Associate producer: Seth Holt. Script by William Rose. Photographed by Otto Heller, in Technicolor. Art direction by Jim Morahan. Music by Tristram Cary. Edited by Jack Harris. With: Katie Johnson (Louisa Wilberforce), Alec Guinness (Professor Marcus), Cecil Parker (Major Courtney), Herbert Lom (Louis—Mr Harvey), Peter Sellers (Harry—Mr Robinson), Danny Green (One-Round—Mr Lawson), Jack Warner (Police Superintendent), Philip Stainton (Police Sgt), Ewan Roberts (Constable), Frankie Howerd (barrow boy), Kenneth Connor (taxi driver), Fred Griffiths (junk man), Harold Goodwin (parcels clerk), Stratford Johns (security guard), Edie Martin (Lettice), Helen Burls (Hypatia), Evelyn Kerry (Amelia), Phoebe Hodgson (4th guest), Leonard Sharp (pavement artist).

Mar 1956: **THE FEMININE TOUCH** (91 mins)
Directed by Pat Jackson. Associate producer: Jack Rix. Script (uncredited) from the novel *A Lamp Is Heavy* by Sheila Mackay Russell. Photographed by Paul Beeson, in Eastmancolor. Art direction by Edward Carrick. Music by Clifton Parker. Edited by Peter Bezencenet. With: George Baker (Dr Jim Alcott), Belinda Lee (Susan Richards), Delphi Lawrence (Pat Martin), Adrienne Corri (Maureen O'Brien), Henryetta Edwards (Ann Bowland), Barbara Archer (Liz Jenkins), Diana Wynyard (Matron), Christopher Rhodes (Dr Ted Russell), Joan Haythorne (Home Sister), Beatrice Varley (Sister Snow), Richard Leech (casualty doctor), Dandy Nichols (Skivvy), Newton Blick (porter). Mandy Miller (Jessie), Dorothy Alison (the suicide), Joss Ambler (Bateman).

Mar 1956: **WHO DONE IT?** (85 mins)
Directed by Basil Dearden. Produced by Michael Relph. Script by T.E.B. Clarke. Photographed by Otto Heller. Art direction by Jim Morahan. Music by Philip Green. Edited by Peter Tanner. With: Benny Hill (Hugo Dill), Belinda Lee (Frankie Mayne), David Kossoff (Zacco), Garry Marsh (Hancock), George Margo (Barakov), Ernest Thesiger (Sir Walter), Thorley Walters (Raymond Courtney), Nicholas Phipps, Gibb McLaughlin (scientists), Charles Hawtrey (disc jockey), Stratford Johns (policeman).

The last comedy made at Ealing, a dull slapstick vehicle for Benny Hill; the casting of Garry Marsh reinforces the sense of a 20-year throwback to the Formby days.

June 1956: **THE LONG ARM** (96 mins)

Directed by Charles Frend. Associate producer: Tom Morahan. Script by Janet Green, Robert Barr; story by Barr. Additional dialogue by Dorothy and Campbell Christie. Photographed by Gordon Dines. Art direction by Edward Carrick. Music by Gerbrand Schurmann. Edited by Gordon Stone. With: Jack Hawkins (Supt Tom Halliday), Dorothy Alison (Mary Halliday), Michael Brooke Jr (Tony Halliday), John Stratton (Sgt Ward), Geoffrey Keen (Supt Malcolm), Newton Blick (Cdr Harris), Ralph Truman (Col Blenkinsop), Joss Ambler (shipping office cashier), Sydney Tafler (Stone), Richard Leech (night watchman), Meredith Edwards (Thomas), Ian Bannen (workman), Maureen Davis (his wife), George Rose (informer), Glyn Houston (Sgt), Nicholas Parsons (P.C. Bates), Alec McCowen (Surgeon), Ursula Howells (Mrs Elliot), John Welsh (estate agent), Gillian Webb (housewife), Maureen Delaney (daily help), Harry Locke (second-hand dealer), William Mervyn (Festival Hall manager), Harold Goodwin (Somerset House official), Sam Kydd, Stratford Johns (constables).

This efficient police film has brought Ealing a long way from Dixon and Paddington Green. Hawkins travels by car beween Scotland Yard and his semi-detached house in a bleak middle-class road in Bromley, where his wife is lonely but cheerful and they worry about their son's schooling. The society he explores in his work is correspondingly fragmented.

Jan 1957: **MAN IN THE SKY** (87 mins)

Directed by Charles Crichton. Associate producer: Seth Holt. Script by William Rose, John Eldridge; story by Rose. Photographed by Douglas Slocombe. Art direction by Jim Morahan. Music by Gerbrand Schurmann. Edited by Peter Tanner. With: Jack Hawkins (John Mitchell), Elisabeth Sellars (Mary Mitchell), Catherine Lacey (her mother), Jeremy Bodkin (Nicholas Mitchell), Gerard Lohan (Philip Mitchell), John Stratton (Peter Hook), Walter Fitzgerald (Conway), Eddie Byrne (Ashmore), Donald Pleasence (Crabtree), Victor Maddern (Joe Biggs), Lionel Jeffries (Keith), Ernest Clark (Maine), Russell Waters (Sim), Howard Marion Crawford (Ingram), Megs Jenkins (Mrs Ingram).

Jack Hawkins as a test pilot for a small company, who decides to try to save the company by landing its damaged prototype rather than baling out as instructed. The film is close to *The Long Arm* in the way it uses Hawkins, both in his embarrassed heroism at work and in the middle-class agonising of the domestic scenes (this time, he and his wife are preoccupied with buying a larger house).

July 1957: **THE SHIRALEE** (99 mins)

Directed by Leslie Norman. Produced by Jack Rix. Script by Norman, Neil Paterson, from the novel by Darcy Niland. Photographed by Paul Beeson. Art direction by Jim Morahan. Music by John Addison. Edited by Gordon Stone. With: Peter Finch (Jim Macauley), Elisabeth Sellars (Marge Macauley), Dana Wilson (Buster Macauley), Rosemary Harris (Lily Parker), Russell Napier (Mr Parker), George Rose (Donny), Niall McGinnis (Beauty Kelly), Tessie O'Shea (Bella), Sidney James (Luke), Charles Tingwell (Jim Muldoon), Reg Lye (Desmond), Barbara Archer (shopgirl), Alec Mango (Papadoulos), John Phillips (doctor).

Leslie Norman had worked on Ealing's first three Australian films, before directing this fourth one. Finch plays a swagman whose marriage breaks up and who then roams the outback with his young daughter, Buster. The supporting cast has more of an imported feeling than on previous occasions, but this is certainly, after *Nowhere to Go*, the most vigorous of Ealing's MGM sextet.

Dec 1957: **BARNACLE BILL** (87 mins)

Directed by Charles Frend. Associate producer: Dennis van Thal. Script by T.E.B. Clarke. Photographed by Douglas Slocombe. Art direction by Alan Withy. Music by John Addison. Edited by Jack Harris. With: Alec Guinness (William Horatio Ambrose/six ancestors), Irene Browne (Arabella Barrington), Maurice Denham (Mayor), Victor Maddern (Figg), Percy Herbert (Tommy), George Rose (Bullen), Lionel Jeffries (Garrod), Harold Goodwin (Duckworth), Warren Mitchell (pier entertainer), Miles Malleson (angler), Frederick Piper (Harry), Richard Wattis (Registrar of shipping), Eric Pohlmann (Liberama consul), Jackie Collins (June), Donald Churchill (Teddy boy), Donald Pleasence (bank teller), Allan Cuthbertson (councillor).

Dec 1957: **DAVY** (83 mins)

Directed by Michael Relph. Produced by Basil Dearden. Written by William Rose. Photographed by Douglas Slocombe, in Technirama and Technicolor. Art direction by Alan Withy. Music: Wagner, Puccini, Mozart, played by the orchestra of the Royal Opera House, Covent Garden. Edited by Peter Tanner. With: Harry Secombe (Davy), Ron Randell (George), George Relph (Uncle Pat), Susan Shaw (Gwen), Bill Owen (Eric), Peter Frampton (Tim), Alexander Knox (Sir Giles), Adele Leigh (Joanna), Isabel Dean (Miss Carstairs), Gladys Henson, Joan Sims, Elisabeth Fraser (tea ladies), Kenneth Connor (Herbie), Campbell Singer (doorkeeper), Bernard Cribbins (A.S.M.).

Mar 1958: **DUNKIRK** (134 mins)

Directed by Leslie Norman. Associate producer: Michael Forlong. Script by W.P. Lipscomb, David Divine, from *Dunkirk* by Ewen Butler and J.S. Bradford, and from the novel *The Big Pickup* by

Elleston Trevor. Photographed by Paul Beeson. Art direction by Jim Morahan. Music by Malcolm Arnold. Edited by Gordon Stone. With: John Mills (Cpl Binns), Bernard Lee (Charles Foreman), Maxine Audley (Diana Foreman), Richard Attenborough (John Holden), Patricia Plunkett (Grace Holden), Anthony Nicholls (military spokesman), Cyril Raymond (General Viscount Gort V.C.), Robert Urquhart (Mike), Ray Jackson (Barlow), Ronald Hines (Miles), Sean Barrett (Frankie), Roland Curram (Harper), Meredith Edwards (Dave Bellman), Kenneth Cope (Lt Lumpkin), Michael Gwynn (Sheerness commander), Joss Ambler, Frederick Piper (small-boat owners), William Squire (Captain), Lionel Jeffries (Medical Colonel), Harry Landis (Dr Levy), Victor Maddern (Seaman), Bud Flanagan and Chesney Allen (themselves).

Part of the pathos of this film as a final Ealing testament lies in the casting of old faithfuls: Joss Ambler and Frederick Piper, uncredited, in tiny parts as boat-owning volunteers, and Patricia Plunkett (of *It Always Rains On Sunday*) as a whiningly resentful wife.

Dec 1958: **NOWHERE TO GO** (97 mins)
Directed by Seth Holt. Associate producer: Eric Williams. Script by Holt, Kenneth Tynan, from the novel by Donald Mackenzie. Photographed by Paul Beeson. Art direction by Alan Withy. Music by Dizzy Reece. Edited by Harry Aldous. With: George Nader (Paul Gregory), Maggie Smith (Bridget Howard), Bernard Lee (Vic Sloane), Geoffrey Keen (Inspector Scott), Bessie Love (Harriet P. Jefferson), Andrée Melly (Rosa), Howard Marion Crawford (Cameron), John Welsh, Arthur Howard (Dodds & Dodds, coin specialists), Lionel Jeffries (pet shop man), Harry H. Corbett (Sullivan), Harry Locke (Bendel), Noel Howlett (Mr Howard), Oliver Johnston (strongroom official), Beckett Bould (gamekeeper).

Aug 1959: **THE SIEGE OF PINCHGUT** (100 mins)
Directed by Harry Watt. Produced by Eric Williams. Script by Watt, Jon Cleary; story by Inman Hunter, Lee Robinson; additional dialogue by Alexander Baron. Photographed by Gordon Dines. Art direction by Alan Withy. Music by Kenneth V. Jones. Edited by Gordon Stone. With: Aldo Ray (Matt Kirk), Neil McCallum (Johnny Kirk), Heather Sears (Ann Fulton), Victor Maddern (Bert), Carlo Justini (Luke), Gerry Duggan (Pat Fulton), Barbara Mullen (Mrs Fulton), Alan Tilvern (Superintendent Hanna), Kenneth J. Warren (Commissioner), Richard Vernon (Under-secretary), Martin Boddey (Brigadier), Grant Taylor (Macey).

The last Ealing film, the only one to be released by the Associated British Picture Corporation after the six-film agreement with M.G.M. came to an end. There was some talk of production continuing when A.B.P.C. bought up the Ealing assets, but this never happened. For *Pinchgut*, Watt had returned to Australia for a thriller set in Sydney. Aldo Ray plays a convict who escapes, determined to establish his innocence; he and his brother hole up on an island in the harbour, with enough bargaining power to put pressure on the authorities. The movement of the film is of Ray being pushed, hard, from a strong non-violent stance towards violence, thereby earning a reflex response of shock and horror from the authorities and then from his brother, who betrays him to them. As with other honourable Ealing films that recoil from violence (*Secret People*), it's hard to express criticism in summary terms without appearing callously pro-violence; but I feel confident in saying that *Pinchgut*'s attitude to its violence is very confused, and that the confusion is typical of the weak side of 'fifties Ealing. The film gives to its police and politicians a moral endorsement which they have not earned. Appropriately, the final image of any Ealing film is of a return to security and the embrace of the law: the brother and the family held as hostages sit together in the launch taking them back from the island to the city community.

CHRONOLOGICAL CHARTS

In the charts on the following two spreads, the film titles are listed in chronological order of their release. The first chart gives the initials of the directors. Each director is given a separate column (except for the last column, as noted below). This makes it easy to read off the set of films made by each individual, and it brings out in diagrammatic form certain overall patterns and continuities in Ealing production, as discussed in the text.

The directors are listed below in order of their first directing credit, together with the years of their first and last films, span of years as an Ealing director, and total number of films (including any co-director credits).

		first	last	years	films
WF	Walter Forde	1938	1940	3	6
RS	Robert Stevenson	1938	1940	3	3
AK	Anthony Kimmins	1939	1939	1	2
PT	Penrose Tennyson	1939	1940	2	3
MV	Marcel Varnel	1940	1941	2	3
SN	Sergei Nolbandov	1941	1943	3	2
BD	Basil Dearden	1942	1956	15	21
CF	Charles Frend	1942	1957	16	12
TD	Thorold Dickinson	1942	1952	11	2
AC	Alberto Cavalcanti	1942	1947	6	4
HW	Harry Watt	1943	1959	17	7
CC	Charles Crichton	1944	1957	14	13
RH	Robert Hamer	1945	1952	8	5
AMc	Alexander Mackendrick	1949	1955	7	5
LN	Leslie Norman	1955	1958	4	3

The final column lists directors who made one film at Ealing:

JPC	John Paddy Carstairs	1940
HC	Henry Cornelius	1949
SC	Sidney Cole	1949
RSm	Ralph Smart	1950
AP	Anthony Pelissier	1953
MT	Michael Truman	1955
PJ	Pat Jackson	1956
MR	Michael Relph	1957
SH	Seth Holt	1958

Although the span-of-years column is only a rough figure, and is misleading in the case of people who left Ealing and then returned (Hamer, Watt and, especially, Dickinson), it does, like the chart on the next spread, demonstrate how, after the initial few years, a long-term group of directors took over. Moreover, many of them—including some of the one-off directors—had already worked for years at Ealing in other capacities. Fuller career details are given in the next section, Biographies.

Abbreviations in the chart for writers on pp.212-213 are given on p.214.

EALING DIRECTORS

*= comedy

DATE	TITLE	DIRECTOR (see previous page for abbreviations)					
1938	The Gaunt Stranger	WF					
	The Ware Case	RS					
1939	* Let's Be Famous	WF					
	* Trouble Brewing		AK				
	The Four Just Men	WF					
	There Ain't No Justice			PT			
	Young Man's Fancy	RS					
	* Cheer Boys Cheer	WF					
	* Come On George		AK				
1940	Return to Yesterday	RS					
	The Proud Valley			PT			
	* Let George Do It				MV		
	Convoy			PT			
	Saloon Bar	WF					
	* Sailors Three	WF					
	* Spare a Copper						JPC
1941	* The Ghost of St Michael's				MV		
	* Turned Out Nice Again				MV		
	Ships with Wings				SN		
1942	* The Black Sheep of Whitehall					BD	
	The Big Blockade					CF	
	The Foreman Went to France					CF	
	The Next of Kin						TD
	* The Goose Steps Out					BD	
	Went the Day Well?						AC
1943	Nine Men						HW
	The Bells Go Down					BD	
	Undercover				SN		
	* My Learned Friend					BD	
	San Demetrio London					CF	
1944	Halfway House					BD	
	For Those in Peril						CC
	They Came to a City					BD	
	Champagne Charlie						AC
	* Fiddlers Three						HW
1945	Johnny Frenchman					CF	
	Painted Boats						CC
	Dead of Night					BD	AC CC RH
	Pink String and Sealing Wax						RH
1946	The Captive Heart					BD	
	The Overlanders						HW
1947	* Hue and Cry						CC
	Nicholas Nickleby						AC
	The Loves of Joanna Godden					CF	
	Frieda					BD	
	It Always Rains on Sunday						RH

DATE	TITLE									DIRECTOR
1948	Against the Wind					CC				
	Saraband for Dead Lovers	BD								
	* Another Shore					CC				
	Scott of the Antarctic		CF							
1949	Eureka Stockade				HW					
	* Passport to Pimlico									HC
	* Whisky Galore							AMc		
	* Kind Hearts and Coronets						RH			
	Train of Events	BD				CC				SC
	* A Run for Your Money		CF							
1950	The Blue Lamp	BD								
	Dance Hall					CC				
	Bitter Springs									RSm
	Cage of Gold	BD								
	* The Magnet		CF							
1951	Pool of London	BD								
	* The Lavender Hill Mob					CC				
	* The Man in the White Suit							AMc		
	Where No Vultures Fly				HW					
1952	His Excellency						RH			
	Secret People			TD						
	I Believe in You	BD								
	Mandy							AMc		
	The Gentle Gunman	BD								
1953	* The Titfield Thunderbolt					CC				
	The Cruel Sea		CF							
	The Square Ring	BD								
	* Meet Mr Lucifer									AP
1954	* The Love Lottery					CC				
	* The Maggie							AMc		
	West of Zanzibar				HW					
	The Rainbow Jacket	BD								
	Lease of Life		CF							
	The Divided Heart					CC				
1955	Out of the Clouds	BD								
	The Night my Number Came up								LN	
	The Ship that Died of Shame	BD								
	* Touch and Go									MT
	* The Ladykillers							AMc		
1956	The Feminine Touch									PJ
	* Who Done It?	BD								
	The Long Arm		CF							
1957	Man in the Sky					CC				
	The Shiralee								LN	
	* Barnacle Bill		CF							
	Davy									MR
1958	Dunkirk								LN	
	Nowhere to Go									SH
1959	The Siege of Pinchgut				HW					

EALING WRITERS

*= comedy

DATE	TITLE	RP	RMc	AMp	JD	AMf	DM	MD	TEBC
1938	The Gaunt Stranger								
	The Ware Case	RP							
1939	* Let's Be Famous		RMc						
	* Trouble Brewing			AMp					
	The Four Just Men	RP		AMp					
	There Ain't No Justice								
	Young Man's Fancy	RP							
	* Cheer Boys Cheer		RMc						
	* Come On George								
1940	Return to Yesterday	RP		AMp					
	The Proud Valley								
	* Let George Do It			AMp	JD	AMf			
	Convoy								
	Saloon Bar			AMp	JD				
	* Sailors Three			AMp	JD	AMf			
	* Spare a Copper		RMc			AMf			
1941	* The Ghost of St Michael's			AMp	JD				
	* Turned Out Nice Again				JD	AMf			
	Ships with Wings					AMf	DM		
1942	* The Black Sheep of Whitehall			AMp	JD				
	The Big Blockade			AMp					
	The Foreman Went to France			AMp	JD				
	The Next of Kin			AMp	JD				
	* The Goose Steps Out			AMp	JD				
	Went the Day Well?			AMp	JD		DM		
1943	Nine Men								
	The Bells Go Down		RMc						
	Undercover				JD			MD	
	* My Learned Friend			AMp	JD				
	San Demetrio London								
1944	Halfway House	RP		AMp			DM		TEBC
	For Those in Peril								TEBC
	They Came to a City								
	Champagne Charlie			AMp	JD	AMf			
	* Fiddlers Three						DM		
1945	Johnny Frenchman								TEBC
	Painted Boats								
	Dead of Night			AMp					TEBC
	Pink String and Sealing Wax	(RP)					DM		
1946	The Captive Heart			AMp					
	The Overlanders								
1947	* Hue and Cry								TEBC
	Nicholas Nickleby				JD				
	The Loves of Joanna Godden			AMp					
	Frieda			AMp					
	It Always Rains on Sunday			AMp					

DATE	TITLE	WRITER					
1948	Against the Wind				TEBC		
	Saraband for Dead Lovers	JD					
	* Another Shore						
	Scott of the Antarctic						
1949	Eureka Stockade						
	* Passport to Pimlico				TEBC		
	* Whisky Galore	AMp					
	* Kind Hearts and Coronets		JD				
	Train of Events	AMp			TEBC		
	* A Run for Your Money						
1950	The Blue Lamp				TEBC		
	Dance Hall			DM			
	Bitter Springs				MD	WL	
	Cage of Gold						JW
	* The Magnet				TEBC		
1951	Pool of London						JW
	* The Lavender Hill Mob				TEBC		
	* The Man in the White Suit	RMc	JD				
	Where No Vultures Fly					WL	
1952	His Excellency					WL	
	Secret People						
	I Believe in You						JW
	Mandy						JW
	The Gentle Gunman	RMc					
1953	* The Titfield Thunderbolt				TEBC		
	The Cruel Sea						
	The Square Ring						
	* Meet Mr Lucifer			DM			
1954	* The Love Lottery			DM			
	* The Maggie						WR
	West of Zanzibar					JW	
	The Rainbow Jacket				TEBC		
	Lease of Life						
	The Divided Heart						JW
1955	Out of the Clouds						
	The Night my Number Came up						
	The Ship that Died of Shame						
	* Touch and Go						WR
	* The Ladykillers						WR
1956	The Feminine Touch						
	* Who Done It?				TEBC		
	The Long Arm						
1957	Man in the Sky						WR
	The Shiralee						
	* Barnacle Bill				TEBC		
	Davy						WR
1958	Dunkirk					WL	
	Nowhere to Go						
1959	The Siege of Pinchgut						

The list on the preceding spread indicates the contribution of the main Ealing scriptwriters—that is, those who have credits on four or more films. They are listed below in order of their first Ealing script credit:

		first	last		years	films
RP	Roland Pertwee	1938	1944		7	5
RMc	Roger Macdougall	1939	1952		14	6
AMp	Angus Macphail	1939	1949		11	23
JD	John Dighton	1940	1951		12	17
AMf	Austin Melford	1940	1944		5	6
DM	Diana Morgan	1941	1950		10	6
MD	Monja Danischewsky	1943	1954		12	4
TEBC	T.E.B. Clarke	1944	1957		14	15
WL	W.P. Lipscomb	1950	1958		9	4
JW	Jack Whittingham	1950	1954		5	6
WR	William Rose	1954	1957		4	5

Again, the span-of-years column is misleading in cases where a writer returned to Ealing after an absence (Macdougall, Morgan, Lipscomb). Directors who took script credit on certain films have been omitted, along with those who wrote, or co-wrote, fewer than four films. No distinction is made between solo and shared credits. Altogether, the analysis is much less definitive than that of the director credits. It does, however, bring out similarly revealing patterns of continuity. Only Clarke has an Ealing career that closely parallels the trajectory of the main directing team in that it runs from mid-war to the late 1950s. Macdougall, Macphail and Dighton are obviously important in helping, like Balcon, to provide continuity between the early and later periods. Experienced Ealing writers were always available to work with debutant directors.

BIOGRAPHIES

This section provides brief notes on the careers of Balcon himself and of all those directors and writers already listed in the two charts of Ealing production: that is, everyone who directed an Ealing film or who had four or more script credits. This also, in effect, includes most of the main Ealing producers, since they tended to function, at some point in their time at Ealing, as writers and/or directors. Film credits are obviously, in most cases, incomplete.

BALCON, Michael. Born 1896. In films as a distributor, then producer from the early 1920s, launching the career of Alfred Hitchcock, and in the 1930s building up a big annual production programme of films for both Gainsborough and Gaumont-British. Head of MGM-British, 1936-38, then in charge of production at Ealing. A regular and committed spokesman for the British film industry, especially in the 1940s. Knighted in 1948. After Ealing, produced some films independently (*Sammy Going South*, 1962), and helped form Bryanston Films, a group of independent film-makers including several ex-Ealing colleagues. After a frustrating period as Chairman of British Lion (1964-68), in which he found it impossible to fulfil his commitment to support a continuity of indigenous production, he became Chairman of the British Film Institute's Experimental Film Fund, retiring 1972. Died 1977.

CARSTAIRS, John Paddy. Born 1910. Prolific writer and director from the early 1930s, mainly of low-budget comedies. Directed only one Ealing feature, the George Formby vehicle *Spare a Copper*, but made a series of short films at Ealing around the same time (early 1940), on the dangers of careless talk: *All Hands, Now You're Talking, Dangerous Comment*. These pioneered the use of the short-story form in propaganda campaigns and were widely distributed. Later films included many with Norman Wisdom. Died 1970.

CAVALCANTI, Alberto. Born Brazil, 1897. 1920-33: worked in French films as writer, art director and avant-garde director (*Rien que les heures*, 1926). To England 1933 to join the GPO Unit under Grierson, mainly as sound expert and then producer. Collaborated with Ernest Lindgren of the National Film Library to produce the lengthy anthology film, *Film and Reality* (completed 1942), which had a strong influence through its screenings

to film societies and educational audiences. Moved to Ealing early in the war, initially as head of Balcon's short-film unit (compiled *Yellow Caesar*, a portrait of Mussolini, 1941); stayed until 1946, working as art editor, producer, and director. Subsequent films in England (notably *They Made Me a Fugitive*, 1947), then worked in Brazil and Europe. Died 1989.

CLARKE, T.E.B. Born 1907. Journalist, policeman, then to Ealing as writer, under contract 1943-57, Intermittent work subsequently in films and television (*Gideon's Day* for John Ford, 1958; *Sons and Lovers*, 1960); also novels and autobiography. Died 1989.

COLE, Sidney. Born 1908. Editor in the 1930s, occasionally at Ealing in Basil Dean's time. Worked with Dickinson on Spanish Civil War films, then as editor on his *Gaslight* (1940) and on Leslie Howard's *Pimpernel Smith* (1941). At Ealing, 1942-52, as supervising editor, producer, and briefly director (one section of *Train of Events*). Then extensive TV and film production, including *The Kitchen*, 1961, and TV co-productions in New Zealand. Active from the 1930s onward in technicians' union (ACT, subsequently ACTT), and took a leading part, as producer and actor, in the union's own pro-Soviet short film entitled *Our Film*, made at Denham in 1942.

CORNELIUS, Henry. Born 1913, in South Africa. Pre-war work in Germany, France and England: editor for Korda at London Films (*The Four Feathers*, 1939). Wartime documentaries in South Africa, then to Ealing in 1944, as producer. Left Ealing after directing one film (*Passport to Pimlico*); most of his later films had some Ealing links (*Genevieve*, 1953). Died 1958.

CRICHTON, Charles. Born 1910. Editor 1935-40 for Korda at London Films (*Sanders of the River*, 1935), then to Ealing, rising rapidly from editor to producer to director (1944). One film outside Ealing (*Hunted*, 1952), and several in the years immediately after Ealing closed (*Battle of the Sexes*, 1959, with many Ealing echoes and collaborators). After steady employment as director on filmed TV series, made a spectacular comeback to features with the Anglo-American comedy, *A Fish Called Wanda* (1988).

DANISCHEWSKY, Monja. Born 1911, in Russia. Publicity work for various companies in England, then in 1938 as publicity director to Ealing, where he developed the company's distinctive policy for poster design. Became a writer (1943) and then producer (1949); left to work independently (*The Galloping Major*, 1951, directed by Cornelius); returned in the mid-1950s as producer/writer, and continued briefly after Ealing closed (*Rockets Galore*, Relph, 1958; *Battle of the Sexes*, Crichton, 1959). Later work in television.

DEARDEN, Basil. Born 1911. Actor and stage manager in the theatre, notably with Basil Dean; joined Dean at Ealing in 1937 and continued to work there when Balcon took over. Collaborated on Formby scripts, co-directed Will Hay comedies, and from 1943 began to direct a much wider range of films. Continued to be extremely prolific, in a continuing partnership with Relph (qv), until his death in 1970 (*The Smallest Show on Earth*, not for Ealing, from William Rose's script, 1957; *Victim*, 1961).

DICKINSON, Thorold. Born 1903. Left Oxford early to work on silent films with George Pearson in Britain and Europe. At Ealing in Dean's time, graduating from editor (*Sing as We Go*, 1934) to director (*The High Command*, 1937). Spanish Civil War films (with Sidney Cole), then features in England including the first film of *Gaslight* (1940) and two widely-spaced ones at Ealing. After the second, *Secret People*, worked in Israel, then took a United Nations film post, before returning to set up pioneering courses in film at University College, London: appointed Professor of Film in 1967. Died 1984.

DIGHTON, John. Born 1909. Prolific 1930s screenwriter: worked for Balcon at Gaumont-British, 1932-35, moved to Warner, then joined Ealing in 1939 for a dozen years of mainly collaborative projects including both *Kind Hearts and Coronets* and *The Man in the White Suit*. Author of the play *The Happiest Days of Your Life* and of its popular film adaptation (non-Ealing, 1950), and writer of some 1950s Hollywood films after leaving Ealing (*Roman Holiday*, 1953, *Summer of the Seventeenth Doll*, 1959). Died 1989.

FORDE, Walter. Born London, 1898. Stage comedian who entered films in 1919, directing many of his own silent comedies in Britain and (briefly) Hollywood. Retired as a performer in 1930 and worked prolifically as a director of British thrillers, musicals, and comedies, many of them for Balcon (*Rome Express*, 1932, *Chu Chin Chow*, 1934, *Bulldog Jack*, 1935). Directed Balcon's first Ealing film (*The Gaunt Stranger*) and five more in quick succession before leaving in 1940. Married to Culley Forde, associate producer of his last two Ealing films. After more British films (*Cardboard Cavalier*, 1949), retired to America. Died 1984.

FREND, Charles. Born 1909. Editor from 1931, mainly with Balcon (four Hitchcock films including

Sabotage, 1936; all three of the big MGM-British productions of the late 1930s, including *A Yank at Oxford*, 1938). To Ealing 1941 as director, remaining until the end. Intermittent film work subsequently for TV and cinema (*Cone of Silence*, 1960; 2nd unit director of *Ryan's Daughter*, 1970). Died 1977.

HAMER, Robert. Born 1911. Editor in the 1930s (*Jamaica Inn* for Hitchcock, 1939), and worked briefly for the GPO Film Unit. To Ealing 1941 as editor, then producer, writer, and, from 1945, director. Films as director outside Ealing: *The Spider and the Fly*, 1949; *The Long Memory*, 1953; *Father Brown*, 1954; *To Paris with Love*, 1955; *The Scapegoat* (produced by Balcon for MGM), 1959; *School for Scoundrels*, 1960. Died 1963.

HOLT, Seth. Born 1923. Brother-in-law of Robert Hamer. Actor; to Ealing 1944 as assistant editor, graduating to editor (1949), producer (1955) and director (1958). Subsequently returned to editing for Crichton's *Battle of the Sexes* (1959) and for *Saturday Night and Sunday Morning* (1960). Films as director outside Ealing: *Taste of Fear*, 1961; *Station Six Sahara*, 1961; *The Nanny*, 1965; *Danger Route*, 1967; *Blood from the Mummy's Tomb*, 1971. Holt died in 1971 before completing this last film.

JACKSON, Pat. Born 1916. Spent a decade in the British documentary movement: assistant on *Night Mail*, 1936; director of various short films and of the feature documentary *Western Approaches*, 1944. Put under contract to MGM, for which he made one film (*Shadow on the Wall*, 1949) before returning to Britain (*White Corridors*, 1951). Only one feature at Ealing (*The Feminine Touch*, 1956), despite other projects. Some modest later films (*The Birthday Present*, 1957), also television.

KIMMINS, Anthony. Born 1910. Playwright; screenwriter and director from 1934. Worked at Ealing in Basil Dean's time: writer for Carol Reed (*Midshipman Easy*, 1935) and for Gracie Fields (*Queen of Hearts*, 1936); writer/director for George Formby (e.g. *Keep Fit*, 1937), and continued in this capacity after Balcon took over; then left for naval service. Several postwar films (*Bonnie Prince Charlie*, 1948). Died 1962.

LIPSCOMB, W.P. Born 1887. Actor, then writer, working in the 1930s both for Dean at Ealing and for Balcon at Gainsborough (*The Good Companions*, 1933); then to Hollywood, initially to adapt his own play, *Clive of India*. After returning to Britain, was briefly scenario editor at Ealing in the early 1950s. Died 1958.

MACDOUGALL, Roger. Born 1910. Cousin of Alexander Mackendrick, with whom he formed a company early in World War II to make informational cartoons. Playwright; in films first as composer, then writer. At Ealing as writer intermittently between 1939 and 1953, meanwhile working for several years in the 1940s as writer and director of documentaries for his own company, Merlin. Two of his Ealing scripts, *The Man in the*

White Suit and *The Gentle Gunman*, were adaptations of his own plays. Later worked for the stage, and occasionally for films (*The Mouse that Roared*, 1959). Died 1993.

MACPHAIL, Angus. Born 1903. Founder-member of the original Film Society in 1925; film critic; writer and editor for silent films. Closely associated with Balcon for two decades: scripts for Gainsborough (1927-31), then story supervisor for Gaumont-British (1931-37) and subsequently for Ealing (1939-48), where all but one of his 23 screen credits were shared with other writers. Several collaborations with Alfred Hitchcock, including two American films (*Spellbound*, 1945; *The Wrong Man*, 1956). Died 1962.

MACKENDRICK, Alexander. Born 1912 in Boston, Mass, of Scottish parents; brought up in Glasgow; cousin of Roger Macdougall. In advertising, and briefly films, in the 1930s (writer on *Midnight Menace*, 1937). Wartime cartoon scripts, then documentary work in Rome. To Ealing 1946, initially as sketch artist, then as writer and director. Left Ealing to make *Sweet Smell of Success* in New York (1956). Other films as director: *Sammy Going South*, 1962, for Balcon; *A High Wind in Jamaica*, 1965; *Don't Make Waves*, 1968, in Hollywood. Subsequently based in America, teaching in the film school at the California Institute of Arts.

MELFORD, Austin. Born 1885. In theatre and revue; author of play on which Buster Keaton's *The Battling Butler* (1926) was based. Then in films as actor, writer and director, mainly of musicals and comedies, often for Balcon: wrote and directed *Oh Daddy*, from his own play, for Gainsborough (1935), and co-scripted *O.H.M.S.*, directed by Raoul Walsh for Gaumont-British (1937). Worked on Formby scripts at Ealing in Dean's time (*I See Ice*, 1937), and continued after Balcon took over, writing mainly for Formby and Tommy Trinder, and leaving Ealing once both of them had gone. Died 1971.

MORGAN, Diana. Born 1913. Author of plays and revues, who became, in the 1940s, the only woman member of Ealing's 'creative elite', contributing to a wide variety of scripts. After leaving Ealing, worked in theatre and occasionally films (*Let's Be Happy*, 1957).

NOLBANDOV, Sergei. Born 1895, in Russia; moved to England in the early 1920s. Silent film editor, then writer in the 1930s (*Fire Over England* for Korda, 1936). Moved with Balcon to Ealing and worked as writer and producer on the three films directed by Penrose Tennyson. After Tennyson's death, directed two films himself, then left in 1943 to produce short films, and subsequently the documentary series *This Modern Age* for Rank (1946-49). Returned to feature films as producer (*The Kidnappers*, 1953). Died 1971.

NORMAN, Leslie. Born 1911. Varied work in the industry from the late 1920s, mainly as editor. To Ealing initially as chief editor: first credit for *The Overlanders* (1946), then producer and writer (1949), and director from 1955. Worked regularly on Harry Watt's Australian and African films, and returned to Australia as director both for Ealing and afterwards (*Summer of the Seventeenth Doll*, 1960). Father of Barry Norman, the presenter of a long-running programme on the cinema for BBC TV. Died 1993.

PELISSIER, Anthony. Born 1912. Theatre director, then films from the late 1940s (*The Rocking Horse Winner*, 1949). One feature only at Ealing: *Meet Mr Lucifer*, 1953. Subsequent work in theatre and television, for instance with the experimental BBC Drama team, The Langham Group. Died 1988.

PERTWEE, Roland. Born 1896. Playwright; entered British films as writer in the early 1920s. Many scripts in the 1930s, some of them for Balcon at Gaumont-British (*The Ghoul*, 1933; *King Solomon's Mines*, 1937). In Michael Powell's first volume of autobiography, *A Life in Movies*, Pertwee is used, without being named, as the epitome of bad British screen-writing, at whose expense Powell teams up with Pressburger—'a member of a famous English theatrical family, who knew all about writing for the theatre and nothing about writing for films' (page 300). Pertwee worked on several early Ealing scripts, and later wrote some Gainsborough melodramas (*Madonna of the Seven Moons*, 1944). He also acted in *The Four Just Men* and *Halfway House*, and was author of the play which formed the basis for *Pink String and Sealing Wax*; his son, Michael, later co-scripted *Against the Wind*. Died 1963.

RELPH, Michael. Born 1915. Entered films in 1933 as assistant art director with Balcon; then art director for Warner and for MGM-British; also theatrical designer. Joined Ealing 1942 as chief art director, working mainly on Basil Dearden's films; producer and occasional writer from 1946. After producing *Kind Hearts and Coronets*, he settled into a prolific partnership with Dearden that survived the studio's closure and continued until Dearden's death in 1971. In some cases the pair were jointly credited at Ealing with 'production and direction', but *Davy* in 1957 was still regarded as Relph's debut as director. Later, he again directed occasionally, with Dearden producing (*Rockets Galore*, 1958), but it was normally the other way round. Relph succeeded Balcon as Chairman of the BFI Production Board (formerly the Experimental Film Fund) and later returned to commercial production with Don Boyd (*An Unsuitable Job for a Woman*, 1982).

ROSE, William. Born 1918. American writer, who worked in British films for a decade from 1948 (*Genevieve*, 1953), and wrote five scripts for Ealing between 1954 and 1957. Returned to America to write for Stanley Kramer and others (*It's a Mad*

Mad Mad Mad World, 1963; *Guess Who's Coming to Dinner*, 1967). Died 1987.

SMART, Ralph. Born 1908. In films from 1927 as editor, writer, and maker of commercial short films; wrote some of Michael Powell's early films for Balcon at Gaumont-British (*The Phantom Light*, 1935). Spent the war producing short propaganda films for the Australian government, then worked on Ealing's first two Australian features, and directed the third, *Bitter Springs* (1950). One more Ealing credit, as writer for *Where no Vultures Fly* (1951); then mainly writer and producer for TV series.

STEVENSON, Robert. Born 1905. Writer and then director with Balcon in the 1930s (*Tudor Rose*, 1936), and moved with him to Ealing, directing three films there in quick succession. Two of these starred his wife Anna Lee, with whom he then left for a successful career in Hollywood (*Back Street*, 1941; *I Married a Communist*/*The Woman on Pier 13*, 1949). All of his later work was for Disney (*Mary Poppins*, 1964). Died 1986.

TENNYSON, Penrose. Born 1912. Like Dickinson before him, left Oxford early in 1932 to enter films, spending his whole career with Balcon, first at Gaumont-British (assistant director to Hitchcock on *The Man who Knew Too Much*, 1934, and *The 39 Steps*, 1935), then MGM-British, then Ealing. After three films as director, he joined the navy to make training films, and died in a 'plane crash in 1941.

TRUMAN, Michael. Born 1916. From 1934, assistant director and junior editor in various studios. Made wartime training films for the army, then joined Ealing as an editor in 1944, becoming a producer in 1951, and directing one film (*Touch and Go*) in 1955. Occasional films as director thereafter (*Go to Blazes*, 1962). Died 1974.

VARNEL, Marcel. Born in Paris 1894. Theatre director in France and America, then films in Hollywood and, from 1935, in Britain. Comedy specialist who worked extensively with Will Hay (including *Oh Mr Porter*, 1937), the Crazy Gang, and Arthur Askey, before joining Ealing for three early-war films: two with George Formby, one with Hay. When Formby left Ealing, Varnel went with him and continued as his regular director. Died 1947.

WATT, Harry. Born 1906. Worked in the 1930s with the GPO film unit, directing several of their most celebrated films (*Night Mail*, 1936). Continued with the unit in wartime when it was renamed Crown and placed under the Ministry of Information's control, and directed the documentary feature *Target for Tonight* (1941); then moved to Ealing along with Cavalcanti. All of his five post-war Ealing films were shot in Australia or Africa. Went to TV briefly in the 1950s, then returned to Ealing, and subsequently to documentary. Died 1987.

WHITTINGHAM, Jack. Born 1910. Playwright; film critic in the 1930s, then screenwriter (*Q Planes*, 1939). Under contract to Ealing in the early 1950s, with screen credit on six films, including three for Basil Dearden. Subsequent work in films (wrote and produced *The Birthday Present*, 1957) and in television. Died 1972.

BALCON AFTER EALING

This is a revised version of an essay originally published in German translation in a book about Michael Balcon that accompanied a retrospective season of his work in Berlin in 1981: 'Der Produzent: Michael Balcon und der Englische Film' edited by Geoff Brown. This is its first publication in English.

I am extremely grateful to Jon Burrows, whose scholarly research on the Bryanston company deserves publication in its own right, for providing data for the filmography that follows, and for prompting some improvements to the text.

Monja Danischewsky, a long-term member of the Ealing team, tells a story in his 1966 autobiography of being summoned urgently one day to Balcon's office:

'I found him slumped in his chair gazing morosely at a painting by Paul Nash propped up against the back of a settee.
' "Sit down, dear boy."
'I sat waiting. He indicated the painting.
' "Do I like it – or don't I?" '

The Robert Morley character in *The Battle of the Sexes* (1959), inspecting the scale model of a factory which his firm may be going to build, calls an employee into his office and asks him: 'Do I like it – or don't I?'

The echo is no coincidence: it was Danischewsky who wrote and produced *The Battle of the Sexes*. Set in Scotland, this was the first film to be released by Bryanston Films, a company formed in April 1959, not long after Ealing ceased production. The Chairman of Bryanston throughout its five years and more than thirty films was Michael Balcon.

The whole film is intensely evocative of Ealing, in terms equally of personnel and of themes. Besides Danischewsky, both its director (Charles Crichton) and its editor (Seth Holt) had worked continuously at Ealing for fifteen years. The main actors (Morley, Peter Sellers, Constance Cummings) all had Ealing experience, while many of the supporting cast are familiar from the Scottish comedies directed there by Alexander Mackendrick, *Whisky Galore* (1949) and *The Maggie* (1954). The casting of the dying head of the firm makes a link with a third Mackendrick comedy: Ernest Thesiger had played Sir John Kierlaw in *The Man in the White Suit*. Chief of the next generation of mill-owners in that film was Cecil Parker, in a role that is the structural equivalent of the Morley one in *The Battle of the Sexes*; Mackendrick revealed in a 1970 TV programme on Ealing ('Kind Hearts and Overdrafts', produced by Harry Hastings) that his unofficial instruction to Parker was to model his performance style on Balcon. History was indeed being replayed.

Thematically, *The Battle of the Sexes* is reminiscent of Ealing in being centred on a conflict between traditional and modern, small-scale and large-scale. As I have argued, many of the films from *Cheer Boys Cheer* (1939) onward contain an unmistakable sub-text about Ealing itself, the small 'family business' struggling to survive in a hard industry. 'Just an old family firm' is how MacPherson junior (Morley) describes his tweed business at the start of *The Battle of the Sexes*. Like the Greenleaf Brewery, it is given a foundation-date of 1789, as if to establish good democratic credentials for it; its small-scale, traditional character is threatened in the course of the film, then triumphantly restored. The first Bryanston film, then, is like a nostalgic celebration: an assurance that things can go on as they used to, both on and off screen, within a new family firm run by the same lovable headmaster-boss who can be affectionately joked about.

My aim here is to consider how seriously Balcon attempted to create a form of Ealing-in-exile, and, more broadly, how this last phase of his career relates to his Ealing work. In the changed conditions of the late 1950s, he had found it impossible either to continue running the studio itself on the old independent basis, or to transplant the Ealing team into a new home. After the partnerships with Rank, MGM and ABPC all proved abortive, he set up simply as an independent producer, making one-off deals. His partner was the production manager from Ealing, Hal Mason, and he used Ealing directors: Robert Hamer for *The Scapegoat* (a Michael Balcon Production for MGM, 1959), and Leslie Norman for *The Long and the Short and the Tall* (ABPC, 1961). By the time this second post-Ealing film was complete, Balcon had become chairman of Bryanston Films.

According to a report in the June 1959 issue of Films and Filming, 'The recent setting up of Bryanston Films – under the chairmanship of Sir Michael Balcon – could dramatically be called a break for freedom.' This sense of 'drama', of a potentially important intervention made at a crucial time of transition in the industry, is borne out in other magazines and trade papers of the period, and also, in a broader context, by Alexander Walker's book 'Hollywood UK' (first published by Michael Joseph, London, in 1974 as 'Hollywood England') – an invaluable account of the British cinema of the 1960s written soon after the decade ended and based on extensive interviews, some of them with Bryanston people. The Films and Filming report went on to quote Balcon himself:

'We know, or we think we like to know, what is right in picture making. But many of our members have had projects rejected because they did not conform to the well tried pattern of making films which slavishly followed the successes of ten years ago.

'We are not an arty crafty experimental organisation but we do want to tackle original and unusual subjects of international importance. We are now in a position whereby, working through a small selection panel, we can give a producer financial backing to make these subjects. And we welcome any outside producer who has an exciting subject.'

Bryanston was not a studio, nor was it a distributor (though Sight and Sound reported that it would 'exercise a good many of a distributor's functions'). All of its members (the number fluctuated between twelve and fifteen) bought their way in with a stake of at least £5,000, and this commitment and the collective film-making authority of the group earned them a guarantee of distribution of their films through British Lion, and, on the strength of this, of bank financing.

Balcon was evidently not the prime mover in creating this company, nor had he foreseen such an arrangement while Ealing was breaking up. In his auto-biography, he introduces the Bryanston period in typically deadpan style:

'Production was in a period of deflation and for the first time I thought seriously about retiring. However, one day I had a conversation with Maxwell Setton . . .'

Setton, himself an independent producer, put up the idea of a consortium: Balcon would come in with his own new production company, and be Chairman. He accepted, and began to draw others in.

It is not unlike what had happened twenty years earlier. In 1938, Balcon was no longer running the companies that he had become strongly identified with (Gainsborough, then Gaumont-British); he had just finished a brief and unhappy period with MGM; and he had begun making some films independently, working with former associates. Ealing happened to become available, and he was invited to take it over. In the late 1950s, he likewise found himself 'the right man in the right place at the right time' (*see* p.43). Just as he had quickly become the main spokesman, in the pre-war and early-war period, for a continuing strong national cinema, so he now moved easily into the Bryanston post and filled a similar role, speaking up for the maintenance of an independent and authentically British school of film-making within a changing industry. At Ealing he had initially used directors familiar to him from his time at Gaumont-British: Walter Forde, Penrose Tennyson, Robert Stevenson. The first group of Bryanston films gave work not only, as we have seen, to Charles Crichton and Leslie Norman from Ealing (and to Danischewsky as writer/producer), but to another old faithful in Charles Frend; subsequent directors included Alfred Shaughnessy, Michael Truman, Pat Jackson, Basil Dearden and Alexander Mackendrick. A year or two after Balcon's arrival at Ealing, important new blood was introduced, from documentary, in the persons of Alberto Cavalcanti and Harry Watt; again, this pattern seemed to repeat itself when Bryanston gave support to the Woodfall group, with its background in Free Cinema and the Royal Court Theatre and its commitment to location shooting. Woodfall's film of *The Entertainer* (directed by Tony Richardson from John Osborne's play – the successor, on film as on stage, to their *Look Back in Anger*) was financed by Bryanston, and Woodfall joined the consortium. Both publicly and behind the scenes, Balcon expressed his delight with this association, and with the quality of the next Woodfall production, *Saturday Night and Sunday Morning* (produced by Richardson, and directed by Karel Reisz).

The board of film-makers discussing each other's projects seemed to recreate Ealing's famous Round Table. The London office of the company even had at its door the commissionaire from Ealing. And films on the old pattern began to be released, starting with *The Battle of the Sexes* and then Charles Frend's *Cone of Silence* (1960), an airline film that fits squarely into the Ealing tradition of modest institutional drama.

But of course Bryanston was not Ealing, nor was Balcon filling quite the same role as he had done there. He acknowledged this from the start (Sight and Sound, Summer/Autumn 1959): 'You couldn't today run a studio in the way Ealing was run – certainly not in this country, and perhaps nowhere in the world.' *The Battle of the Sexes*, then, represents less a renewal of the old ways than a nostalgic farewell to them. There is evidence that Balcon found the transition less than easy to accept. Danischewsky (in a conversation in 1980, from which the quotes that follow are taken) recalled as a turning-point the time when Balcon attended the first private showing of one of the Woodfall films. As the lights went up, he started to give his opinion in the way he had always been accustomed to, only to be told curtly by one of the Woodfall team that they were not interested in what he thought. It is likely that this film was *The Entertainer*, on which Balcon and Woodfall disagreed publicly in 1960; just before the scheduled première, it was withdrawn for some re-recording and re-editing to be done, and replaced, with a pleasing neatness, by *Cone of Silence*. Bryanston became 'a camp divided', with Balcon more inhibited and less dominant than at Ealing, 'very careful not to offend or dictate'. In Danischewsky's words, 'One never felt the same kind of relationship with the other directors on the board as we had at Ealing.' Projects were accepted (or not accepted); then the film-makers got on with it. A variety of people have written about the experience of working on Ealing films, and their accounts always foreground the ethos of the company and of Balcon himself, but one can read accounts of the making of films that bear the Bryanston label and find no reference at all to that company, or to the name of Balcon.

Nevertheless, Bryanston did remain a coherent and significant operation; there was a pattern in the kind of project that it attracted, and approved, and Balcon continued as its committed chairman and spokesman to the end. The last Bryanston film was released in 1964, and the company was sold to the television company Associated Rediffusion in early 1965.

It seems indisputable that the turning point in Bryanston's commercial fortunes was the Woodfall production of *Tom Jones*. Walker's chapter on the film is entitled 'The One That Got Away', i.e. got away from Bryanston. As members of the board, Woodfall applied for, and received, backing for this ambitious period film in colour (all previous films both from Bryanston and from Woodfall had been black and white). An already high budget was then revised upwards, and Bryanston hesitated. Despite the film's very unEaling bawdiness, and despite the element of tension that had developed between Balcon and Woodfall, the evidence is that Balcon was a sincere and vigorous supporter of the project and was frustrated by the caution of his fellow directors. Woodfall quickly submitted the project to the new London office of United Artists, and gained 100% finance at the new figure. *Tom Jones* became a huge financial success. Not only did Bryanston fail to benefit from this, but a whole new system became established for the financing of British-made films. American companies, after *Tom Jones*, were much keener than before to invest in British production, and could generally offer a more attractive deal – more money, fewer strings – than British companies such as Bryanston or British Lion could manage. As Walker's book lucidly recounts, the centre of gravity in British film finance was shifting radically, with results that would be far-reaching. Increasingly, companies like Bryanston became the last resort, attracting the parochial and the unambitious project – which was, in a sense, what they had preferred all along. Like Ealing, Bryanston favoured projects that were modest in scale, and 'responsible': embodying, that is, serious treatment of social issues, or innocent diversion. This policy was both its strength and its downfall.

It's interesting to speculate about what would have happened if Balcon and Bryanston had in fact financed, and then profited from, *Tom Jones*. Would they, with an access of power and confidence and magnetism, have backed the *Blow-Ups* and *Ifs* of the next few years, and established for the new British cinema a less brittle foundation that in fact developed, making it less vulnerable to the turning-off of the American tap that came as abruptly as its turning on? Somehow, one doubts it. One of the reasons Bryanston lost *Tom Jones* may have been that it had just taken advantage of a deal with the American-based company Seven Arts to set up another big-budget colour film, Balcon's own production of *Sammy Going South* (directed by Mackendrick), and was nervous of a second expensive commitment. For all its merits, *Sammy Going South* was a commercial failure. As his whole career demonstrates, Balcon was always more comfortable with modest, tightly-budgeted films than with gambles on international stars and markets. Nor did Woodfall and Richardson go on to do much of significance, artistically or commercially, with the profits and status that *Tom Jones* brought them.

By his own account, Balcon never ceased to regret Bryanston's loss of *Tom Jones* and its profits, and the subsequent domination of the British industry by American money, yet he quickly returned with all the old zest to advocating and practising a policy of modest parochialism. There is a certain inconsistency here, as there is in the article he wrote as chairman of Bryanston in the trade paper Kinematograph Weekly on 25th July 1963, while *Tom Jones* was still enjoying its triumphant first run in the West End. It is the last, as far as I know, of the ringing statements of policy he was to make as an active film producer, and begins thus:

'It has long been customary in the world of film production for anniversaries to be regarded as a time when production executives announce, with the largest possible fanfare of trumpets, the Greatest Ever Programme of Box Office Smash Hits.

'I should like to mark the fourth anniversary of the Bryanston organisation by one simple statement: We have survived.'

He goes on to discuss with pride two aspects of the company's record, its provision of 'better quality supporting features', and its regular 'flow of product' – a certain number of films each year, maintained on the principle that this is an end in itself, that

'. . . if a producer holds up until, say, Peter Sellers is available to him, he may ultimately have a profitable picture on his hands, but he will have done nothing in the meantime to provide a sufficient supply of workmanlike pictures to help keep the country's cinemas open and operating successfully.'

The problem here is that, by 1963, the consistent supply of 'workmanlike' pictures had long ceased to satisfy audiences or to keep cinemas 'open and operating successfully'. With at least half his mind, Balcon knew this and knew its implications – indeed, elsewhere in the same article, he was complaining about the difficulty of finding dates for his films to play the circuits. Some of them had to wait unshown for many months, and it was this delay in getting money back, while interest charges accumulated, that led to the halting of Bryanston production soon after the article was published.

Balcon's chairmanship of Bryanston overlapped with his brief chairmanship of British Lion (early 1964 to early 1966), a bitter episode in his career which plays out in a shorter term some of the same conflicts. Partly owned by the government, British Lion had long been seen as a potential 'third force' in the industry alongside the two vertically integrated combines, Rank and ABPC: it comprised a production company (with some experienced film-makers on its board) and a distributor (by whom Bryanston's product was handled) but lacked, crucially, a circuit of cinemas. When the Conservative government sold its controlling share in British Lion, it was a group gathered and headed by Balcon whose bid for control was successful; it included film-makers from the former board (Launder and Gilliat, the Boultings), from Bryanston (Woodfall, Balcon himself), and from elsewhere (e.g. Joseph Janni). In Balcon's words, from his 1969 autobiography (p.206):

'I saw in this group a strong force of creative talent, and with their full approval I accompanied our offer to buy with the statement that we "envisaged an annual production of somewhere between ten and fifteen first feature films a year".'

Lion would thus have been a kind of super-Bryanston, committed to keeping up the 'flow of product'.

It is hard not to sympathise with him over what then happened: having gained entry on Balcon's ticket, as it were, his colleagues left him isolated, holding back on production and working to replace him as chairman. At the same time, it is hard to be optimistic about the prospects of the more substantial programme of films that Lion might have cobbled together if Balcon's policy had prevailed. To maintain the flow of product by making more of the same kind of film would be to risk adding to the number of films accumulating on the shelf – to what *Movie* magazine characterised as 'a logjam of mainly dull movies'. This *Movie* article (in issue 14, Autumn 1965) provides a useful analysis of Lion's problems during Balcon's brief chairmanship. It questions the timidity of their policy both as producers, making films with 'little appearance of adventure' about them, and as entrepreneurs, failing to match the drive with which American companies encouraged imaginative independent projects. What is particularly interesting is that the article's author, Mark Shivas, was on the brink of a long and successful career as a producer of drama and film for television.

The impact of television is something with which Balcon seems never really to have come to terms. At Bryanston he continued mainly (even allowing for the relevant Woodfall productions, of which there were only four) to promote modest, unstarry films in black and white, many of them uncomfortably close to the type of drama that TV's regular 'flow of product' was already providing. For all their modest virtues, this can be said of films like *The Big Day* (1960), a competent drama of office and domestic life that was selected for archival preservation as 'an outstanding British second feature', and the likeable *Girl on Approval*, directed by Ealing's Charles Frend, of which the Monthly Film Bulletin commented ominously in December 1962:

'It is the sort of affectionate, well-observed picture of lower middle-class life that occasionally crops up in television drama, where it must be admitted it often gets slicker and more technically assured treatment.'

Compare the critic of The People (3rd November 1963) on *Girl in the Headlines*, made by another Ealing man, Michael Truman: 'If you haven't got a Television set this is gripping entertainment'. Every year, however, sets were being installed in hundreds of thousands more homes.

Looking down the list of Bryanston films and film-makers, one is struck by the Ealing connections, by the TV-like modesty of many of the projects, and by a third factor that is equally thought-provoking. Directors include Freddie Francis, John Gilling, John Krish, Vernon Sewell, Don Sharp, Alfred Shaughnessy, and Leslie Norman. All of these men directed horror films in the period between 1955 and 1965, but for companies other than Bryanston.

'You couldn't today run a studio in the way Ealing was run – certainly not in this country' (Balcon in 1959, quoted above). He was wrong. The Hammer company, with its own studio at Bray, operated in ways quite similar to Ealing. As noted earlier (p.18), Hammer rose to prosperity at precisely the time Ealing was declining, and flourished during the 1960s as a tight operation by a closely-knit team turning out a steady flow of product. The idea, however, of Michael Balcon launching a programme of Dracula and Frankenstein films is inconceivable; indeed, one of the first proposals brought to the Bryanston board was Michael Powell's for *Peeping Tom*, which they turned down with unanimous distaste. The categories of respectable film and 'exploitation' film continued, in a manner that has been characteristic of British film culture, to be kept rigidly separate. Not only Balcon but critics too seemed unable fully to grasp the fact, and the implications, of Hammer's success; witness the remarkable omission of any mention of Hammer from Alexander Walker's book.

What, finally, is the legacy of this last stage of Balcon's career in the commercial industry? Nothing as enduring as the Hitchcock and Victor Saville films he produced in the '20s and '30s, or as the best Ealing films of the '40s and '50s. Only two of the films carrying the Bryanston tag have the kind of vitality that makes them, similarly, of continuing interest to other than specialist audiences: *Saturday Night and Sunday Morning*, in whose production Balcon was not closely involved, and his last personal production, *Sammy Going South*, which has an honourable place in the distinguished, unlucky career of its director, Alexander Mackendrick. (Some might want to add one or more of the three other Woodfall films to this list.) But the body of films is still of great interest as a product of its time, as a coherent attempt by the respectable side of the indigenous cinema, represented supremely by Michael Balcon, to engage with a changing industry and a changing society, one stage on from Ealing. As with late Ealing, the mechanics of its honourable failure make an instructive case study.

I noted above that when the première of *The Entertainer* had to be postponed, the film that replaced it was another Bryanston one, *Cone of Silence*. The latter attracted little critical attention, but the comparison is worth exploring. Derek Hill, praising *The Entertainer* in his weekly Tribune column (5th August 1960) when it eventually emerged, called it, with rather fatuous partisanship, 'the most professionally handled production this year', but *Cone of Silence* looks in every sense more professional, more controlled and eloquent in structure and in *mise-en-scène*. What seems even more apparent now about *The Entertainer* than it did at the time is the amount it has in common, for all its superficial freshness, with the most depressing tendencies of mainstream British cinema, such as clumsiness in handling theatre-based actors, and wilful drabness of tone and structure. The start of this book discusses the paradoxical-seeming links between the original Osborne play and Ealing's 1957 film *Davy*; the film version of *The Entertainer* is even closer, and also recalls the 1955 comedy *Touch and Go*, with its central characters who talk endlessly about breaking free of their stagnant environment but never look like succeeding, or genuinely wanting to.

It also has an Oedipal structure that is closely paralleled in *Cone of Silence*. The moral centre of both films is an only daughter, played by an excellent young stage actress (Joan Plowright in *The Entertainer*, Elisabeth Seal in *Cone of Silence*), who protects her father (Laurence Olivier, Bernard Lee) when he is in agonising professional difficulties. Both have conventionally worthy boyfriends with whom their relationship is much less intense (Daniel Massey, Michael

Craig). It seems to me that *Cone of Silence* does more with this structure, in a variety of ways.

One aspect of it is this. The father figure in *Cone of Silence* is an airline pilot who has survived a disastrous crash. An inquiry decides, to his daughter's indignation, that he is to blame, but he is allowed to go on flying. Eventually he crashes a second time in similar circumstances, and is killed. A second inquiry begins, and seems to have no option but to find that he again failed to keep to the rules of 'the book' for taking off. His daughter insists that, on the contrary, he always kept obsessively to 'the book', in every aspect of his professional and domestic life.

There are last-minute revelations which resolve the matter: he did keep to the book, but the book was wrong. The reason he, and not others, had the crashes, was that he kept more strictly to the book than they did. The father is vindicated; but the father was wrong. Without him, these crashes would not have happened; but his crashes allowed others to see more clearly. The book was wrong; the book will be rewritten. The daughter goes off with her boyfriend, who will help to rewrite it.

Cone of Silence achieves a seductive balance between the support of authority – the book, the law, the father – and their undermining. Like so many of the Ealing films, and like *The Battle of the Sexes* in its cruder way, it works as a story that is at some level 'about' the company and the film industry, and the Bernard Lee character, less consciously but more profoundly than the Robert Morley one, is like Michael Balcon himself: an authority figure of massive integrity who keeps to the book, but the book by now is wrong, and needs rewriting.

MICHAEL BALCON'S POST-EALING FILMS

Outline details follow of the feature films in which Michael Balcon had a production interest after Ealing closed, including all those that were financed by Bryanston; unless another company is indicated in brackets after the title, the film is a Bryanston one. The list includes a small number of films that bear the name of two sister companies, both of them also chaired by Balcon: Bryanston Seven Arts (set up in association with the American company Seven Arts, with the aim of financing higher-budget films), and Pax: these films are designated (BSA) or (Pax) after the title. Because of the importance of the link with Woodfall, that company's four titles are also identified. The month given before the title is (except in the case of the films that Balcon produced for MGM and for Associated British) the month of completion; since the release of many of the Bryanston films was delayed or aborted, this is the clearest way of indicating the sequence of production.

Names in italics indicate writers, producers, directors and actors with Ealing experience.

Aug 1959: The Scapegoat (MGM-British)
Directed by *Robert Hamer*. Produced by *Michael Balcon*. Script by *Hamer*, Gore Vidal, from novel by Daphne du Maurier. With *Alec Guinness*, Bette Davis.

Dec 1959: The Battle of the Sexes
Directed by *Charles Crichton*. Produced and written by *Monja Danischewsky*, from short story by James Thurber. With *Peter Sellers*, *Robert Morley*.

April 1960: The Entertainer (Woodfall)
Directed by Tony Richardson. Produced by Harry Saltzman. Script from his own play by John Osborne. With Laurence Olivier.

April 1960: Cone of Silence
Directed by *Charles Frend*. Produced by Aubrey Baring. Script by *Robert Westerby*, from novel by David Beaty. With Michael Craig, Peter Cushing.

May 1960: Light up the Sky
Directed and produced by Lewis Gilbert. Script by Vernon Harris, from play by Robert Storey. With Ian Carmichael, Tommy Steele.

July 1960: The Wind of Change
Directed by Vernon Sewell. Produced by John Dark. Script by Alexander Doré. With Donald Pleasence.

July 1960: The Big Day
Directed by Peter Graham Scott. Produced by Julian Wintle, Leslie Parkyn. Script by Bill MacIlwraith. With Donald Pleasence.

Aug 1960: Saturday Night and Sunday Morning (Woodfall).
Directed by Karel Reisz. Produced by Harry Saltzman, Tony Richardson. Script from his own novel by Alan Sillitoe. With Albert Finney.

Sept 1960: The Boy Who Stole a Million
Directed by *Charles Crichton*. Produced by George H.Brown. Script by *Crichton*, *John Eldridge*. With Virgilio Texeira.

Nov 1960: **Linda**
Directed by Don Sharp. Produced by Julian Wintle,
Leslie Parkyn. Script by Bill MacIlwraith. With
Carol White.

Jan 1961: **The Long and the Short and the Tall**
(Associated British)
Directed by *Leslie Norman*. Produced by *Michael
Balcon*. Script by Wolf Mankowitz from play by
Willis Hall. With Richard Todd, Laurence Harvey,
Richard Harris.

Feb 1961: **Double Bunk**
Directed and written by C.M.Pennington-Richards.
Produced by George H.Brown. With Ian Carmichael.

Mar 1961: **Spare the Rod**
Directed by *Leslie Norman*. Produced by Victor
Lyndon. Script by John Cresswell, from novel by
Michael Croft. With Max Bygraves, Donald Pleasence.

May 1961: **The Impersonator**
Directed by *Alfred Shaughnessy*. Produced by
Anthony Perry. Script by *Shaughnessy*, Kenneth
Cavender. With John Crawford.

July 1961: **A Taste of Honey** (Woodfall)
Directed and produced by Tony Richardson.
Script/play by Shelagh Delaney. With Rita
Tushingham, Dora Bryan.

Sept 1961: **Dangerous Afternoon**
Directed by Charles Saunders. Produced by Guido
Coen. Script by Brandon Fleming, from play by
Gerald Anstruther. With Ruth Dunning.

Sept 1961: **The Day the Earth Caught Fire** (Pax)
Directed and produced by Val Guest. Script by
Guest, Wolf Mankowitz. With Janet Munro.

Oct 1961: **Two and Two Make Six**
Directed by Freddie Francis. Produced and written
by *Monja Danischewsky*. With George Chakiris.

Nov 1961: **Girl on Approval**
Directed by *Charles Frend*. Produced by Harold
Orton, Anthony Perry. Script by Kathleen White.
With Rachel Roberts.

April 1962: **Strongroom**
Directed by Vernon Sewell. Produced by Guido
Coen. Script by Max Marquis, Richard Harris. With
Derren Nesbitt.

May 1962: **The Quare Fellow**
Directed and written by Arthur Dreifuss, from play by
Brendan Behan. Produced by Anthony Havelock-
Allan. With Patrick McGoohan, Sylvia Syms.

June 1962: **A Prize of Arms**
Directed by Cliff Owen. Produced by George
Maynard. Script by Paul Ryder. With *Stanley Baker*.

Aug 1962: **The Loneliness of the
Long-Distance Runner** (Woodfall)
Directed and produced by Tony Richardson.
Script/short story by Alan Sillitoe. With *Michael
Redgrave*, Tom Courtenay.

Dec 1962: **Don't Talk to Strange Men**
Directed by *Pat Jackson*. Produced by Derick
Williams. Script by Gwen Cherrell. With Christina
Gregg.

Dec 1962: **Dilemma**
Directed and written by Peter Maxwell. Produced
by Ted Lloyd for A.C.T. Films (Association of Cine
Technicians). With Peter Halliday, Ingrid Hafner.

Dec 1962: **Lunch Hour**
Directed by James Hill. Produced by Harold Orton,
Alfred Shaughnessy, John Mortimer. Script from his
own play by Mortimer. With Shirley Anne Field,
Robert Stephens.

Jan 1963: **Sammy Going South** (BSA)
Directed by *Alexander Mackendrick*. Produced by
Michael Balcon, Hal Mason. Script by Denis
Cannan, from novel by W.H.Canaway. With
Edward G. Robinson.

Feb 1963: **The Small World of Sammy Lee**
(BSA)
Directed and written by Ken Hughes, from his own
television play. Produced by Hughes, Frank
Godwin. With Anthony Newley, Robert Stephens.

Feb 1963: **Calculated Risk**
Directed by Norman Harrison. Produced by
William McLeod. Script by Edwin Richfield. With
William Lucas.

June 1963: **A Place to Go**
Directed by *Basil Dearden*. Produced and written by
Michael Relph, from novel by Michael Green. With
Rita Tushingham.

June 1963: **Ladies Who Do**
Directed by C.M.Pennington-Richards. Produced
by George H.Brown. Script by Michael Pertwee.
With Peggy Mount, *Robert Morley*.

June 1963: **Girl in the Headlines**
Directed by *Michael Truman*. Produced by John
Davis. Script by Vivienne Knight, Patrick Campbell,
from novel by Laurence Payne. With Ian Hendry.

July 1963: **A Matter of Choice**
Directed by Vernon Sewell. Produced by George
Maynard. Script by Paul Ryder. With *Anthony Steel*.

Sept 1963: **Panic**
Directed and written by John Gilling. Produced by
Guido Coen. With Janine Gray, Glyn Houston.

Nov 1963: **A Jolly Bad Fellow** (Pax)
Directed by Don Chaffey. Produced by *Michael
Balcon*, Donald Taylor. Script by *Robert Hamer*,
Taylor, from novel by C.E.Vulliamy. With Leo
McKern, *Dennis Price*.

Dec 1963: **The Wild Affair** (BSA)
Directed and written by John Krish, from novel by
William Sansom. Produced by Richard Patterson.
With Nancy Kwan, Terry-Thomas.

Dec 1963: **The Silent Playground** (Pax)
Directed and written by Stanley Goulder. Produced
by George Mills. With Bernard Archard.

Feb 1964: **The System**
Directed by Michael Winner. Produced by Kenneth
Shipman. Script by Peter Draper. With Oliver Reed.

BIBLIOGRAPHY

This brings together the books of clearest direct relevance to Ealing, while omitting both magazine articles and books about (or by) actors. There is a full, and lucidly organised, Balcon bibliography, including magazine material, in the last of the Balcon books listed below (1984), and an excellent, if narrower, one in Philip Kemp's 1991 book on Mackendrick (also listed in section 1). The 1983 collection edited by Curran and Porter (section 3) has a general bibliography of British cinema that is impressive in size and depth of research, if harder to find one's way around.

1) books by, or about, Ealing personnel

Michael Balcon (and others): *Twenty Years of British Films 1925-1945*, Falcon Press, 1947.

Michael Balcon's 25 Years in Films, edited by Monja Danischewsky, World Film Publications, 1947.

Michael Balcon: autobiography, *A Lifetime of Films*, Hutchinson, 1969.

Der Produzent: Michael Balcon und der Englische Film, edited by Geoff Brown, Volker Spiess, Berlin, 1981. Collection of essays, and of interviews with associates of Balcon (in German).

Michael Balcon: The Pursuit of British Cinema, edited by Jane Fluegel, main text by Geoff Brown and Laurence Kardish, Museum of Modern Art, New York, 1984. Extensive factual apparatus.

John Paddy Carstairs: early autobiography, *Honest Injun*, Hurst & Blackett, 1942.

Alberto Cavalcanti, edited by Lorenzo Pellizzari and Claudio Valentinetti, Locarno Film Festival, 1988. Extensive collection of interviews and articles (in French).

T.E.B. Clarke: autobiography, *This Is Where I Came In*, Michael Joseph, 1974.

Monja Danischewsky: autobiography, *White Russian, Red Face*, Gollancz, 1966.

Thorold Dickinson: The Man and his Films, by Jeffrey Richards, Croom Helm, 1984.

Walter Forde, edited by Geoff Brown, British Film Institute, 1977.

Lethal Innocence: The Cinema of Alexander Mackendrick, by Philip Kemp, Methuen, 1991.

Penrose Tennyson: A Memoir, by C.T. [Charles Tennyson, his father], A.S. Atkinson, 1943.

Harry Watt: autobiography, *Don't Look at the Camera*, Elek, 1974.

2) books exclusively on Ealing

Lindsay Anderson: *Making a Film: The Story of Secret People*, Allen & Unwin, 1952.

Ealing Studios, edited by Emanuela Martini, Bergamo Film Meeting, 1988. Collection of essays (in Italian).

Penelope Houston: *Went the Day Well?*, monograph in the series on Film Classics, British Film Institute, 1992.

George Perry: *Forever Ealing: A Celebration of a Great British Film Studio*, Pavilion/Michael Joseph, 1981.

Projecting Britain: Ealing Studios Film Posters, edited by David Wilson, British Film Institute, 1982.

Valladolid Film Festival: *La Comedia Ealing*, 1990. Anthology of articles and interviews (in Spanish).

3) other books containing chapters on Ealing, or interviews with Ealing personnel

Anthony Aldgate and Jeffrey Richards: *The Best of British: Cinema and Society 1930-1960*, Blackwell, 1983. Includes chapter on *The Ladykillers*.

Anthony Aldgate and Jeffrey Richards: *Britain Can Take It*, Blackwell, 1986. Includes chapters on *Let George Do It*, *The Next of Kin* and *Went the Day Well?*

All Our Yesterdays: 90 Years of British Cinema, edited by Charles Barr, British Film Institute, 1986. Collection of essays, including Pam Cook on *Mandy* and Jim Cook on *The Ship that Died of Shame*.

British Cinema History, edited by James Curran and Vincent Porter, Weidenfeld and Nicolson, 1983. Collection of essays, including two that deal with Ealing, by Porter and Ian Green.

British Council: *The Years's Work in the Film, 1950*, Longmans Green, 1951. Includes chapter by Thorold Dickinson on 'The Work of Sir Michael Balcon at Ealing Studios'.

Film and Theatre Today, edited by Gavin Lambert and Clifford King, Saturn Press, 1949. Includes chapter by Lindsay Anderson on Ealing, 'The Studio that Begs to Differ'.

Mass Observation at the Movies, edited by Jeffrey Richards and Dorothy Sheridan, Routledge, 1986. Includes data on the reception of a number of Ealing's wartime films and devotes chapters to *Let George Do It* and *Ships with Wings*.

Sixty Voices: Celebrities Recall the Golden Age of British Cinema, edited by Brian McFarlane, British Film Institute, 1992. Interviewees include Sidney Cole, Pat Jackson, Michael Relph and many actors who refer to their Ealing work.

Elizabeth Sussex: *The Rise and Fall of British Documentary*, University of California Press, 1975. Book based on interviews with veterans of the British documentary movement, including Cavalcanti, Jackson and Watt.

4) some other historical works with material on Ealing

Roy Armes: *A Critical History of British Cinema*, Secker & Warburg, 1978.

Britain and the Cinema in the Second World War, edited by Philip Taylor, Macmillan, 1988.

Robin Cross: *The Big Book of British Films*, Charles Herridge, 1984.

Raymond Durgnat: *A Mirror for England: British Cinema from Austerity to Affluence*, Faber & Faber, 1970.

Marcia Landy: *British Genres: Cinema and Society 1930-1960*, Princeton University Press, 1991.

Robert Murphy: *Realism and Tinsel: British Cinema and Society 1939-48*, Routledge, 1989.

National Fictions: World War Two in British Films and Television, edited by Geoffrey Hurd, British Film Institute, 1984.

James Park: *British Cinema: The Lights that Failed*, Batsford, 1990.

Basil Wright: *The Long View*, Secker & Warburg, 1974.

INDEX

Page numbers in italics refer to picture captions. The last reference given for each film is for its entry in the Film Credits and Notes section.